Charles William Super

A History of the German Language

Charles William Super

A History of the German Language

ISBN/EAN: 9783337085131

Printed in Europe, USA, Canada, Australia, Japan

Cover: Foto ©ninafisch / pixelio.de

More available books at **www.hansebooks.com**

A HISTORY

OF THE

GERMAN LANGUAGE

BY
CHARLES W. SUPER, A. M., PH. D.,
President of the Ohio University; Translator of Weil's Order of Words, Etc.

"Glib is the tongue of man, and many words are therein of every kind, and wide is the range of his speech hither and thither."
— *Iliad* xx: *248-9*.

COLUMBUS, OHIO:
HANN & ADAIR,
1893

"*Von allen Organismen gehen die sprachlichen unser innerstes Wesen am nächsten an; macht doch die Sprache erst den Menschen.*"—SCHLEICHER.

"*In dem Menschen liegt ein Etwas, eine qualitas occulta, wenn man so will, das ihn von allen Thieren ausnahmslos sondert. Dieses Etwas nennen wir Vernunft, wenn wir es als innere Wirksamkeit denken, wir nennen es Sprache, sobald wir es als Äuszeres, als Erscheinung gewahren und auffassen. Keine Vernunft ohne Sprache, keine Sprache ohne Vernunft. Die Sprache ist der Rubicon, welcher das Thier vom Menschen scheidet, welchen kein Thier jemals überschreiten wird.*"—MAX MÜLLER.

"*Alle Geschichte beruht bei uns auf dem Gegensatz des religiösen und politischen Lebens, auf der Anerkennung beider als selbständig neben einander; nie hat der Glaube uns die irdischen Aufgaben vergessen lassen, die dem Menschen doch auch obliegen und die ihn beschäftigen, so lange er im Schweisz seines Angesichts sein Brot essen musz. Diese irdischen Aufgaben verlangen vor allem eine wirtschaftliche Ordnung, in der sie allein gelöst werden können, ein Recht, wodurch das äuszere Leben gepflegt und geschult wird, und einen Staat, der den zeitlichen Bedürfnissen entspricht und das Recht im innern wie auch nach auszen zur Erfüllung bringt.*"—ARNOLD.

TABLE OF CONTENTS.

	PAGE.
PREFACE,	7
INTRODUCTION,	11

GENERAL PART.

PRELIMINARY OBSERVATIONS,	25
THE GERMAN LANGUAGE CONSIDERED CHRONOLOGICALLY AND TOPOGRAPHICALLY,	26
PRE-GERMANIC PERIOD — SHIFTING OF SOUNDS AND ACCENT,	29
THE GERMANIC AND ITS SUB-DIVISIONS,	38
THE OLD HIGH GERMAN PERIOD,	44
THE MIDDLE HIGH GERMAN PERIOD,	59
LANGUAGES AND DIALECTS,	66
THE NEW HIGH GERMAN PERIOD —	
1. Extent of Territory,	69
2. The Written Language and Folk-Speech,	72
3. Unification in a Common Literary Language,	77
4. Uniformity in the Spoken Language,	101
5. Some Disadvantages of Uniformity,	110
6. Characteristics of the New High German,	113
THE INNER HISTORY OF THE GERMAN LANGUAGE —	
The Influence of Analogy, (What is Analogy?)	122
INADEQUACY OF THE TRADITIONAL VOCABULARY,	137
AMPLIFICATION OF THE MATERIALS OF SPEECH,	156
1. Changes of Meaning,	156
2. Coinage of New Words,	174
3. The Influence of Foreign Language on the German	181

SPECIAL PART.

THE NEW HIGH GERMAN ORTHOGRAPHY,	215
THE ACCENT OR INTONATION OF THE GERMAN,	217

THE DOCTRINE OF SOUNDS IN THE GERMAN,	222
THE INFLECTIONS OF THE NEW HIGH GERMAN	
1. The Noun, or Substantive,	237
2. The Pronoun,	250
3. The Adjective,	253
4. The Verb,	255
WHAT IS ANALOGY IN LANGUAGE?	269
THE SYNTAX OF THE NEW HIGH GERMAN,	271
THE PARTS OF SPEECH,	272
The Noun,	280
The Verb,	285
PROPER NAMES—	
Names of Persons,	292
Names of Places,	306

APPENDIX.

PREFACE.

I WAS led to prepare this volume under the conviction that there are persons enough in this country interested in the historical development of the German language to justify the undertaking. My object has been to produce a book that would be read with interest, and could be read with profit, by people whose knowledge of German does not extend much beyond the rudiments and who know next to nothing of comparative philology. While not primarily intended as a manual for the classroom, it is believed that it can be used with advantage in connection with any German grammar. It has been my constant aim to make duly prominent the common origin of the English and German languages, and to use the facts of the one to elucidate, as far as possible, the facts of the other. It is only by the study of what *has been* that we are able to understand what *is*. I have now and then called attention to those general phenomena which all languages exhibit in common, and have thus, in a slight measure, invaded the domain of the comparative philologist. It has also been my special object to show the relation of dialects to the language of literature, so that I would fain hope this volume may contribute somewhat to dissipate the erroneous notions so widely prevalent on this subject. The importance and persistence of the dialects of the German make it particularly well fitted for exhibiting the relation of the two modes of speech to each other.

My original plan was to prepare a translation of Behaghel's Geschichte der deutchen Sprache. But I soon became convinced that the author's point of view ought not to be that of one who has before his mind's eye an English-speaking public. One who writes for Germans can count on a more thorough and more general knowledge of phonetics, and on a larger measure of popular interest in the exposition of its laws. Professor Behaghel accordingly confined himself more closely to, and expressed himself more briefly on, this part of his subject than seemed to me advisable in an English work. Besides, I am inclined to believe that most of my readers will share with me the belief that a word or a sentence is of more general interest as the visible expression of a thought than as an exemplification of a phonetic law. Though the statement may seem to involve a contradiction, the literary and pedagogical sides of my subject have been made more prominent than the scientific and technical. It seemed to me better, in the long run, to arouse an interest in the subject that would stimulate further inquiry than to furnish indisputable facts, even supposing such a thing to be possible. When we recall that Comparative Philology has been several times rewritten, both in general and particular, during the last two or three decades, and that many of its problems are still unsolved, such a course must be regarded as decidedly advisable.

The result has been that while my book is based on that of Professor Behaghel, it contains a good deal of matter that he might not approve, and for which it would be unjust to hold him responsible. I desire, however, to express my great obligations to his excellent volume and to the clear manner with which he treats his theme. I know no German writer on this subject who combines in an equal degree both learning and lucidity. I have also made some use of Kluge's Etymologisches Woerterbuch der deutschen Sprache; Socin, Schriftsprache und Dialekte im Deutschen; Welker's Dialektgedichte, Skeat's Principles of English Etymology, first and second series; Paul's Grundriss der germanischen Philologie; and Balg's

Glossary of the Gothic Language. I have likewise profited by the lectures of the late Professor von Keller, of Tuebingen, with whom I read the Heliand more than a score of years ago. Several other works have been named where they throw light on special subjects discussed in the volume. I am under special obligations to my brother, O. B. Super, Professor of Modern Languages in Dickinson College, for suggestions and assistance. His co-operation has, I feel sure, added no little to the value of my work.

It is probable that I have fallen into some errors in tracing the origin and development of words. The path of the linguistic sciences is thickly strewn with defunct and decaying etymologies, and that I have added some to the number is more than probable. Nevertheless, I have adopted none for which I did not have competent — I would fain believe the best — authorities, so that I have reason to believe my mistakes will be found to be comparatively few. It should be remembered, too, that the necessity of being brief, may now and then lead the reader to think that I have been mistaken, where a fuller discussion of the point in question would show that I am probably correct in the conclusion I have accepted. Against premature verdicts of this sort I know of no remedy except a careful examination of the evidence on which I have proceeded. The chain may occasionally seem to be broken merely because some of its links have not been exposed to view.

I would fain believe that under more favorable conditions I could have produced a better book than I have. Most of it was written at long intervals, in brief periods of an hour or two in length. The official demands of a laborious position; daily recurring duties as a teacher; frequent calls for editorial work in another field, made such large drafts on my time that but little was left for any self-assumed task. What could have been done under fairly favorably conditions in a little more than a year, occupied me nearly four years. All this can be no excuse for any errors of fact the volume may contain, but it may be some palliation for minor defects in their arrangement and for infelicities of style of which I fear attentive readers will find only too many. For these the generous indulgence of the reader is asked. My experience is but a counterpart of hundreds, perhaps thousands, of American teachers: whatever they do in the line of systematic study except so far as it serves the immediate purposes of the school and class-room, is generally at the sacrifice of no little personal ease and at the expense of hours of rest and recreation.

If this volume contributes somewhat to the better knowledge of a language, which, in my opinion, embodies a larger number of excellencies than any other of ancient or modern times, except the Greek, I shall feel that my labor has not been in vain.

I am not unaware that we have a number of American scholars whose attainments in Germanic Philology are much superior to mine, and who are in position to produce a better book than this. As they have not, however, thus far undertaken the task, at least so far as the public is informed, I am led to put forth this modest work in the hope that it may, at least, prepare the way for something more excellent. CHARLES W. SUPER.

Athens, O., June, 1892.

INTRODUCTION.

SO far as we know, the Germans from the remotest times have lived substantially in the same place where we now find them. It was formerly believed that they had originally emigrated from Asia, but many of the best authorities at present favor the theory that the Aryans originated in Europe; and if this is true, the Germans must have come into existence on or near the territory which they now occupy.

When we ask the question intelligently, What was the original abode of the Aryan race? we can only mean, What part of the earth's surface did they occupy before splitting up into the fragments that subsequently developed into a number of nationalities? To answer this we have nothing except the slender evidence of a very limited vocabulary which was formed in accordance with the fauna, flora and general topographical conditions among which the race originally dwelt. But if in their unity they wandered about, as it is universally admitted they did, over countries having substantially the same physical characteristics, their vocabulary would not change either by increase or elimination. If these conditions changed, new words would be formed, which would correspond to the new habitat. But how are we now to distinguish these from the older stratum, if the people who used them were still homogeneous? Do the primitive words that still survive, date from the beginning of their career, or from the time when they had become comparatively stable? The inquiry must always remain barren of trustworthy results, fascinating as it is for the student of language.

The first mention that is made of the Germans is found in a description of a voyage made by Pytheas of Massilia about 340 B. C. He speaks of them as Teutones and calls them a part of the great Skythian stock. This mistake on his part in confounding Germans and Skythians is attributable to the ignorance of the writer. To the Greeks all the people of northern and eastern Europe were Skythians,—wherever definite knowledge ended there the

Skythians began. For the name "German" we are directly indebted to the Romans, who received it from the Kelts. It probably means "neighbors," the Germans being for a long time the only foreign nation with whom the western Kelts came into contact. There are other significations of the name proposed, one of the best authenticated being "dwellers in the forest."

Pytheas probably advanced along the coast of the North Sea as far as the mouth of the Eider, and in the region of the Elbe, according to his account, was the dividing line between Kelts and Teutons. Later investigations tend to show that Pytheas was correct in this matter, for many of the proper names in northwestern Germany, especially in the valley of the Ems, are now known to be of Keltic origin.

The dividing line on the south of the Germans was the Hercynian Forest, which is merely a general term for the range of hills and mountains extending entirely through central Germany. *Hercynia* is itself a Keltic name allied to Kymric *erchymiad, elevation*. Precisely at what time they extended their boundaries westward, it is impossible to say, but the extension in that direction occurred earlier than in a southern direction, for in Cæsar's time the Rhine was substantially the boundary between the two nations, the Menapii being the only Keltic tribe still remaining east of the Rhine, and they only in part. It was about this time that the Volcæ, who were then living in the valley of the Main, were driven out by the Marcomanni and Chatti. Near the same time three German tribes, the Vangiones, Nemeti and Triboci settled along the Rhine, occupying the territory in the above order from the mouth of the Neckar to the Swiss boundary. Shortly before this (about 72 B. C.) Ariovistus had led his Germans across the Rhine and settled in eastern Gaul.

On the east, the Germans were shut in by the Slavs who were pressing westward. A line drawn from Koenigsberg, in Prussia, to the confluence of the Bug and Vistula and then following the latter to its source, will indicate the boundary between Slavs and Germans.

Although Sweden has been regarded by some as the original home of the Germans, it is more likely that that country was at one time inhabited entirely by Finns, and that these were gradually driven northward by the encroachments of the Germans, who crossed over either from Germany or Denmark. Certain it is that Finnish antiquities have been found in almost every part of Sweden.

But this limited space soon proved too small for a people who increased so rapidly as the Germans, and emigration became a necessity, especially since their eastern neighbors not only prohibited expansion in that direction, but were actually crowding them westward. However, there is not much doubt that the rapid increase of population common among the Germans will furnish a sufficient explanation of these vast swarms of emigrants.

The first of the German tribes to leave their homes *en masse* was the Bastarnæ, who are found north and west of the mouth of the Danube as early as the second century B. C. Next came the great emigration of the Cimbri and Teutons. The latter started from the shores of the North Sea, and there is a tradition that they were compelled to leave their homes on account of an incursion of the ocean; which is not improbable, since the whole northwest coast of Germany is so little elevated above the sea level that the tide can only be kept out by artificial means. Notwithstanding the dykes, about 15,000 persons perished in a single night in 1634 by a high tide on the west coast of Schleswig-Holstein. These Teutons moved toward the southeast, and the Cimbri, who lived on the left bank of the Elbe in the region of the present Magdeburg, joined them in their expedition and formed its van-guard. On their march they came in contact with the Boii, a Keltic tribe living in what is now called Bohemia (i. e. home or land of the Boii). Prevented from settling here, they continued their journey to the southeast, across the Danube, through Pannonia until they came into the land of the Scordisci, a Keltic tribe living about the junction of the Save and the Danube. They must have arrived here about 114 B. C. Defeated in a battle with the Scordisci, they retreated toward the northwest, and on their way met and defeated the Roman Consul, Papirius Carbo, at Noreia, 113 B. C. They then advanced westward, passing apparently unhindered through the territory of the Helvetians, and arriving on the Rhone, on the confines of the Roman Province, 109 B. C. Here they defeated the Consul Silvanus, but instead of marching directly into Italy, they began to plunder Gaul, which they subjugated almost entirely. In the year 105 they gained another great victory over the Romans at Arausio (Orange) after which the Cimbri separated from the Teutons and returned into the heart of Gaul. They soon afterwards made an expedition into Spain and plundered the northwestern part of it, but having been defeated by the Keltiberians, they returned to Gaul in the year 103 B. C. In the year following, the Teutons were defeated and nearly annihilated by Marius at Aquæ Sextiæ, in the Province, and the Cimbri at Vercellæ, in northwestern Italy, in the following year.

It does not lie within the scope of the present volume to give in this Introduction a history of the various German tribes. Such a history must, from the nature of the case, consist largely of the discussion of obscure points and contradictory, or, at least, apparently contradictory statements made by ancient writers about them. But it will be proper to give a brief account of those tribes that made expeditions beyond the German territory, and for a while exerted an influence upon the destinies of the countries through which they passed, or in which they sojourned for a greater or less time. We shall thus get a fuller insight into the character of the German people than their language alone is able to give us. Such a preliminary sketch is the more important for the reason that it relates, for the most part, to a period from which the existing linguistic remains are very scanty.

The German nation as such is some eight hundred years old; but during most of this time it was broken up into an almost countless number of different governments under many different names, and varying greatly in extent of territory. At the beginning of this period the tribal differences had been to a considerable extent obliterated, and tribal affinities no longer formed a bond between the subjects of the different rulers.

The Bastarnæ were, according to Zeuss, the first German tribe of whom we have any fairly definite knowledge. At this time they dwelt about the headwaters of the Vistula. They are subsequently found north and west of the Danube. In the reign of Perseus, king of Macedon, they formed an alliance with this monarch against the Romans. Still later they are found in the service of Mithridates, king of Pontus. In fact, they appear several times among the enemies of Rome, until the time of the emperor Probus, toward the close of the third century, when they disappear from history.

We first hear of the Burgundians in the present province of Posen. In the third century of our era they emigrated toward the southwest, and lived, during nearly the whole of the fourth century, along the upper Main. Toward the end of the century they came to the Rhine, where they founded a kingdom with Worms as its capital. It is here that the legends of the Nibelungen find them. In consideration of their services to the Romans as mercenary troops, they were permitted to establish themselves in eastern Gaul, especially in the basin of the Rhone.

Toward the close of the ninth century we find in this region two Burgundian kingdoms, one of which was called the "cisjuran," the other the "transjuran." These existed separately for some twenty-five years, when they were again united. For more than four centuries Burgundy was regarded as at least nominally a part of the German Empire. The dukedom of Burgundy lay north of these two kingdoms, and under a succession of ambitious rulers played an important part in the history of France. Though varying considerably, at different times in extent of territory, it had a separate existence until near the close of the seventeenth century, when it shared the destiny that had befallen the larger part of the Burgundian kingdoms much earlier, and was absorbed by France.

The Lombards, whose tribal affinities allied them with the Suevi, first appear about the lower course of the Elbe. They were probably the last of the German tribes to leave their homes *en masse*. For a long time they do not seem to have played a prominent part in the various tribal wars and expeditions. So late as the middle of the fifth century they were subjects of the Heruli in Moravia. Subsequently they defeated these and made themselves masters of considerable territory in what is now Hungary. Later still they formed a union with a horde of Saxons with whom they marched across the Alps, and before the end of the sixth century they had made themselves masters of all northern Italy. Here they founded a kingdom, with Milan as its capital, that lasted two hundred years. Their history, which is a turbulent one, can be traced until the time of Karl the Great, who made their territory a part of his empire. Though never numerous, they maintained their supremacy by their valor. Few traces of them now remain, the most conspicuous being the name Lombardy, which is still applied to that part of Italy which they once held in subjection.

The Vandals first emerge into the dim light of history

dwelling along the mid-course of the Oder. Like most of their brethren they joined various expeditions against the Romans, but subsequently adopted a more settled life in Pannonia. About the beginning of the fifth century they forced their way across Gaul into Spain, where they founded a kingdom, the name of which is still preserved in that of the province Andalusia. They afterward passed over into Africa, subdued its northern portion, captured Carthage, which they made their capital, built large fleets with which they plundered the islands of the Mediterranean, as well as the adjacent coasts, and finally took Rome itself. As is wont to be the case, they now began to degenerate by reason of their prosperity and fancied security. In the year 524 their King Gelimer was defeated by the Roman general Belisarius, and taken to Constantinople to grace his triumph, while the kingdom of the Vandals was made a part of the Eastern Empire.

The Goths had a tradition that their original home was on an island called Scandzia, and there may be some connection between their name and that of the southernmost province of Sweden. In the time of Tacitus they lived along the lower course of the Vistula. Probably about the middle of the second century they started on their long march toward the southwest, which ended by their settling in the regions north and west of the Black Sea. Here they soon appear as Eastern and Western Goths, these appellations designating the relative geographical positions which their two main divisions occupy to each other. For a period of nearly two centuries they made occasional incursions into the Roman empire. It was in one of these raids that they burned the splendid temple of Artemis in the year 260. (See Acts of the Apostles, chapter 19.) A few years before the beginning of the fifth century the Eastern Gothic tribes were subdued by the Huns, but the Western Goths continued to plunder southeastern Europe, and crossing over into Italy they finally captured Rome itself in 410. Still continuing to move westward they are found for three centuries longer in France, Spain, and Africa, when they disappear from history. The remembrance of their former presence is still preserved in the name of the Spanish province, Catalonia (Gotalonia). The Eastern Goths, as subjects of the Huns, took part in several of the expeditions of their king Attila. After the death of this monarch they achieved their independence, and settled in what is now Austria proper. Somewhat later they made an expedition into Italy, the northern portion of which they brought under subjection, and finally extended their rule over the entire peninsula. After varying fortunes they disappear as a separate people, toward the end of the sixth century.

A glance at the map of Europe in the last quarter of the fifth century, when their power was at its zenith, shows the following territory in the possession of the Germans: The Suevi were masters of the northwestern portion of the Iberian peninsula. Their kingdom was about as large as Portugal. The Western Goths possessed the remainder of the peninsula and France as far northward as the river Loire. The kingdom of the Burgundians lay in the basin of the Rhone. The Franks held sway over an extensive territory lying on both sides of the Rhine between Treves, Mayence and the North Sea. North and east of them were the Saxons. Toward the south between the Franks and the Burgundians were the Alemani, and east of the Saxons, Franks and Alemani were the Thuringians, a people whose eastern boundary cannot be defined. The head-waters of the Oder were occupied by the Longobardi; directly south of them dwelt the Heruli; and still further south, between the Danube and the river Aluta, were the lands of the Gepids. West of the last two tribes lay the kingdom of the Ostrogoths, some of whom were, however, in Illyria and subjects of the Eastern Empire. The Rugians had settled in the Grand Duchy of Austria on both sides of the Danube. From here to the Mediterranean, including Italy and Sicily, stretched the kingdom of Odoacer, while the Vandals held in subjection most of Africa west of the Great Syrtis, Corsica, Sardinia, and the Balearic Isles. The Saxons and Angles had just begun to make settlements on the coast of England.

After this brief survey of the earliest history of the Germans we next proceed to define the relation of the Teutonic to the other most important languages of the world. It seems important to do so here, though we shall find it necessary to repeat some of our statements farther along.

The German is an important member of the great family of languages variously designated as the Aryan, the Indo-Germanic and the Indo-European. This family is usually divided by philologists into nine different groups or branches of which three belong to Asia and six to Europe.

The Keltic, the most westerly of these groups, is at present the native speech of three or four millions of people in Scotland, Wales, Ireland and a few departments of France. Aside from a small number of inscriptions found chiefly in the region of the central Saone little is known of the Keltic in its earliest forms. The oldest monuments of the Welsh dialect date from the eighth century and consist chiefly of legendary poems and chronicles. The Breton, another dialect of the Keltic, was probably transplanted into France in the fifth century. It closely resembles the Welsh though its literary monuments are not older than the fourteenth century. Somewhat later it is largely represented in glosses to Latin authors and in the Middle Ages it possessed an extensive literature in the form of Chronicles, Legends, and Laws.

The Slavic is the most easterly of the European groups and is spoken by about ninety millions of people. Numerically it is the first in importance of the exclusively continental groups. It is the principal language of Russia in Europe, and to it belong the Polish, the Bohemian (or

Czech), the Servian, the Bulgarian and a number of less important dialects. The earliest monuments of the Polish language date from the tenth century, and Bohemia had an extensive literature dating from the Middle Ages and extending to the time of the Hussite wars. The alphabet of the Slavic was adapted from the Greek though very inadequate to its intended purpose, by the brothers Cyrillus and Methodius who first preached Christianity to the Bulgarians in the ninth century. Its oldest literary remains are the Gospels translated by the missionaries and some liturgical works in the Old Bulgarian, which, though not the mother of the other Slavic tongues, stands in the relation of an older sister. Where this language was spoken has not been definitely determined, but probably somewhere in the region between the Black and Adriatic Seas. Slavic dialects are still used to some extent in Saxony and Prussia and at one time a considerable portion of what is now Germany was occupied by Slavs.

The Lithuanian group is spoken by about two and a half millions of people in northeastern Prussia and the adjoining territory of Russia. Its literature is of very little importance and it hardly at any time attained the dignity of a written language. But this group is of great interest to philologists because it has conserved in a remarkable degree some prominent characteristics of the primitive Indo-European language.

The Italian group has no extant literature of any importance of earlier date than the comedies of Plautus, though there are some fragments of older date both in Latin and other Italic dialects. Its most important extant representatives are the French, the Spanish, the Portuguese, and the Italian.

The Greek group has been confined from the remotest times to substantially the same territory it now occupies. Its literary monuments are several centuries older than those of any other European language. It has never been spoken by a very large number of persons, but its influence upon the civilization of the world has been much greater than that of any other group. Its dialects have diverged less, generally speaking, from the parent language than has been the case with any other member of the Indo-European stock, and modern Greek is still substantially the same language it was nearly three thousand years ago.

The Germanic or Teutonic group embraces the German proper, the Dutch, the English, the Danish, and the Swedish. German proper is the native language of about sixty millions of people in continental Europe, but the Teutonic group of languages is not only spoken by a larger number of persons than any other of the Indo-European stock, but it represents the most potent influence in literature, science and all the arts of civilized life. Its oldest extant literature is represented by the Maeso-Gothic dialect and dates from the close of the fourth century. This dialect was at that time spoken in the region of the lower Danube, probably in what is now Bulgaria.

The earliest literary monuments of the German language, aside from the translation of the Bible by Ulfilas, are confined, roughly speaking, to southwestern Germany. We first meet with the so-called glosses or interlinear translations of Latin texts into German, and lists of Latin words arranged either alphabetically or according to subjects with their equivalents in German. These were prepared for pedagogical purposes. There are extant two longer poems dating from the ninth century — the old Saxon Heliand, a sort of New Testament history by an unknown author, and Otfried's Harmony of the Gospels. Toward the end of the eleventh century we meet with several longer religious poems. Nevertheless, the literature of the ninth, tenth and eleventh centuries, must be called scanty, and all of it together makes a volume of but moderate size. To the close of the eighth century belong likewise some brief translations of liturgies and catechetical writings. The ninth century adds some other religious writings and translated portions of the Bible. The Commentary of Notker is usually assigned to about the year 1000, and it is believed that Willeram's Paraphrase of the Song of Solomon is about a century younger. Both these contain a liberal intermixture of Latin.

This literature is somewhat widely distributed, but it belongs chiefly to Austrian Germany, Bavaria, eastern Switzerland, Alsatia and Fulda, once an independent bishopric, but now a part of Prussia. The Heliand above mentioned is of a more northern origin. With the twelfth century German poetry entered upon a career of rapid development and toward its close the culmination of the first classical period had been attained. It was, however, still confined chiefly to South Germany, and it is only in the two following centuries that there is an intellectual movement northward. The prose literature of the twelfth century consists chiefly of sermons, and its mass is largely increased during the thirteenth and fourteenth centuries. To the first part of the thirteenth century must be assigned the so-called Sachsenspiegel, a collection of provincial laws, and this is a few decades earlier than the Schwabenspiegel, a similar collection. These are the first legal writings in German. Of about the same age is the first historical work in the native language, a Chronicle of the World, in Low-German. Toward the close of the thirteenth century we begin to meet with German title-deeds and other official documents. With the fourteenth century they increase in number rapidly. The earliest of these belong to southwestern Germany, but before the end of the thirteenth century they are met with in almost all parts of the nation, except the eastern parts of what is now Prussia. The German is employed to considerable extent for purposes of historical narration, and in the fifteenth century literature proper (belles lettres) is extensively cultivated. During this period many devotional books and translations of portions of the Bible were published and widely read. The rise of Protestantism was favorable to the cultivation of German, and in the sixteenth century it had become the recognized medium for the adherents of this faith, while the Latin continued to be the official language of the Church of Rome. But the rise of the German universities was unfavorable to the German language. The Latin continued to be the means of communication among the learned in all the professions, and the use of the German was considered unworthy of the scholar. According to Paulsen seventy per cent. of the books printed in Germany about the year 1570 were in the Latin language. At no other time does the German seem to have been so far in the background, and from this point it begins to move slowly to the front. But not until 1680 were more German books published than Latin. In 1730 only about one-third of the issues from the press were Latin, and toward the close of the century this language had virtually ceased to be in general use even among scholars. The proportion of Latin and German seems to have varied considerably in the writings pertaining to the different professions and departments of learning. In the domain of Protestant theology German probably predominated from the first, except in purely doctrinal discussions. In historical works German was chiefly used as early as the end of the seventeenth century; it also predominated for philosophy and medicine at the beginning of the eighteenth century. For writings on jurisprudence Latin continued to be chiefly employed until about the middle of the eighteenth century, when for the first time German works are in the majority. At the universities Latin was exclusively used in the lectures until 1687. From this time German came into use gradually, but Latin was not entirely superseded until quite recently. It was largely owing to this preference for

Latin as the language of books that the Germans were the latest of all the important nations of Europe to develop a modern classical literature. For about two hundred years anterior to the appearance of Goethe, Germany produced hardly a single work belonging to the department of belles lettres. The best intellects devoted themselves to the study of antique life, and the literature in which it is embodied, in apparent ignorance of the unlimited capabilities of their mother tongue. This unwise and almost exclusive devotion to foreign languages had a deleterious effect on even those authors who wrote in German. Not having had the rhetorical training of the writers of antiquity their sentences are generally long and lumbering, inartistically constructed and heavy.

During a part of the eighteenth century this predilection for foreign languages and literature manifested itself in a new direction, and French was cultivated to a considable extent. This was especially the case among the nobility, and those who aped their manners. It is chiefly due to the influence and writings of Lessing, Goethe, and Schiller that modern German literature attained the high place it now holds.

GENERAL PART.

PRELIMINARY OBSERVATIONS.

THERE is, perhaps, nothing that we can study and investigate that is more mysterious than language. We may divide and subdivide, and analyze as much as we please, there always remains a residuum that defies our closest scrutiny. We know that a word belonging to an unfamiliar foreign language affects the mind, the sensorium, differently from one to which we are accustomed. We may say that one enters the intellect, while the other only enters the ear. We talk about an awakened image, a responsive chord; but there is no real image and no actual chord. These are but figures of speech taken from the material world intended to illustrate, as well as they may, psychic processes. They are symbols of which the value is pretty generally understood, but they are only symbols. We have no name and no designation for the thing itself,—no words that in the first instance were used, only of mental operations. Language is something with which we operate, something of which the power and functions are well known, but of its essence we know little or nothing. We often talk of language as if it was something external, or as if it were the dead matter that we find written or printed, when in truth it has no existence, is not language in the proper sense of the word, if it is not vitalized by life and thought. The body of language, the living and only real word exists but the moment it is uttered; its imperfect image is sometimes fixed on the printed page, or on some plastic substance; which, however, tells us nothing until brought in contact with the living, thinking mind.

There are languages that are not written; *tens of thousands* of dialects exist, or have existed, that were never put in books or on paper, and yet they were or are as truly human speech as those that are the custodians of the most extensive literature. We are too apt to regard the language we find written or printed as the only real language, when, in fact, it is nothing more than its faint image. I look at the instrument with which I write. I think of it as the pen, *die Feder, la plume*, designating it by a different name in each language with which I am acquainted. Here the thing awakens in my mind what I may call a vocal image, even though I do not necessarily give it voice. Or I hear some one pronounce the name of the object, and it at once brings before my "mind's eye" the concept of the pen, and so there goes on incessantly in the world, and has gone on for countless ages, this transition from concept to vocal expression,—this translation of thought into words; and from vocal expression to concept, the transmutation of vocal expression into thought. We think, then speak or write; others speak or write, and their words stimulate thought in us.

THE GERMAN LANGUAGE CONSIDERED CHRONOLOGICALLY AND TOPOGRAPHICALLY.

Matters of every day occurrence rarely attract our attention or stimulate us to reflection. Nothing is more common than the words that make up our speech—the sentences we meet in our ordinary reading. These things are, however, rarely the subject of remark among the illiterate, to whom language is something that exists as a matter of course. But among people of intelligence there is a lively interest in the phenomena of speech or language, and they are frequently the theme of friendly discussion. How are certain facts to be explained? If we ourselves always used the same form of expression for the same thought, or saw others doing so, there is no doubt that questions of language would interest us as little as the observation that water flows down hill, or that iron rusts. But the phenomena of speech do not have this uniformity; our attention is continually drawn to differences in the time, the place, and the personality of the speaker.

While it may seem perfectly natural for the educated man of the present day to take note of these phenomena, and in accordance with the scientific spirit of our time, to arrange them so far as may be in categories, the world has made slow progress toward this attainment.

The Hebrews had no grammar of their language until more than a thousand years after Christ. The Greeks made no scientific study of their language during its Golden Age; and not till it had sunk far in decay, or about half a century B. C., was the first Greek grammar composed. This became the basis of nearly all subsequent grammars of both the Greek and Latin languages. The grammatical study of the Teutonic languages, in a truly scientific spirit, dates from the appearance of Grimm's Deutsche Grammatik, at the beginning of the present century. But good grammars of either English or German for young learners are hardly older than the present generation. It is the different ways in which the same thought may be expressed that more than anything else awakens reflection upon language. These differences are not merely casual, but are the necessary phenomena which make up the life of a language. To record and explain, as far as it can be done, the changes which a language undergoes, is to write its history. This present work is intended to be a brief *resumé* of the most important changes the German language has undergone from the earliest period within our knowledge up to our day; for it is only after a study of its growth that we are in a position to understand its present structure.

The German language, as the term is generally understood and as it is here employed, is the speech used by the different members of the German family, but this should be carefully distinguished from the Germanic family, which is more comprehensive. Its territory is in the main, that embraced within the German empire, but extending somewhat beyond its borders so as to include a part of Switzerland, German Austria, contiguous portions of Russia, and settlements in other parts of the world. The language of the Netherlands may also be reckoned as belonging to the German.

Authorities differ considerably as to the number of persons whose native speech is German. Meyer's Lexicon gives the number of Germans in the empire as 42,000,000, and a recent writer in the London Times, as 47,000,000. Hovelacque estimates those in Austria at 9,000,000, and in Switzerland at 2,000,000. Morfill puts the number of Germans in the Russian empire at about 1,240,000, and Meyer-Waldeck at 2,000,000. The following table is believed to be substantially correct:

Number of Germans in the Empire	45,000,000
Number of Germans in Austria	10,000,000
Number of Germans in Switzerland	1,800,000
Number of Germans in Russia	1,500,000
Number of Germans in France	150,000
Number of Germans in Holland	100,000
Number of Germans in Italy	30,000
Number of Germans in all other lands	100,000
Total	58,680,000

The Allgemeine Erdkunde, published by Tempsky, in Prague, says that Europe contains one hundred and five millions of people belonging to the Germanic race; ninety-eight belonging to the Romanic; ninety-six belonging to the Slavic; and three millions belonging to other Indo-European races. About thirty millions are not of Indo-European stock.

The census of the United States for 1880 shows that there were in this country at that date about two million persons who were natives of the German Empire. The number of persons whose father or mother was a native German was considerably larger. These should be added to the table given above.

If we wish to examine the beginnings of the German language and to trace its historical development from its inception it will not suffice to confine ourselves within the limits above prescribed. Our first and introductory chapter will take us far beyond these. It will be necessary to consider the language in its remotest discoverable relationships.

PRE-GERMANIC PERIOD—SHIFTING OF SOUNDS AND ACCENT.

The different members of the German family are only a fragment of a larger whole ; they are a portion of the great Germanic stock to which belong, among the nations of our time, the English and the Scandinavians. The separation of the Germans proper from their remaining kinsfolk, necessarily brought with it a change in their language. If, therefore, there is an agreement on any point in the structure of the German and Scandinavian languages, it may in most cases be assumed with confidence that it takes us back to a period anterior to that separation. A comparative study of the different Germanic dialects enables us then to form a pretty correct idea of the language used by all the Germanic tribes in common. This language is called the General Germanic or Primitive Teutonic speech.

But the science of language enables us to do more. By it we are placed in position to prove that just as the English and Scandinavians are related to the Germans in a certain degree of kinship, so the latter are in turn related, but more remotely, to a larger circle of people of the same blood. This larger circle embraces the natives of India, of Iran, of Armenia, as well as the Greeks, the Italians, whose chief representatives were the ancient Romans, the Kelts, the Slavs and the Lithuanians. All these formed, at one time in the far distant past, a homogeneous nation, and spoke a common language, now generally known as the Indo-Germanic. The people themselves are called Indo-Europeans or Aryans. It is possible to form a fairly definite idea of this language by a comparison of the various languages that are descended from it. No amount of research can take us further back than this point. The attempt has been made by several different scholars to show that ultimately a relationship existed also between the Indo-European and Semitic languages, the best known of which is the Hebrew, and the most important, the Arabic, but the results of their labors have convinced few competent scholars.

See, for instance, Andreas Raabe, Gemeinschaftliche Grammatik der arischen und der semitischen Sprachen, Leipzig, 1874; Delitzsch Studien ueber Indogermanisch-Semitische Wurzelverwandschaft, Leipzig, 1873; and von Raumer, Die Urverwandschaft der semitischen und der arischen Sprachen, in Kuhn's Zeitschrift, Band XXII. More accessible are the articles Philology and Shemitic Languages in McClintock and Strong's Cyclopedia. They are written by different authors and maintain radically different views. The belief seems to be gaining ground that all languages are descended from one parent speech, though it is at present held for anthropological rather than linguistic reasons.

But if it is as yet impossible for the most thorough investigation to penetrate beyond the point above indicated, this does not prove or even make it probable that the Indo-European bore a close resemblance to the primitive human speech. It was, on the contrary, a highly developed language that postulates a long period of formation and development, and, so far as structure is concerned, there is no radical difference between Indo-European (or Indo-Germanic) and Germanic. The former had about the same and an equal number of sounds as the latter; in richness of grammatical forms it was superior. In the structure of the complete sentence it was, however, inferior, though it already exhibits the principle of subordinating one sentence to another by means of conjunctions.

The following pages set forth the most important sounds of the Indo-European tongue, together with the specific terms used to designate them. It is customary to divide them into vowels and consonants. The vowels were:

Simple { a, e, i, o, u, short.
         ā, ē, ī, ō, ū, long.

Compound (or diphthongs) ai, au, ei, eu.

Until a few years ago, philologists, almost without exception, held to the opinion that the vowel system of the Indo-European had but three sounds, namely, a, i, u. Herein they followed such leaders as Grimm, Schleicher, and Curtius. The investigations of the so-called "Junggrammatiker" (neo-grammarians) have, however, caused this view to be generally abandoned by all except those whose long service in defense of the old theory has made it morally impossible for them to adjust themselves to the newest discoveries.

The consonants are divided into sonants (voiced) and surds (voiceless). Of the former class the Indo-European possessed the semi-vowels j (English y) and w, the liquids r and l, and the nasals m and n; of the latter there were two classes:

(a) Simple and momentary, because they did not admit of lengthening;
(b) Continuative, or enduring.

The momentary or explosive consonants are further sub-divided into gutturals, k and g; labials, p and b; and dentals, t and d; or into tenues k, t, p; and medials, g, b, d.

The continuative consonants, or those that may be indefinitely prolonged, sometimes called fricatives or spirants, are chiefly represented by s.

The compound consonants are combinations of the media with the letter h, thus forming gh, dh, and bh.

These two letters were, however, sounded separately, somewhat as in log-house, god-head, etc.

At a time, which cannot now be determined, the Germanic language separated from the primitive Indo-European tongue—in other words changes began to take place in one part of this tongue, from which the remaining portion continued free. When we examine the list of words which the Germanic has in common with the Greek and Latin, we notice that the vowels and sonant consonants are, in the main, the same in all three, but that the surds, except s, have, in all cases, undergone a change; however, with such regularity and consistency that we commonly find a certain consonant in Greek and Latin represented by a certain other consonant in the Germanic. This phenomenon of sound-shifting is usually called Grimm's Law, for the reason that Jacob Grimm, acting on a suggestion of the Danish philologist Rask, first clearly stated the conditions under which it takes place This law, however, expresses only the first of two similar changes that took place during the life of the Germanic language. The facts may be ranged under three general heads:

(1) The tenuis of the Indo-European, which is represented for us by the Greek and Latin, becomes a spirant (fricative) in the Germanic. It is necessary to make a distinction here which could fitly be omitted in describing the sounds of the Indo-European. Just as there are surd and sonant, or voiceless and voiced—momentary-consonants, so there are likewise surd and sonant fricatives. Now, the spirant that represents the Indo-European tenuis is voiceless. It is also to be remarked that the guttural spirant is represented in the Germanic by h. Accordingly k becomes h, p becomes f, and t becomes th, pronounced as in "third." The following words illustrate this law:

A History of the German Language 33

PRIMITIVE INITIAL K-SOUNDS BECOME H.

GREEK.	LATIN.	GERMAN.	ENGLISH.
καρδία	cord-is	Herz	heart
κέρας	cornu	Horn	horn
κυνός	cauis	Hund	hound
κώπη	capulum	Heft	haft

PRIMITIVE INITIAL P-SOUNDS BECOME F.

GREEK.	LATIN.	GERMAN.	ENGLISH.
πατήρ	pater	Vater (fater)	father
πέτ-ομαι	penna (petna)	Feder	feather
πλέω	pluit	flieszen	fleet
πλώω		Flotte	float

PRIMITIVE MEDIAL T BECOMES TH.

GREEK.	LATIN.	GERMAN.	ENGLISH.
φράτηρ	frater	Bruder (bruodar)	bro-ther
μήτηρ	mater	Mutter (muotar)	mo-ther
πατήρ	pater	Vater (fatar)	fa-ther

NOTE.—These three examples are given because they illustrate the phonetic law in a general way, though they do not all strictly belong to the same category. See also page 51.

These lists might be considerably extended, and the student will do well to search for other examples. It needs to be kept in mind that the object here is to give equivalents in form, as far as possible, though not in meaning; for the farther we go from the parent speech the more widely do the significations of words generally part asunder. The four words for "father" and "mother" have precisely the same meaning in the four languages above given, but the Greek φράτηρ is not the same in sense with the other words placed opposite. So "canis" and "Hund" mean the same thing, but the meaning of "hound" is more restricted. The words placed with πετ- and πλε- or πλο-, are all related both in form and signification, but the minor differences are important. It will be noticed that the English often bears a closer resemblance to the primitive Germanic than the modern German.

(2) The law, stated in its most general terms, is that the Indo-European aspirates appear as mediæ in the Germanic. We need to remember, then, that the primitive gh, dh, and bh correspond to the Greek χ, θ and φ, and to the Latin h, f and f. We thus get:

PRIMITIVE INITIAL GH BECOMES G.

GREEK.	LATIN.	GERMAN.	ENGLISH.
χόρτος	hortus	Garten	garden
χηνός	(h)anser	Gans	goose

INITIAL DH BECOMES D.

GREEK.	LATIN.	GERMAN.	ENGLISH.
θύρα	fores	Thüre, Thor	door
θυγατήρ		Tochter	daughter
θηρός	ferus	Tier	deer

INITIAL BH BECOMES B.

GREEK.	LATIN.	GERMAN.	ENGLISH.
φέρω	fero	ge(bären)	bear
φηγός	fagus	Buche	beech, buck (wheat)
φρακ-	farcio(frac-)	Burg	burg, bury

We saw above that the Greek word for "brother" is not derived from the same root with the Latin and Germanic, but from one entirely different, as is evident from the word ἀδελφός. We notice a similar omission in the Latin, where the place of the missing word for daughter has been taken by "filia." There are comparatively few words of the original Aryan that have representatives, or descendants, in all the branches into which it subsequently split.

But the facts do not, in all cases, accord with the law stated above. Some dialects have g only at the beginning of words or not at all ; in its stead they have a voiced guttural spirant. Some dialects again, especially the Low German, do not have a labial middle mute (b) in the interior of words, but supply its place with a sonant spirant, a sound lying between the German f and w, and which may be represented by bh. These spirants have not proceeded from mediæ; they maintain their original place. It is evident that our second law is not of universal application. It is probable that all the aspirates of the Indo-European first become spirant, and these afterward in part passed into mediæ, or middle mutes, and in part have persisted to the present time.

(3) The mediæ become tenues (the middle mutes become smooth).

INITIAL G BECOMES K.

GREEK.	LATIN.	GERMAN.	ENGLISH.
γένυς	gena	Kinn	chin
			cild (?)
γένος	genus	kind	kin
			kind

INITIAL D BECOMES T.

GREEK.	LATIN.	GERMAN.	ENGLISH.
δάκρυ	lacruma (dacruma)	Zähre	tear
δύο	duo	Zwei	two
δαμάω	domao	Zahm	tame

PRIMITIVE MEDIAL B BECOMES P.

GREEK.	LATIN.	GERMAN.	ENGLISH.
τύρβη	turba	(Dorp) Dorf	-thorpe -throp

And, perhaps,

| κάνναβις | cannabis | Hanf | hemp |

There is no example where this change occurs initially.

The syllable -thorp or -thorpe is found as an affix in many names of persons and places, as Ibthorpe, Althorpe, Wilstrop. In England these names occur chiefly in those portions where the Danes made permanent settlements. The metathesis of r is very common in the Indo-European languages, and is often found in words that have passed from Anglo-Saxon into English, as urnan - run, brid — bird, etc.

Owing to these shiftings a marked change passed over the vocalization of the Indo-European. The Germanic no longer, possesses aspirates; but the number of spirants, the only representative of which was s in the primitive tongue has considerably increased.

These three sets of consonant shiftings had no connection with each other, and were not contemporaneous. In fact, it can be shown that the transformation of media to tenuis is much more recent than the other two changes. Neither is there any connection of cause and effect between them. It cannot be said that the media shifted to tenuis because the aspirates became media in order to avoid the concurrence of certain sounds; that is, in order to prevent the coincidence of the old sound with a different new one; for, to say nothing of other causes, such a trend toward differentiation which should operate to prevent the coming together of certain sounds and verbal forms, is entirely foreign to the language. It has hitherto been impossible to assign any valid reasons for the shiftings we have just explained; and every theory that has been proposed is too fanciful to merit a place here.

But the laws that we set forth underlie an apparent exception. We find that the Indo-European k, t, and p are represented not only by h, th, and f, but also by g, d, and b. Besides the correspondence exhibited in (1) above, we find also the following:

GREEK.	LATIN.	GERMAN.	ENGLISH.
δείκνυμι	dico	zeigen	
κλυτός	(in)clytus	laut	loud
	capio	heben	heave

In the first series we have the Latin and Greek k-sound represented by the German g; in the second, the Latin and Greek t by the English d; and in the third, p by b. How shall these exceptions be accounted for?

A study of the laws of accentuation in the different languages furnishes an explanation. We shall have frequent occasion to show that the accent plays an important part in the fortunes of words. Now, the Indo-European accent and the Germanic are not the same; that is, the original accent was not persistent. The Germanic tongues now place the chief stress on the same syllable, both in radical and derivative words. In such words as *Häuser*, *häuslich* and *Häuslichkeit*, the accent remains on the word *Haus*, from which they are derived. So in English we say head, heady, headstrong, headstrongness, and even interest, interesting, interestingly and disinterestedness; for, though these words were not originally English, there is a constant tendency to naturalize loan-words by bringing them under its own laws of accent. As a rule, the first syllable of a word carries the accent. The case was otherwise in the Indo-European where it shifted from one syllable to another in the same word. A familiar illustration is furnished by the nominatives μήτηρ and ἄνδρες which become in the genitive μητρός and ἀνδρῶν. Any syllable may receive the accent. This mobility of the Indo-European accent continued into the Germanic period, and had an influence on the displacement of the smooth mutes. If it preceded one of these letters, or sounds, which may be represented thus —k, —t, —p, the tenuis was changed into a spirant; if it followed, the result was a middle mute (media). This law will be further exemplified on the following pages.

These laws are of great importance because they enable us to distinguish the words of pure Germanic stock from those of later introduction. Only words in which these consonantal shiftings have taken place are of native origin; but those in which gutturals correspond to gutturals, labials to labials, or dentals to dentals, are not originally related. The German *Kopf* cannot, therefore, be cognate with the Latin "caput," nor *Fuchs* with "fuscus." It is true *Kammer* and "chamber" are identical with the Latin "camera," but this is not a word of German origin, but simply borrowed from the Latin. In like manner *Dom* is the Germanized form of the Latin "domus."

By means of Verner's Law—as the law just given is called from the name of its discoverer--we are enabled to determine the place of the accent in Aryan words. In those cases where an Indo-European k or t or p corresponds to German sonant the accent must have followed these letters; where they are represented by a spirant it preceded them. Or, more fully: Indo-European k, t, or p are sometimes represented by h, th, or f, and sometimes by g, d, or b. How the accent determines which of the two it shall be may be seen by the following examples: The Latin pater, mater and frater all have the original medial t; but in German the words appear as *Vater*, *Mutter* and *Bruder*. We find, however, that the two former had in the pre-Teutonic period the accent on the final syllable, while the latter had it on the first.

The Greek ἐπ-τά represents the original accent. Here ἐπ- alone would, according to Grimm's Law, become sef, and we find, for example, capt-us appear as haft. But the exception above noted gives us the O. H. G. *sib-un*, a word that also has the Gothic consonants, while regularly we should get *sif-un*. The cases where h stands in place of the regular g are comparatively rare.

An article in the Eclectic Review for July, 1892, by Max Muller, reprinted from the Nineteenth Century, and entitled, "On the Enormous Antiquity of the East," incidentally discusses the effect of the shifting accent on certain English words.

THE GERMANIC AND ITS SUB-DIVISIONS.

These two processes, namely, the rotation of the consonants above given, and the shifting of the accent, achieved the independent existence of the primitive Germanic tongue. It still possessed considerable wealth in forms. The verb had a separate form for the passive voice and the noun one to be used in answering the questions, where?

whence ? wherewith ? The verb has also suffered considerable curtailment in its tenses. But the Germanic verb exhibits a mode of expressing time that is peculiar to itself; i. e., it did not exist in the earlier language. This is the so-called weak preterit, *klagte*, *legte*, and corresponds to what most English grammarians call the regular verb. In the structure of its sentences the primitive Teutonic used methods no longer in use in the German. To express cause or time the latter is obliged to employ a subordinate sentence; but the primitive Germanic, like the Greek and Latin, could do this by means of a noun and participle : *als der vater kam* was *faderi kumondi*. In like manner where the modern German employs *als* or *denn* to designate a comparison, the parent tongue could, like the Greek and Latin, make use of a case. *Niu saiwala mais ist fodeinai jah leik wastjom ?* Matt. vi. 25. Here "than food" and "than raiment" (garments), is expressed by nouns in the dative case.

The Germans and the primitive Germanic language first broke up into three grand divisions, each embracing three groups of tribes whose members were more closely related to those within than to those without. The first is called the Gothic, the second the Scandinavian. These two probably resemble each other more closely than either resembles the third group. They are usually called the East Germanic, and the third group the West Germanic. It is reasonable to suppose that the last named, though still constituting a homogeneous people, separated from the main s'ock some time before it split into two branches.

The first appearance of the ancient Goths on the stage of history is a brilliant episode in the national life of the Germans. In the plentitude of their native power they founded a monarchy on Roman territory. Not long, however, were they able to resist the seductive influences of Roman civilization. Rome yielded to the superior culture of Greece, though her all-conquering arms and invincible valor easily destroyed her political independence. So the Germans all along the line of contact were in their turn subdued by Roman arts and Roman letters. The language of the Goths fell into decay; though doubtless a considerable portion of its vocabulary passed into Italian, Spanish and Portuguese, where it is still preserved. The syntax of these languages likewise bears traces of Germanic influence. But no written memorials exist from which we may learn the language in which Gelimer sang the sorrows of captivity; we know next to nothing of the speech of the Gepidæ and the Bastarnæ; nor have the Ostro-Goths left us any written memorials of their existence. Of the Visi-Goths—the branch that once dwelt in the Balkan peninsula—we possess somewhat extended literary monuments in their own tongue. These are the oldest existing remnants of any Germanic language. They comprise fragments of a translation of the Bible made for the most part by Wulfila or Ulfilas, the first bishop of the Goths, about A. D. 350.

This translation, while to some extent under the influence of the Greek and Latin, from which it was made, furnishes a fair sample of the language of the Goths. In its sounds it does not differ materially from the primitive Teutonic type, and affords us in the main a true picture of the same. In richness of etymological forms, it has, however, suffered some losses, and is somewhat less primitive in certain regards than the West Germanic dialects that have come down to us from a much later period.

Speaking accurately, the extant remains of Gothic literature comprise the larger portion of the four Gospels, Paul's Letters to the Romans, Corinthians, Ephesians, Galatians, Philippians, Colossians, Thessalonians, to Timothy, Titus and Philemon. There are a few fragments of Ezra and Nehemiah, of a Commentary on the Gospel of John, some charters of the time of Theodoric the Great, and a few additional trifles. As an interval of several centuries lies between the Gothic as we know it and any other German dialect, it may interest the reader to compare a specimen with modern German. We accordingly subjoin a sample of each:

Atta unsar thu in himinam, veihnai namo thein; quimai
Vater unser du in Himmeln geweihet werde Name dein komme
thiudinassus theins; vairthai vilja theins, swe in himina, jah
Herrschaft dein werde wille dein sowie in Himmel, auch
ana airthai; hlaif unsarana thana sinteinan gif uns himma
auf Erden Brod unseres dies fortwahrende gieb uns diesen
daga, jah aflet uns thatei skulans sijaima svasve jah veis
Tag und erlasse uns das Schuldige wir seien sowie auch wir
afletam thaim skulam unsaraim; jah ni briggais uns in
erlassen diesen Schuldigen unseren und mcht bringest uns in
fraistubnyai, ak lausei uns of thamma ubilin; unte theina ist
Versuchung sondern lose uns ab diesem Uebel denn dein ist
thiudangardi jah mahts jah vulthus in aivins. Amen.
Herrscherhaus und Macht und Glauz in Ewigkeit. Amen.

" The remnants of the Gothic consist of about 3,000 native words; of which, however, a large majority are compounded out of a comparatively small number of simpler words. Some of the simpler words are not preserved ; but their existence in the time of Ulfilas or previously is certified by their compounds. Unfortunately the 3,000 and odd words are but a fraction of the whole Gothic vocabulary. Of the language of native song and saga, of war and sport, of political, social, and family life, of the older national religion, of commerce, agriculture, and other arts; and of the terminology of natural objects, celestial and terrestrial, animal, vegetable, and mineral; either very scanty specimens or none at all are preserved. This loss is the more to be regretted because Ulfilas shows, in the treatment of alien subjects and events, not only ease and elegance, but sometimes an exuberance and sometimes a precision and refinement of expression that even surpass his model." Douse, An Introduction to the Gothic of Ulfilas. London, 1886.

Only a small fragment of the Goths preserved a separate existence until comparatively recent times. These dwelt in the Crimea where they were visited in the sixteenth century by a Belgian physician named Busbecq, who has left some record of their language, and a list of words which he heard, in Constantinople.

We do not have the Scandinavian or Norse in its unified form, but only in the various languages into which it subsequently broke up ; from these, however, it is possible to construct the original. It embraces the Swedish, the Norwegian, the Danish and the Icelandic. There are no manuscripts in these languages of earlier date than the twelfth century. Neither have we access to the third and, for us, most important branch of the Germanic languages in its primitive unity. We have no means of knowing when the Visi-Goths separated from their brethren, nor where this separation took place. Neither is it possible to ascertain the extent of territory covered by the various languages during the first centuries of our era before the time when the literary monuments begin. In that proto-historic period the Germanic tribes were a mass that was almost constantly in motion.

Ancient tribes and tribal names disappear; new confederacies and new names appear on the pages of history. It is not until the sixth century, or about the time when the conquest of Britain was achieved, that the shifting masses become to some extent stationary. At this period the West Germanic tribes embraced the following sub-divisions as nearly as can now be made out: The Lombards, the Bavarians, the Alemanians, the Burgundians, the Franks, the Hessians, the Thuringians, the Angles, the Saxons, the Jutes, and the Frisians. The German tongue anciently extended over a larger territory than at present. It included Great Britain about as far north as the river Clyde, while in the west and south of the European continent it was bounded by the Atlantic ocean and the Pyrenees. Its southern limit was the summit of the Alps. It must be remembered, however, that the German occupation of much of this territory was not exclusive. It was still settled by other nationalities, chiefly Kelts, over whom they had gained the supremacy by conquest. On the other hand its eastern boundary was considerably farther westward than it now is. Here the Elbe was the limit, and the country lying east of this river was settled by Slavs.

If we had documents written in the dialects of the various tribes above named, dating from the fourth or fifth century, they would, in all probability, exhibit but slight divergencies from each other and from the Gothic.

The main difference between the Gothic and the Scandinavian on the one hand, and the West Germanic on the other, lies in the inflection of the verb. In the former the second person of the singular number of the preterit of the strong verb ends in t. For example, *namt* (*du nahmst*), *gaft* (*du gabst*)=(thou gavest). In the West Germanic tongues the equivalent forms end in i, as *nâmi*, *gâbi*.

But at the period from which we possess MSS. written in the West Germanic, or at least a number of verbal forms, the various branches of the original tongue diverge considerably from each other, and likewise from the Gothic; and these divergencies kept getting wider. The Germanic language of Britain has gone farthest from the primitive type. This is the speech of the Angles, Saxons and Jutes, generally known as the Anglo-Saxon, but which is also called " English " by those who insist that the language of England has remained substantially unchanged since the conquest of Hengist and Horsa. This difference was caused partly by the insular position of Britain and partly by the subsequent fate of its inhabitants. The Norman conquest tinged the vocabulary of the natives with a considerable admixture of Romanic words; besides which the frequent irruptions of the Danes, and their subsequent temporary occupation of the island, were doubtless not without their effect on the language.

The English, however, does not further concern us here; nor does the Frisian, a language, or rather a dialect, still spoken on the islands and along the coast of the North Sea. It differs considerably from the other Germanic dialects of the continent. There remain, therefore, for our further consideration : the Lombards, the Bavarians, the Alemanians, the Burgundians, the Franks, the

Hessians, the Thuringians, and those of the Saxons and Angles who remained behind when their fellow-tribesmen crossed over into Britain. The history of the German language naturally falls into three great epochs or periods, an older, a middle, and a modern.

THE OLD HIGH GERMAN PERIOD.

This period closes about the year 1100; but the reader should remember that in a matter so largely subject to the laws of growth and decay as language, to assign definite dates that are of much value, is impossible. The beginning of this period is not coincident with any particular year. We can hardly say more than that it may be put about the time when credible history begins, and is in the main coeval with the epoch from which the earliest contemporary literary and historical documents have come down to us. These documents are, however, by no means entitled to the epithet "literary," in the proper sense of that term; often they do not even consist of connected discourse. The oldest German poetry, like that of all other nations, had its life in oral tradition; and, if now and then, a fragment was written down, it would have been little short of a miracle if it had survived the hostility of the clergy to the national songs and sagas and the reminiscences of heathendom which they perpetuated. The language of science and learning, of public intercourse, of law, was the Latin, and continued to be for several centuries longer. It is true, Charles the Great (Charlemagne) made earnest efforts to place his mother-tongue in honor. He gave German names to the months, caused a German Grammar to be compiled, and took great pains to collect from German minstrels the ancient heroic songs of his countrymen. But his son Lewis, who was wholly under the influence of the priests, was zealous in undoing the work of his father. The Latin has, however, preserved a quantity of material that is valuable for the history of the German language; this is especially true of the records and title-deeds pertaining to persons and places within the German territory. These documents contain a large number of German words; chiefly proper names, it is true, furnished with Latin terminations. By a judicious use of this material we are enabled to some extent to recover the native pronunciation and the inflection of the substantive, and to get some idea of German word-formation. But its greatest value is historical because of the dates and names of places given. Many of the words in these Latin parchments are accompanied with glosses, that is, translations of single Latin words for pedagogical purposes. These are either written over the words in the text which they are designed to elucidate, where they are called interlinear glosses, or are brought together into little lexicons or glossaries. With the age of Charles the Great connected and continuous records begin. They consist chiefly of translations of biblical and ecclesiastical works, a number of Christian hymns, and some meager remnants of popular poetry. This literature, if we choose to call it by so dignified a name, is by no means equally distributed among the various Germanic tribes. The Angles have no share at all in it, and of their dialect only a few words of uncertain authenticity now remain; neither have the Hessians, nor the Thuringians, nor the Lombards, nor the Burgundians. The Saxon portion is small; still less that of the Franks along the lower Rhine. The largest portion falls to the rest of the Franks, the Bavarians, and Alemanians, or territorially to the country along the Rhine from Constance to the Moselle, and about the head-waters of the Danube. This is the section of Germany in which Christianity first gained a firm foot-hold.

There is a special reason for the absence of records in the language of the Lombards and the Burgundians. At the beginning of the period that here concerns us the territory embraced by the Germanic tongues had been considerably curtailed. The fate that overtook the Goths on Roman soil was shared by the Burgundians, the Lombards and the Western Franks; their language was displaced by the Latin and its descendants. Still, these languages did not remain free from Teutonic influence, least of all, the French. Many French military terms are derived from the German, and also words relating to feudalism and law. The French word *la guerre* is itself of Germanic origin, and related to *wirren*, the O. H. G. being *werra*. Strangely enough in this case the English word "war" clearly bears the family traits, while the modern German has displaced it by *Krieg*, a vocable of obscure ancestry. The gender of an entire class of French words— those ending in eur, such as "la fureur," "la couleur"— that would according to the rules of the language to which they belong be masculine, has been changed to feminine by the influence of the German.

With these facts before us, we are now able to draw the southern and western boundary of the German language. The line begins on the shores of the North Sea near the straits of Dover between Gravelines and Dunkirk, runs southward almost to the river Lys, then eastward between Maestricht and Liege as far as the river Meüse, thence southeastward toward Malmedy, thence southward toward Longwy, but leaving both these towns on the French side. From here it passes southward as far as Pfalzburg (Phalsbourg), thence southward, west of Colmar, to the point where the little river Lützel crosses the boundary between the German empire and Switzerland. From here it runs eastward to the river Birs, then follows the western boundary of the Swiss canton of Solothurn (Soleure) in a direct line to Lake Biel (Bienne) and the foot of Lake Neuchâtel, thence it passes across Lake Murten (Morat) and the town of the same name, through Freiburg, thence almost directly south toward the Matterhorn, crossing the Rhone at Siders (Sierre). From the Matterhorn its course is eastward by Monte Rosa, then northeastward as far as the St. Gotthard, whence it follows the northern boundary of the Grisons, about as far as the town of Tamins, thence eastward past the city of Chur (Coire) in the direction of Klagenfurt in Austria. It will thus be seen that the present eastern boundary of France is very nearly the line that for many centuries separated the French from the German language.

The internal changes that took place in the language during this period were chiefly confined to the consonants. Here, too, a process of shifting took place, it being the second of a similar character. This is like the first in the fact that the transitions took place independently of each other, and at different times. In the case of the second shifting we are able to follow its course and observe its results almost step by step by means of contemporary documents still in existence. The two shifts, however, differ in so far that the second affected a much smaller number of consonants than the first.

The different parts of the territory occupied by the German, participated in the second shift in a much more unequal degree than the first. Its influence was earliest felt and is the most marked in the south. The farther we come north the feebler is the wave-beat of the movement. The extreme north exhibits but faint traces of it. By this fact we are enabled to distinguish the various dialects, each being marked by the distance its characteristic consonants have moved away from their original value.

The earliest and most complete shifting was that made by the smooth mutes (tenues) k, t, and p. This began and went farthest with the Germanic t. But it is necessary to make a distinction between initial t on the one hand, and medial or internal, and final t on the other. The former did not pass into a simple sound, but into a compound of tenuis and spirant, a so-called affricative. In old documents this is usually indicated by z which was pronounced tz or ts. The Low German *teihn* became *zehn* in High German. Here the English has preserved the original sound in the word ten. Medial and final t was changed into a spirant. But while the Indo-European t was transformed into the German th (See ante, p 33), the new spirant of the second shift had passed into a sound which the MSS. also generally indicate by z. Its pronunciation probably bore a close resemblance to the German s, or rather ss, with which it subsequently became identical It is by this change of t to z, which took place about the year 600, that a most important dialectic difference was marked, namely, that between Low German and High German, between the north and south of Germany. In the Low German it is retained; in the High German it has been superseded by the other sound. Where "that" or "dat" was regularly used in the territory of the former; where *dasz*, that of the latter. The philologist Schleicher was in the habit of designating the one class as "dat-languages," and the latter as "dasz-languages;" for it must not be forgotten that there were, as there still are, many other minor divergencies between them. Generally speaking, the consonants of the Low German underwent few changes, and we shall often have occasion in the future to employ words from its vocabulary as representatives of the General Germanic.

The fate of k like that of t depends upon its position in a word. When initial or final it was aspirated throughout the entire High German territory to ch; for the English "to speak" we get the High German *sprechen*, Low German *sprecken*. The L. G. *ik*, A.-S. "ic," corresponds to the H. G. *ich*. Only in one dialect of the L. G., the West Franconian, it becomes ch when final. Initial k generally persists over the whole region, except in certain districts belonging to the Bavarian and Alemanian where it has given place to kch and ch.

P both initial and medial becomes f whenever k changes to ch: Low German, *schap*, *slapen*, Eng. "sheep," "sleep," are equivalent to H. G. *schaf*, *schlafen*. When initial, it becomes *pf* in the Alemanian, Bavarian and part of the Franconian. The linguistic province of the latter lies along the river Main and south of its eastern portion. The dividing line between the two sections, the northern p and the southern pf, runs between Bruchsal and Heidelberg, so far as it lies in Baden. In respect to the dialects of middle Germany, which we shall consider more at length further on, it may be here remarked incidentally, that pf is likewise one of the characteristics of the Thuringian, the Upper Saxon and the Silesian.

Of spirants the hard h and f remain unchanged; but th passed into d everywhere, even in the Low German. For example, brother is equivalent to *Bruder*, in which case the English has preserved a close resemblance to the Gothic bróthar. The sonant labial mute was turned into an explosive (the same sound it already had as an initial letter) in the Alemanian, the Bavarian and some of the other High German dialects. Here it was the same sound that had already taken its place initially. The transformation of this labial mute is of prime importance for a general characterization of the Germanic dialects. Throughout the territory occupied by the Low German, the difference between b and p was the same as in the Romanic languages; the vocal chords were at rest while the sound represented by p was produced, but in the case of b they were in a state of vibration and a faint *m* was heard in connection with it. In Central Germany the attendant sound was gradually lost; as a result, a distinction ceased to be made between p and b. The habit is still almost universal among the illiterate, and even the educated often unwittingly fall into it. But still farther south the distinction is again observed; in the Alemanian and

Bavarian the b is pronounced with less and the p with greater force. This state of things prevailed as early as the O. H. G. period. The effect of this phonetic change was to displace b as the representative of the weaker labial mute on High German territory, though it remained on Low, as it no longer represented the Romanic b; but p was used in its stead. For example, the N. H. G. *Buch* and the Eng. " book " have the same initial, but its O. H. G. equivalent is *puoh*. The late Latin " bedellus " still survives in our " beadle," but its O. H. G. representative is *petil*. N. H. G. *Pedell*. Between the Bavarian and the Alemanian there was this further difference that the latter generally retained initial b while the former turned it into p here also.

The fate of the soft guttural mute (g) was similar to that just described, in so far as it was developed out of the spirant. In the districts possessed by the Low German, the distinction between the Romanic g and k was preserved, but in Middle Germany the former lost its sonancy and then became virtually identical with k. In the Bavarian, Alemanian and the South Franconian there is some difference in the energy with which the two letters are uttered. In the oldest stage of the two former this middle mute is sometimes written g and sometimes k. This indicates that these letters were intended to represent a sound which partook of the nature of both. In the High German the d loses its sonancy under all circumstances and is replaced by t. The Gothic *dags* and English " day " is *tac* and *tag* in O. H. G.

These differences prevail during the entire further development of the language represented by the three stages pointed out above. In view of these divisions it is customary to speak of Old, Middle and New Low German, and of Old, Middle and New High German.

With these facts before us we are now prepared to see how the principle of consonantal mutation or shifting appears when applied to individual words. This plan is preferable to the mere presentation of literal equivalents. It may be well to call attention again to an important fact in the history of words, namely, that widely diverse meanings are often developed from the same radical syllable.

Indo-European k corresponds to Greek or Latin k or c, Germanic h. Sanskrit kalamas; Greek καλάμη; Latin calamus; English halm or haulm.

Indo-European t corresponds to Latin t, Low German th, High German d. Sanskrit tarsh; Latin torreo; Gothic thaursjan; English thirst; High German Durst.

Indo-European p corresponds to Greek or Latin p, Germanic f. Sanskrit padas; Greek Latin πεδ-, ped, pod-; Gothic fôtus; English foot; High German Fusz.

Indo-European gh corresponds to Greek Latin g, Germanic g. The primitive form would probably be ghans, but Sanskrit hansas; Greek Latin χήν, (h)anser; A.-S. gôs; English goose, gander; High German *Gans*.

Indo-European dh corresponds to Greek θ, Latin f, Low German d, High German t. Hypothetical dhur; Greek θύρα; Latin fores; Gothic daur; English door from A.-S. duru; O. H. G. *tor*.

Indo-European bh corresponds to Greek φ, Latin f, Low German b, High German b or p. Sanskrit bhag; Greek φηγός; Latin fagus; Gothic bôka; English book, buckwheat and beech; A.-S. bôc; O. H. G. buoh and puoh; N. H. G. Buche and Buch. It should, however, be mentioned that the original identity of these two words in Teutonic is not quite certain.

Indo-European g corresponds to Germanic k or ch. Sanskrit gaus, where the Greek and Latin are βοῦς and bos; Gothic kôs (hypothetical); English cow from A.-S. cû; O. H. G. chuo; N. H. G. Kuh.

Indo-European d corresponds to Greek-Latin δ and d, Germanic t, N. H. G. z. Sanskrit daçan; Greek-Latin δίκω, decem; Gothic taihun; English ten, from A.-S. tyn; N. H. G. *zehn*.

Indo-European b corresponds to Latin p, Germanic p, N. H. G. p or pf. Latin pondo; Gothic pund and English pound; N. H. G. Pfund; but Gothic slêps, English sleep; O. H. G. slâfan and slâf; from which it will be seen that the mutation of a consonant at the end of a syllable is sometimes different from that at the beginning.

Very few words can be found that have congeners in a majority of the languages of the Indo-European stock. This will explain the gaps in our series above. In a few instances the phonetic laws here set forth are subject to slight modifications. These I have not thought necessary to exhibit because my object is to show general principles rather than minute facts. A mute does not generally undergo the same transformation at the beginning, the middle and end of a word.

When philologists speak of the Indo-European—the *Ursprache*—as having split up into the various branches still represented in different languages of Europe and Asia, they do not mean that this took place simultaneously. Neither did the General Germanic break into several linguistic fragments. That phonetic changes always take place slowly is abundantly proved by the testimony of those that have taken place within historic times. The oldest records of the Sanskrit probably do not go further back than the sixteenth century B. C. At this period it had already diverged considerably from the primitive stage. Where the people who spoke this language dwelt we do not know. Very likely they were wanderers with no fixed place of abode. Of the Greek we have no remains earlier than the eleventh or twelfth century B. C., while those of the Italic dialects

A History of the German Language 53

are several centuries younger. The history of both Greeks and Italians before these dates rests on a very insecure foundation. Of the Germanic tongues, as we have seen, there are but faint traces earlier than the fourth century after Christ. But we have occasional notices of German tribes in the fourth century B. C. These, too, appear now at one place, now at another, in both Europe and Asia. The various consonantal shifts that play so important a part in the history of the Aryan languages must be regarded as having taken place from the parent speech, and not from any of its branches. Yet it is possible and even probable that this primitive speech broke up into two or more different parts, one or more of which were again further sub-divided. Nor do we know the causes of this differentiation. They were probably climatic and topographical—the result of slight changes in the vocal organs of the different people. We do not know when the Primitive German languages shifted from the Aryan, but it was at a prehistoric period; for we find the process almost complete in the earliest Gothic known to us. The bifurcation of the Primitive Germanic into High and Low German was much later, and took place in historic times. It seems to have been in progress during the period lying between the sixth and the tenth centuries after Christ. It began, as we have seen, in South Germany and moved northward until its energy had gradually spent itself before it reached the region of the lower Rhine. It could be proven by the testimony of the German language, if no other were forthcoming, that those who spoke it were originally a homogeneous mass when they began their independent career which first separated into two main divisions. The minor divergences that still exist partake more or less of the chief characteristics of one or the other of these divisions.

The lines which bound the various dialects have changed but little from the earliest times except that the L. G. has been gradually losing ground before the encroachments of the H. G. We shall, therefore, not go far wrong if we supply the missing links in the older boundaries by the linguistic facts gathered from more recent observations. The dividing line between Low and High German passes nearly east and west. Beginning on the Meuse at a point midway between Liege and Mæstricht it passes down the Meuse as far as Roermonde (Ruremond) and from here eastward past Düesseldorf to Elberfeld. Here it turns south and runs parallel with the Rhine almost to the little river Sieg. Bending thence to the northeast it passes in an almost direct course past Minden, and thence to Magdeburg on the Elbe. This line marked off the territory of the O. L. G. which embraced the Saxons and a portion of the Franks. Their two dialects are called the Old Saxon and the Low Franconian.

The boundary between the Franconian and the Upper German in the valley of the Rhine is formed by the forest of Hagenau in Northern Alsace and the lower course of the Murg, a small river that flows into the Rhine from the southeast, a short distance from Carlsruhe. Following the Murg a little way it turns nearly east a little south of the city of Calw in Würtemberg, crossing the river Nagold it runs northeast as far as the Neckar, near Besigheim, thence directly east to Ellwangen. Here it turns northeast again to Feuchtwangen, then southeast to Wassertrued, whence it runs off in the direction of the Fichtel mountains.

The dividing line between the Alemanian and Bavarian is formed in the main by the rivers Woernitz and Lech, the one flowing southward, the other northward into the Danube, at no great distance from the city of Augsburg, though the Alemanian is also spoken on the right bank of the Lech in its upper course.

The differences between the dialects were in earlier times much less marked than at present. Taking them as a whole and comparing them with the Gothic on the one hand and the German as written to-day on the other, they are found to be more closely akin to the former than to the latter or N. H. G. Compared with this the dissimilarity is greatest in the form of the individual words. A majority of these now end in a monotonous *e*, but in the olden time almost any of the long or short vowels might terminate a word. The sensuous impression produced by the older language with its plenitude of sonorous vowels is very different from the modern.

There is one other peculiarity to which it is proper to call attention. A number of words that now begin with l were in the O. H. G. preceded by an h. The modern *Ludwig* (Lewis, Louis), for instance, was *Hludwig*. This combination of consonants is not found in the Romanic tongues, and when those whose native language was French tried to reproduce it they employed chl. For this reason Chlodwig is no other than *Ludwig*; Chlotar, than *Lothar*.

In the course of the tenth and eleventh centuries the German language gradually assumes a different character. The vowels of the final syllable that had been long, began to be shortened, while the weakening of the short vowels to *e* becomes more and more general. This movement does not begin over the whole German territory at the same time, and advances more rapidly in some parts than in others. The South is, generally speaking, more conservative than the North. The transformation is about completed by the middle of the twelfth century. By this time a leading feature of the O. H. G. has accordingly been obliterated, and the period of the M. H. G. and the M. L. G. begins. But here, too, it is impossible to assign definite dates to what was a continuous organic development. The Upper German, for example, conserved some of its vowels in certain positions until far into the middle period.

The surviving literary monuments of the O. H. G. period are the following, though they do not all belong to O. H. G. dialects. The oldest and most important is the translation of the Bible by Ulfilas, which has already been spoken of. There is a tradition that he included the whole of the Old and New Testament in his work except the Book of Kings, and that he omitted this because he feared lest its narration of military achievements might tend to excite the martial spirit of his countrymen, to which they were, in his judgment, already too prone.

The history of the only existing codex of Ulfilas is sufficiently remarkable to merit a brief notice here. It is one of the many instances where our knowledge of important facts of antiquity is wholly dependent upon the existence of a single record, often imperfect, as in this case. Nothing was known of this codex until the sixteenth century when it was discovered in the Abbey of Werden, a town not far from Duesseldorf in Prussia. It came into the possession of the emperor Rudolf II. In Prague; and when this city was taken by the Swedes in 1648, it was removed to Stockholm. Not long afterward it was transferred to Holland, but was again acquired by a Swede, count de la Gardie, who had it bound in silver, and subsequently presented it to the library of the University of Upsala, where it now is. The letters with which the MSS. is written are chiefly of silver, but partly of gold on purple colored parchment, whence it is called the codex argenteus. It originally consisted of 330 leaves; but all except 177 have been lost. A few fragments of the same translation are in other European libraries.

All the extant literature of the O. H. G. consists of translations and is consequently of little value except for the language. A nearly complete list is here given. We name first, The Rule of St. Benedict, translated about 780 by a monk of St. Gall, and Tatian's Harmony of the Gospels made about a century later. A very important document, both linguistically and historically, are the reciprocal oaths of the kings and people, often called the Strasburg oaths. In the year 842 the kingdom of the Franks was divided between Lewis the German, who received Austrasia (Germany), and Charles the Bald, who received Neustria (France). The latter took an oath in French, the former in German. The old and the modern German are as follows:

In godes minna ind in thes Christianes folches ind unser bedhero·
Aus Liebe zu Gott und zu des Christlichen Volkes und unser beider

ge(h)altnissi fon, thesemo daze frammordes so fram so mir got
Erhaltung von diesem Tage fortan so weit als mir Gott

gewisci indi mahd furgibit, so haldih tesan (thesan) minan bruodher,
Wissen und Macht gibt so halte ich diesen meinen Bruder

soso man mit rehtu sinan bruodher scal, in thiu thaz er mig
sowie man mit Recht seinen Bruder soll, in dem dasz er mir

so sama duo ; indi mit Ludheren in nohheiniu thing. ne gegango,
ebenso thue; und mit Lothar in kein Ding nicht gehe ich,
the minau willon imo ce scadhen werdhen.
das meines Willens ihm zu Schaden werde.

This fragment illustrates some of the phonetic changes that have already been discussed.

A translation and elucidation of the Psalms by Notker Labeo, of the end of the tenth century.

A translation with commentary of the Song of Solomon by Williram, a monk of Ebersberg, made in the eleventh century.

The oldest German poetry extant consists of fragments of the Song of Hildebrand. It is composed in Low German mixed with High German. Its form is alliterative verse, and commemorates the combat of one Hildebrand with his son Hadubrand. It seems to have been committed to writing near the beginning of the ninth century, but it is evidently a reminiscence of an earlier age.

Of uncertain date, but probably belonging to the beginning of the ninth century, is another Harmony of the Gospels in the Old Saxon, known as the Heliand. This also is in alliterative form and in the opinion of Grimm represents the dialect spoken in the district lying between Münster, Essen and Cleves. A specimen is given below chiefly for the purpose of exhibiting the form of versification in general use among the ancient Germans:

Tho ward thar so managumu manne
    mod after Kriste
gihuorben, hugiskefti, sidor sie is
    helagon werk
selbon gisahon, huand eo er sulic ni ward
wundar on weroldi. Than was eft thes
    werodes so filu,
so modstarke man, ni weldun the maht godes
antkennien kudliko, ac sie wid is craft mikil
wunnun mid iro wordun ; Warun im waltendes
lera so leda.
5

The alliteration is not only plainly marked in the above brief extract, but might easily be retained in an English translation. In each line there are three or more principal words having the same initial sound. We may cite current words that have but slightly or not all varied from the meaning they had more than a thousand years ago: Many, man, mood, holy, work, self, saw, so, like, were, wonder, world, and numerous others.

Ekkehard, a monk of St. Gall, who died in 973, when a young man composed a poem called "Waltharius," patterned after Vergil and Prudentius. It commemorates the flight of Walter of Aquitaine and his beloved Hildegunde. Though written in Latin it is valuable for its reminiscences of German heroic poetry.

To the O. H. G. belongs the so-called Wessobrunn Prayer, the distinctive epithet of which is due to the fact that the MS. was discovered in the monastery of Wessobrunn (Weiszenbrunn) in Bavaria. Though Christian in sentiment its form is distinctly pagan, and it is the first known attempt to unite the new and the old religion in this way. Similar in poetic form, that is, alliterative, equally fragmentary and belonging to about the same epoch— about A. D. 900—is another poem called Muspilli. This, though a Christian composition, is pervaded with mythological reminiscences. There is some reason to believe that it was composed by King Lewis the German. The only secular production proper belonging to this period is a fragment of a description of the earth, commonly known as Merigarto (see-girt garden) of the eleventh century. When complete this poem seems to have been very long. The extant portion treats chiefly of the earth and certain miraculous fountains.

Krist, a poem composed by a monk named Otfried, completed about 868, is the first example in German of the use of rhyme. It embraces five books or cantos and owes its form probably to early Latin hymns. The author seems to have been an Alsatian or a Swabian, and this work is probably the first attempt of a German to construct an artificial epic. There exists also a Song of King Lewis (III.), the pæan of victory over the Normans in 881. Its probable author was one Hucbald, who died in 930, and who was during his lifetime a favorite of Charles the Bald and his son Lewis

The above enumeration includes everything in the form of connected discourse, except a few fragments belonging to the O. H. G. period. Though generally included in histories of German literature all this matter belongs rather to a history of the German language, because its literary value is slight, and its linguistic value inestimable. The extant remains of the Anglo-Saxon are more extensive than that of any other Germanic dialect, and the language differs little from the Old Saxon. But as it existed for the most part separate from the rest, it may be left out of account here. It is, however, true of both the continental and the insular Teutonic that it was committed to writing under the impulse of Christianity. For the former, the inspiration proceeded primarily from two literary centers, the school at Fulda in Germany, and St. Gall in Switzerland. The latter monastery was founded about 600, the former nearly 150 years later.

THE MIDDLE HIGH GERMAN PERIOD.

The middle period is usually designated as the Middle High German from the dialects that played the most important part during this time. The picture which the provinces occupied by the German language present during this period, is much more varied than before. The causes that brought about this greater activity are various. In the first place those districts which hitherto have furnished us few linguistic monuments, or had taken no part at all in the literary movements of the times, now come under observation. This is true of the Low German territory, and of the northern portions of the High German, Franconian from Mainz to Cologne, the Hessian and the Thuringian. ' The latter dialects, spoken between the Main and the Low German border, are now called Middle German At the same time the whole area embraced by the German language was a good deal enlarged. In proportion as the Slavic power was forced back by German valor and the conquered land occupied by German settlers their language gained a firm footing east of the Elbe. Saxony and Silesia and, in part, Bohemia are won for the Teutonic tongue, so that in the fourteenth and fifteenth centuries German literature was cultivated to a considerable extent in the latter country. Brandenburg, Mecklenburg, Pomerania and Prussia were likewise germanized.

The ancient kingdom of Prussia had, however, never been, properly speaking, Slavic territory, but was inhabited by German tribes from the earliest times, though it was not subdued and Christianized until the thirteenth century, the two processes going hand in hand. At this time the German outposts toward the east were pushed forward as far as the Niemen. In the southeast the German language also greatly extended its boundaries at the expense of the Magyar, and planted a number of linguistic oases in this region.

The newly acquired lands, nevertheless, did not form a continuous and homogenous whole, a statement that is especially true of the north. In some of the settlements the Low German was the spoken language; in others the High German. But the latter bears traces of the Middle German. Saxony and Silesia are now to be regarded as belonging to Central Germany, and likewise the lands of the Teutonic Knights. The 'Marches, or Viceroyalties, and the coast region, on the other hand, were colonized by Low German immigrants.

But the German language gains during this period not only in extent of territory, but likewise in what may be called intensity. Until now its sway was not fully acknowledged in its own home; in several departments the language used was exclusively Latin. Hitherto prose writings that were not translations were few and of limited extent. In the M. H. G. period this condition of things is changed. German pulpit oratory receives a great impetus through the zealous labors of the Mystics, particularly from about the middle of the thirteenth century. The language of jurisprudence, too, begins to put on a German garb. About 1230 a famous book of laws known as the *Sachsenspiegel* was published. This Saxons' Looking-glass is a compilation of observances and customs to which immemorial usage had given the sanction of laws. It was first written in Latin, a fact that is significant of this transition period, and afterward translated into German by the compiler, a nobleman named Eike or Eko of Repgow. City archives now begin to be kept in German. In Switzerland those dating from the seventh and eighth decades of the thirteenth century are quite numerous. Their frequency in Germany proper is nearly half a century later. It should be noted that the writings of this period were called into existence by the needs of practical life, and belong in no sense to literature. Nevertheless, literary prose is not wholly lacking for there are beginnings of written history both in this form and in verse. We may even speak of works of a scientific character, if we include under this head the philosophical and theosophical treatises of the Mystics that were written in the vernacular. In the main, however, the language of scientific investigation and discussion is still the Latin. The more general cultivation and the larger use of the German during these periods are not the outgrowth of a conscious or unconscious national impulse; they are rather the result of slackening interest in the monasterial education of the times,—the effect of a sort of torpidity that gradually creeps over the civil life of the community.

It were a mistake to suppose that this more extensive use of the German language is a matter of small import to its inner life. When any member of the human body is drawn into new and unaccustomed activity its muscles and sinews are called into requisition to an extent not before experienced There is growth and development where there was little or none before. So, too, language grows with extended usage; every new task assigned to it exercises an influence upon its words and upon the structure and arrangement of its sentences. The more numerous and manifold the written materials belonging to the periods under consideration become, the more clear and distinct do the features of the various dialects stand out, and the more definitely are we able to trace the boundary lines between them.

The dividing line between the Middle and Low German dialects did not remain permanently the same during the period under discussion; the latter retreated slowly before the former. This is true more especially of the territory between the Harz mountains and the river Saale. In 1300 the east and west boundary line was not far from the 50th parallel of north latitude, passing the Saale above Merseburg; but two hundred years later it was, as it is to-day, a good deal farther north, and crossed the Saale below the mouth of the Bode, not far from its confluence with the Elbe. The entire Mansfeld district, and particularly Halle, has undergone a change in its folk-speech. The linguistic character of the Middle German, as might be inferred from its geographical position, make it a bond of union no less than a stage of transition between the Upper and Lower German. The consonants have not in all cases shared in the High German rotation of mutes, while the vowels have remained substantially as in the Upper German. In a large number of syllables long vowels in the Low German correspond to diphthongs in the Upper German, though less in the Lower Franconian than elsewhere. We thus get the following scheme:

M. H. G.	M. L. G.	ENG.
stein	stên	stone
weisz	wêt	wot
zwei	twê	two
boum	bôm	beam
ouch	ôk	
stoup	stôf	
brief	brêf	brief
fiel	fêl	fell
heisz	hêt	hight
gout	gôd	good
huon	hôn	
truoc	drôg	

In all cases the exceptions are confined to the border territory. The Middle German exhibits the Upper German sounds in both vowels and consonants. It is not until pretty well along in our period that a tendency becomes manifest to simplify certain double sounds, as, for instance, where the Upper German has *brîf, huon*, pronounced almost like two syllables, we find in the Middle German such forms as *brêf, Hun*, etc.

We have some contemporary documents intended to describe the salient characteristics of the different dialects. One of these is in poetic form, written about 1300 by a schoolmaster of Bamberg. But such descriptions are of little value, even when an honest attempt is made to represent the living sounds. Speaking generally, and applying the remark to other languages as well as German, it may be said that the number of signs in common use is almost always and everywhere inadequate to represent the sounds in actual use. A single sound is sometimes indicated by two or more characters, examples of which are particularly abundant in English, while sometimes the same character is pronounced in two or more different ways, as may be seen in the case of our letter a. Still it must be said that the English is more anomalous than any other language, but it exhibits, though in excessive degree, a common tendency. The result is that we have a greater conformity in written characters than is warranted by the underlying phonetic facts.

We are led to conclude that there must have existed a clearly recognized difference between the living speech inherited by every individual and the language of our written memorials. It would seem that there grew up gradually a written language apart from the various dialects in current use, in part as a medium of literary intercourse, and in part as the fashionable speech of the upper classes. We even read of three such written languages, a M. H. G. which is regarded as the language of court circles, a M. G. and a L. G. The view that postulates the existence of a L. G. or M. G. written tongue is undoubtedly erroneous, and it is very questionable whether there was a M. H. G. The Switzer Ulrich of Zazichoven; the Swabian Hartmann of Aue; the Alastian Godfrey of Strasburg; the Franconian Wolfram of Eschenbach, all of whom flourished about the year 1200, exhibit divergencies enough in their vocabulary to preclude the possibility of a recognized unity of speech. But be this as it may, many facts come to our notice indicative of the general tendency that the German mind is in process of preparation for such a language; a mingling of dialects becomes evident, and the attempt is made by one writer here and another there to use a dialect that is foreign to him, while the language of certain districts evidently preponderates over that of others. The more actively the various sections of Germany interest themselves in fostering poetry, the more frequent literary intercourse becomes, the more attention is given to the multiplication of manuscripts, the oftener it happens that the native tongue of the copyist is different from that of his copy. As a result the MS. he produces will be a mixture of different dialects. The resulting text may in turn be used by a copyist from another part of Germany, which will make his work a mixture of a still greater number of elements. Not only are poems transported from place to place, but poets also lead a sort of nomadic life. We are informed that Wolfram of Eschenbach spent some time in Thuringia; his writings embody peculiarities that are foreign to his native Upper Franconian. The fairest flowers of German mediæval poetry blossomed on H. G. soil. The political supremacy and the literary centers that attract rising talent from all parts of the land are on H. G. territory. We accordingly find several poets who, though natives of L. G. districts, nevertheless aspire to the use of H. G. or M. G. speech. The preponderance of the H. G. is also shown by its encroachment upon L. G. territory—a fact of which we have before spoken. Occasional records in L. G. that exhibit a style of expression somewhat above the mere local folk-speech betray a leaning toward the M. G. Alongside of these main lines of development growing out of the circumstances of the times, certain preferences for this and that dialect manifest themselves that are merely a passing fashion. It was, for example, good form at certain periods during the 13th century, in Upper Germany to intersperse one's speech with words and phrases from the L. G. This was called *zu flaemen*. Ulrich of Lichtenstein says *bluomekin* instead of *blüemelin*, and Meyer Helmbrecht, the courtly son of a peasant addresses his sister with *vil liebe susterkinderkin*, *suster* being the Lower Franconian for *Schwester*. In Austria, on the other hand, it was regarded as an evidence of good-breeding, about the middle of the 14th century, to use the Swabian idiom.

LANGUAGES AND DIALECTS.

Few people of this country know how great is the lack of homogeneity existing among all the more widely spoken languages of Europe. This diversity of speech, however, prevails only among the illiterate, and not among the educated. Those who are of the present generation in the United States and whose education has been sufficient to enable them to read and write their mother tongue fairly well, speak English so nearly alike that the peculiarities are rarely sufficient to betray the particular section to which they belong. Even the speech of the wholly illiterate has but little local color. But in Germany the birth-marks inhere, as a general thing, in the speech of all, no matter what their education may have been. It is only the language of the stage that is entirely free from localism. Almost every university in Germany contains one or more professors from all parts of the empire, and in almost every case an expert would detect their native province after listening for a short time to their lectures. Public sentiment is strongly against obliterating these local peculiarities. This pride of birth is so generally felt and recognized that to speak without any traces of a dialect is regarded as a mark of affectation.

Most Americans who study German and many native Germans are unaware of the great variety the language presents. But the same is true as regards French, or Italian, or Spanish, or any of the more widely spoken languages. The local French of Normandy and that of Provence are widely dissimilar, and both are unlike the literary French. The Italian of Lombardy and Calabria are unlike in many respects, and both differ from the native speech of the Tuscans. The illiterate natives of these provinces have great difficulty in understanding the natives of every other, though, as would be expected, the most widely sundered dialects have the fewest points in common. A Pomeranian cannot understand a Bernese, while an Oldenburger finds less difficulty in comprehending good Saxon English than good New High German, because there is a greater similarity between the two languages or dialects lying close together than those that are farther apart. It is a well established fact that Lessing and Schiller spoke with a marked dialectic accent and adhered as tenaciously to their local German as Carlyle did to his "broad Scotch." But the only difference in their written German is that of style.

While the divergences are greatest at the two extremes, they shade off into one another so gradually that it is almost impossible to discover where they begin or end. This is not only true of the varieties of the same speech, but also of languages that are wholly unlike when scientifically examined. Border languages partake of a more or less mixed character. The boundaries between two distinct governments may mark the limits of the official language, but they cannot prohibit the intercourse of the people and the use of a medium by means of which they make themselves mutually understood. Perhaps the only circumstances under which two contiguous languages are kept from commingling at all, is when they are separated by natural barriers that are almost impassable. Within the territory of the same language the dialects shade off into each other by almost imperceptible degrees. Careful observers claim that they can detect differences in the speech of the people of two villages that are only a few miles apart. From the nature of the case this must be so. If the extreme eastern and extreme western or the extreme northern and extreme southern portions of a country having the same language are yet linguistically wide apart it is evident that this must result from almost imperceptible gradations between points lying close together.

The historical study of dialects, as well as the history of primitive peoples, proves beyond a doubt that they began in a unity from which they diverged more and more without, however, entirely obliterating their native characteristics. But after a time the centrifugal force has spent itself and a centripetal force begins to make itself felt. The latter is sometimes moral, sometimes political, often both. In the case of the Greek, the moral force predominated. It was the intellectual preponderance of the Attic dialect that in the course of time made it the basis of the Greek of the civilized world. It was the political power of Rome that gradually carried the language of a small district into every country subdued by Roman arms. The same cause made the language of Northern Gaul the language of classic French literature. Farther along it will be shown how moral causes brought into existence the New High German. Finally, however, moral causes produce the most lasting effects. Military force alone will not permanently hold in subjection a people who are intellectually the superiors of their conquerors. In the end the victory remains with civilization and culture. These survive because human experience has demonstrated that they are the fittest. Power in the end remains where there is the most knowledge.

Among modern languages the German embraces the largest number of dialects that are interesting to the student of language. The Germans themselves have assiduously studied many of them, while several embody a literature of considerable extent and value. This is chiefly owing to the absence of a strong central government and the existence of a large number of capitals scattered over Germany. Natural jealousies were fostered by these means, though they could not obliterate race characteristics. Dialectic differences are chiefly of two kinds, for they rarely affect the structure of the sentence. They may consist in the use of different words for the same object, or they may consist in differences of pronunciation of words that are written precisely alike. Sometimes a word is the same in two or more dialects, but has not the same gender. The Germans themselves are not agreed as to how certain letters of their language are to be pronounced. But here, too, as has so often happened in the course of human events, political power and intellectual preponderance are gradually deciding the question. The pronunciation of the more conservative Prussians is destined to become the norm for all students of German. This is not, however, saying that a time will ever come when there will no longer be German dialects. The persistence of local peculiarities of speech among a comparatively stationary population is one of the best attested facts of history. So far as the German is concerned some of these can be traced back more than a thousand years, and they are likely to be still in existence a thousand years hence. The fact that it can be traced in almost unbroken continuity for fifteen centuries and has a longer career of uninterrupted development than any other language of western Europe, gives to German a unique place among the languages of the civilized world.

THE NEW HIGH GERMAN PERIOD.

EXTENT OF TERRITORY.

The changes in the territorial boundaries of the German language during this period are not as great as during the former, nevertheless several of considerable importance took place. The loss of French Flanders is a serious one for the German. In the seventeenth century the Flemish tongue extended beyond Boulogne; at the beginning of the eighteenth the dividing line between it and the French was near Calais; now it is, as before stated, east of Gravelines. In Alsace-Lorraine the German suffered losses at different times by the encroachments of the French. Since 1870 these have ceased. In the south, the German is slowly retreating before the

Romanish and the Italian. The German oases upon Italian territory known as the *setti communi* and the *tredeci communi* have become almost obliterated. In the s'ruggle between the German and the Czech, which took place where the outposts of the former had pressed upon the territory of the latter, the German was not able to hold what it had gained. Here the opposition to the German is particularly strong. In Poland the Teutonic has been slowly but steadily gaining ground for about two centuries. Northward the German has likewise acquired some territory at the expense of the Danish during the last two decades. The oasis in Lusatia inhabited by Wends is gradually becoming smaller. A remarkable restriction in the use of the German language took place within German territory in the time under consideration. During the M. H. G. period there was a clearly marked tendency toward the use of German prose in scientific and literary discussion. This tendency not only ceased, but a strong reaction set in. At no period in the history of the German tongue is the popular mind so active as in the sixteenth; no other has called into being such masterpieces of native eloquence and popular satire. Church hymns of the very highest merit and folk-songs of the same order belong to this period. This impulse was due to Luther more than to any other man; but he was only the leader of a movement in which a large portion of the German people took part. The most tangible evidence of his labors in behalf of his mother-tongue is his translation of the Bible, completed in 1534. Of this about forty editions were published in the next twenty-five years, and nearly twice as many of the New Testament portion alone.

But at the same time the use of the Latin language is revived both in prose and poetry. The Humanists—as the friends of liberal culture based on a knowledge of Greek and Roman antiquity are commonly called—carried on their controversies and their correspondence in Latin.

Terence was raised from the dead, as it were, to see his comedies performed on the stage of the Latin schools. Almost every scholar translated his name into Latin or Greek as nearly as it could be done. In this way a great deal of talent and literary ability that would naturally have been employed in the development of the German language was wasted; for scholars sought their models in the past, chiefly in Cicero, under conditions which made even an approach to him impossible. A dead language, like a cadaver, may be useful for dissection and study, but growth and development are as far from the one as from the other. But in the course of the seventeenth century the unlimited authority of the Latin begins to be questioned and signs of a linguistic rebellion appear here and there. We see a conscious effort on the part of German patriots to restore their grand old native tongue to its place of honor and to rescue it from under the haughty dominion of the foreigner. The situation was in this respect different from what it had been in the preceding period, where the increasing use of German was the almost unconscious but natural result of the conditions of society. The foremost German savant of the seventeenth century—Leibniz—stands on the dividing line between what may be called the old and the new era. Though his principal works were written in Latin, his German writings give clear evidence that he appreciated the worth of his mother tongue, and in them he champions its cultivation, albeit his pleas failed to produce the effect they might have had from the importance and influence of their author had they been published during his life. Younger contemporaries took more decisive steps than he. In the winter of 1687-8, Christian Thomasius gave at Leipzig the first course of lectures ever delivered in the German. During the latter year he also began to issue the pioneer of German literary periodicals. This step required no little courage, for as was to be expected, his colleagues with few exceptions raised an outcry against such a "desecration" of the professional office. Christian Wolf—born in 1679—made German the language of Philosophy. In the wake of Philosophy appeared critical and historical writings. By the middle of the eighteenth century the German language is master of the field. Since that time the importance of Latin has been on a steady decline. In larger works it is only used when the writers expect to be read beyond the boundaries of Germany; and even then but rarely, because the most valuable contributions to science, history and literature are soon translated into the chief languages of Europe. The use of Latin is now confined almost exclusively to dissertations on subjects connected with classical philology.

THE WRITTEN LANGUAGE AND FOLK-SPEECH.

The most important difference between the M. H. G. and the N. H. G. is not mainly one of pronunciation, as we have seen was the case in the transition from the O. H. G. to the M. H. G., although there is considerable difference in this respect between the M. H. G. and the N. H. G. The salient features of the language of the New High German period are of a different kind. In this period for the first time we observe a definite and designed purpose to create a uniform written language which shall be above all the existing dialects. We now distinctly recognize two currents in the German language. The one is, to use Behaghel's figure, that of the dialects or folk-speech, each of the latter flowing in its well-worn and natural bed, and each resembling the other only in its general features. In fact, every one of these may be likened to a separate rivulet, small and unimportant when compared with the main stream. The other is the written language moving in an artificial channel, provided with many sluices and filters for the purpose of keeping out the scum, the sediment and the earthy taste. The difference between the natural and the artificial is here as in every other case very marked. The process of unimpeded development is seen only in the dialects. The water that flows in a channel made by the hand of man—the written language, is a preparation found in nature no oftener than brooks that flow with distilled water.

No belief could be more erroneous, yet it is one held even to-day by many intelligent persons that dialects are a corruption of written speech. Continuing the metaphor, we may say that the fall of the two channels is very unlike ; the development—to drop the figure—in a language that is merely spoken is, generally speaking, much more rapid than where a language is both spoken and written. The former is facilitated by the natural conditions of the situation. A dialect or patois is handed down from generation to generation by means of the mobile and quickly vanishing spoken word, and at most but two or three generations act upon the child by their manner of speech. With a written language the case is otherwise; he who learns it is in a certain sense under the spell of the written or printed character. This continually calls him back to an established norm, and not only brothers and sisters, parents and grandparents are the instructors of the young, but often words and modes of speech are held up for imitation that belong to former centuries. We should, however, guard against supposing that the printed character does more than fix a language to the eye; it cannot check changes of pronunciation. These take place in spite of it. The French and English languages, and to a less extent the German, as printed, exhibit their status as it was in the main one or more centuries ago, but we do not pronounce as we write. We still write English substantially as Shakespere did, yet it is doubtful whether he pronounced three consecutive words, taken at random from his plays, as they are pronounced to-day. In many cases, nevertheless, the dialects are more conservative than the written language, and the uneducated use words that are unknown to those who have always been accustomed to the language of books. Such words have generally been preserved through oral transmission, though they have not been admitted into books, except for special purposes. When, then, we say that a written language is more conservative than one that is spoken, it is well not to take the statement as unconditionally true.

To characterize generally the development of the dialects of the N. H. G. period it may be said that the inflections suffer abrasion as the inflected words are handed down from generation to generation. But the fate of the different dialects was widely diverse, and their number is at present, legion. In the single canton of Bern, which contains less than 2,700 square miles, or about one-third as many as New Jersey, and not much above half a million of inhabitants, not less than thirteen different dialects have been recognized. One who has accustomed himself to note minute differences of language is generally able to discover the native district of a German from his mode of speech. Some dialects are marked by a peculiarity of intonation. Those of the Saxons, the Thuringians and the German Russians are characterized by a sort of sing-song tone. Then, too, the general impression made by a language differs from that of another according as the voice moves in longer or shorter intervals; that is, the distance between the rising and falling inflections is greater in some cases than in others. In this regard the intervals are in general less among the North Germans than among those of the South. There is also a difference in the rapidity of utterance; in the North, the people talk faster than in the South. We have already, in speaking of the rotation of mutes, called attention to the fact that from time immemorial diversities have existed between the individual sounds, or tones. The same tone has not everywhere the same color. So far as the consonants are concerned these differences are substantially the same as they were in the O. H. G. and M. H. G. periods. The vowels, on the other hand, especially the long ones and the diphthongs, have undergone many mutations. We may cite, as a case in point, the M. H. G. diphthong ei, that is pronounced in the different H. G. dialects as ëi, as ai, as âi, and â, and oi or ōi and oa. Less numerous than the diversities in the vowel sounds, that often vary as one passes from village to village, are the variations in the word formation, the manner of composition and derivation, and in the structure of the sentence. The Low and Middle German makes diminutives by affixing -*ken* and -*chen* to the regular designation, as *Händeken*, *Händchen*; the Upper German by means of -*li* or -*le*, as *Händli*, *Händle*. It is only in the Low German that we find terms of endearment terminating in -*ing*, as *Valting*, *Multing*,- *Lining* and *Mining*. To represent the same ideas the Alemanian has words ending in -*i*, as *Aetti* (compare Gothic *Atta*), *Büebi*, *Ruodi*. In many of the Upper German dialects the verbs formed with the prefix *zer*- are lacking; instead of *zerbrechen*, *zerschlagen*, *zerreiszen*, we find *verbreche*, *verreisze*, etc. In place of the prefix *er*- the Bavarian has *der*-, making *derschlagen*, though it may be that this comes from an original *er*-, just as *minder* was originally *minner*. The Alemanian, excepting the Swabian and some of the Franconian dialects, make no distinction between the nominative and the accusative case, except in the personal pronoun. *Ich hab der vatter net gsehe* means *ich habe den vater nicht gesehen*. On the other hand, the L. G. is without the ending *er* in the nominative case of the adjective and puts in its stead the accusative, *hei is en gauden Mann, en wohren Heid*, for *er ist ein guter Mann, ein wahrer Heide*. The personal pronoun of the third plural *hen*, *sie*, has generally been displaced in the L. G. by the dative (*h*)*em*, *ehr*, a fate similar to that which has overtaken the English accusatives for which we have the datives him, her, them. The Upper, or South German, dialects have all given up the imperfect tense of the verb and put in its place the perfects with *sein* and *haben*. In the use of this perfect the L. G. shows a much stronger preference for the auxiliary *haben* than the H. G. In the former we hear, *dat hett slicht gahn*, for, *das ist schlecht gegangen;* and even *dat hett gaud west*, for, *das ist gut gewesen*. The use of the prepositions with the dative case has, in most of the L. G. dialects, suffered considerable loss to the gain of the accusative: *dat was in dat johr* 1829, for *das war in dem jahr*, or, *ut dit holt*, for, *aus diesem Holz*, or, *an de Bost*, for, *an der Brust*. The Alemanian no longer, or at least rarely, uses the relative pronoun; in its place he has substituted the adverb *wo*, as *'s Hus, wo abbrennt isch*. In dependent sentences the L. G. and M. G. dialects employ the preterit tense, subjunctive mood, as, *mer secht er wär gstorbe*; on the other hand the Bavarian and the Alemanian use the subjunctive present, as, *mer seit, er sig gstorbe* (it is said he has died). What would be expressed in book-German by, *hieraus war nicht viel zu entnehmen*, would be in L. G. with a change in the order of the words, *hir was nich vel ut tau nemen*. The diversities in the vocabulary are great and numerous. Almost every community employs words that are not understood at a few leagues distance; other words again are peculiar to large sections of country. To this class belong for the Upper German *losen* for *hören*, *lupfen* for *emporheben;* for the L. G. *kiken* meaning *sehen* and *trecken* meaning *ziehen*. Often when the same words are found in different dialects they have not the same signification. In the Alemanian the verb *lehren* is equivalent to the H. G. *lernen* as well as to *lehren;* in the South Franconian both significations are included in *lernen*. It is well known that in English the word "learn" often does duty for both itself and the verb "teach". It is characteristic of the L. G. that he uses *all* in the sense of *schon*, and that he applies *schön* not only to things visible, but also to objects that have an agreeable taste or an agreeable smell. Peculiar to the South or Upper German is the use of *Schmutz* for *Fett*, and *schmecken*, which can properly be applied only to the taste, instead of *riechen*. Quite remarkable is the displacement which the meanings of the verbs signifying "to go" have experienced on Upper German territory: in one section the simple verb *gehen* is used as about equivalent to *fortgehen* (depart); here *gehen*, meaning to be in motion, is expressed by *laufen*, but for the H. G. *laufen* (go quickly) we find *springen* used, while for *springen* (leap) a number of different verbs are employed. There is not space here to define with any approach to completeness the local peculiarities of the various German dialects; nor have they as yet been thoroughly investigated and the results recorded. Many words have, doubtless, perished beyond recovery with the generations that used them. A large number of careful observers are however busy in this field and not a day passes which does not contribute its increment to the vocabulary of the German language in its widest sense.

UNIFICATION IN A COMMON LITERARY LANGUAGE.

The same considerations of incomplete investigation hold good when we turn to the artificial structure of the N. H. G. and its history, which we found to be true in regard to the dialects. Nevertheless it is possible to sketch a picture of its development in its most important outlines. It is customary to designate Luther as the creator of the German language as it is now written and to place its beginning about the commencement of the sixteenth century. Taken literally, the statement is not true. For, strictly speaking, Luther did not create the language that he reformed and brought to honor; besides Germany had not, by a good deal, even after he entered upon his public career, a real and recognized unity of speech. The roots of the German book-language lie farther back, and extend into the preceding period. In order that a certain type of speech may gain the ascendency over another, or over every other, it must be supported by some generally recognized authority, and this authority must be sufficiently continuous to produce a permanent impression. It may be chiefly political as in the case of ancient Rome, or modern France and Spain; or it may be chiefly moral and literary as in the case of ancient Greece and modern Italy. It will then obtain recognition in proportion to its similarity to other types. Such authority the official German of the empire must of necessity have had. It was the language in which records were kept, edicts promulgated, charters granted, and so on, beginning with about the year 1325. Before this time the Latin was chiefly used, or German bristling with Latin. Luther himself leaves us in no doubt as to his method of procedure. He says in one place, "I use the common German tongue in order that both North Germans and South Germans may understand me. I speak according to the Saxon chancery which is followed by all princes and kings in Germany. The emperor Maximilian and the elector, duke of Saxony have drawn the German languages into one language in the Roman empire." It proved to be a fact of great significance in the development of the German language that the German emperors belonged to the same dynasty, with one brief interregnum, for almost a century, from the accession of Charles IV. in 1347. Their court was in the capital of Bohemia, a land upon which bordered Middle and Upper German territory, as well as the Upper Saxon and Austrian dialects. The official language or *Kanzleisprache* of the Bohemian metropolis was a sort of compromise between two elements, and the type had become so firmly fixed that when the imperial crown passed from the house Luxemburg to that of Hapsburg in 1438, there was no change made in the official language. And not only was this language used in the imperial chancery for official communications; for while formerly those documents which bore the official signature of the emperor were of a very varied character so far as their language was concerned and contained many provincialisms, those beginning with the era of Frederick III., especially those dating from the time of Maximilian and bearing the official signature, exhibit a designed uniformity in language no matter in what part of Germany they were composed. It followed from the nature of the conditions that the official records of the minor courts or chanceries were patterned after these. That of the Elector of Saxony, who was one of the most influential of the subordinate sovereigns, exercised an important influence. The linguistic territory within its jurisdiction belonged to the Middle German, and its official language accordingly bore the same character until the middle of the fifteenth century when it begins to approximate very plainly to that of the imperial chancery. This is owing partly to the introduction of Upper German peculiarities, and partly to the fact that the development of the Middle German exhibits a tendency to approximate in its pronunciation to the same speech. Both these tendencies progressed more rapidly because they were recorded in the official language than they would have done without such support. Here, then, we have two courts that form, in a sense, the nucleus of a unity that was destined to draw others to itself. This was the first step and a long one; but it was nothing more. The unification was entirely superficial and affected the speech of but a small portion of the people. It was not organic. One fact is of itself weighty evidence in this distinction. The very sovereigns whose chancery-jargon had become a pattern for their peers in official communications still used their native dialect in their private correspondence. But further, this official language was ill-suited to become the medium through which a national literature should find utterance, because the thoughts therein set forth had a rather narrow range and it exhibited a preference for traditional formulas and stereotyped expressions. Its influence was thus limited almost exclusively to the domain of sounds and word-formation. For a reconstruction of the language as a whole and to bring about complete unification much was still lacking.

It was Luther who did the decisive deed. The authority inherent in legal documents is relatively weak and limited; not many persons read them. Luther's imposing figure moved the German people to its deepest depths. He dealt with questions that laid hold upon their hearts and feelings, no matter what their social condition. How mightily religious questions move the Teutonic mind may be seen in the effect produced by the English translation of the Bible made about half a century after Luther's. Its phraseology has made such an impression on English diction that it is still plainly discernible. Of necessity the weighty thoughts with which Luther's words were freighted and which gave them such wide currency had an important influence on German style. Not only his thoughts but the form in which they were expressed were well calculated to make a lasting impression on the minds of his readers. This is true in the largest measure of his translation of the Bible and of his hymns. The particular form in which Luther expressed himself was thus, in its very nature, the pledge of a far-reaching influence; for with clear discernment he selected those words and expressions that had already, in a certain sense, gained more or less currency. This has already in part been pointed out. But the more one studies his life and career the more one becomes impressed with the fact that he was a genius of the highest order. Not only was he a man of transcendant ability in certain directions, but he was great in a variety of senses. He possessed what rarely accompanies genius—extraordinary tact. The task which he undertook was no light one, yet he executed it with a skill never equalled before or since on an equally large scale. In the first place he made himself an authority, and did so by the force of natural talents alone. To do this he had to gain the confidence and affection of his countrymen. When he had gained the needed authority he knew how to use it effectively; or perhaps it would be more correct to say that by a wise use of his influence he kept on increasing it. The times, the man, and the occasion all came together, that made him in a sense the creator of a language. How clearly he discerned one phase of the work before him may be seen from some of his remarks on translating. Says he, "One who would talk German does not ask the Latin how he shall do it; he must ask the mother in the home, the children on the streets, the common man in the market-place and note carefully how they talk, then translate accordingly. They will then understand what is said to them because it is German. When Christ says, "ex abundantia cordis os loquitur,' I would translate, if I followed the papists, *aus dem Ueberflusz des Herzens redet der Mund*. But tell me is this talking German? What German understands such stuff? No, the mother in the home and the plain man would say, *Wesz das Herz voll ist, des gehet der Mund über*.

"Luther came from the elemental class of society; not from the ranks of abject, degraded poverty, the proletariat, but from the class which earns its daily bread in the sweat of its brow, and which—next to the peasant class—is the basis of the social structure. Hence, he retained throughout life a sympathy with the laborer and the peasant, and a power of adapting his expressions to their shrewd, idiomatic, and terse idiom, and hence, of course, the naturalness and vigor of his diction. Furthermore, his experience in the matter of dialect was greater than that of any other man. No one of his contemporaries was brought in contact with so many men of such varied conditions and such varied modes of speech. He was for years the father-confessor, in the truest and best sense, for all Protestantism. Whoever was in doubt of mind or distress of body or estate wrote or went in person to the great reformer and was sure of a full and honest answer. Luther's modest and quiet abode was the goal of a pilgrimage second to none of the Crusades. All the secrets of the soul, all the troubles of social and political life, were poured into his sympathizing heart in every German jargon, from the rasping gutterals of the Swiss Rhine to the lisping sibilants of the half-Slavic Drina. Let us add to this an inborn gift of expression, a delicate ear for proprieties of speech and vocal utterance, a quick perception of what was most available, and a sturdy common sense in recognizing what was attainable, and we shall begin to realize how it was that Luther became the Luther who personifies to us the abiding element of German thought and speech."

There are nevertheless certain points connected with the spread of Luther's German upon which we are not yet fully informed. But it is safe to say that its triumphal march was not so rapid as the phrase " Luther, the creator of the N. H. G. language" would lead one to suppose. It met with vigorous opposition in several quarters. To separate Luther's language from his personality was no easy matter. It was the bearer of Protestant ideas. This circumstance made its progress in Roman Catholic countries a slow one. How closely his language was associated with the doctrines he taught may be inferred from the single fact that Gottsched's *Sprachlehre*, published just before the middle of the eighteenth century, was for some time a prohibited book in countries that still adhered to the old belief. Nay, even in Protestant lands progress was slow. German particularism, not unfrequently a synonym for the narrowest sectionalism, sometimes entered the lists in defense of local peculiarities in language, no less than in other affairs. Even as late as the middle of the seventeenth century or after, Thomas Platter, in Protestant Basel writes his autobiography in the Alemanian dialect. In 1671 the authorities of the Canton of Bern issued a rescript to the clergy in which they are exhorted to refrain from the use of an uncommon and novel German, " which only annoys the intelligent and neither instructs the common people in the truths of Christianity nor edifies them."

On L. G. territory the spread of Luther's language was more rapid than farther south. But here too we find oft-repeated efforts to raise the local speech to the dignity of a literary language; and these have not yet entirely ceased. A number of periodicals and almanacs are still printed in L. G. Besides the designed opposition there was that also which was unintentional. There are still extant letters written in the sixteenth and seventeenth centuries that exhibit a strange mixture of book-German and folk-speech. Specimens of this may be seen in the correspondence of the duchess Elizabeth of Saxony with her brother the landgrave Philip of Hesse. They show that the spirit was willing but the flesh weak.

<small>Those who are interested in a fuller discussion of this subject will find it somewhat briefly but lucidly treated by Professor Kluge, in his *Von Luther bis Lessing* and more fully in an unfinished work by Professor Rueckert, *Geschichte der neuhochdeutschen Schriftsprache.*</small>

It is evident from what has been said, and much more might be said, that despite the zealous efforts of grammarians and the appearance of prominent writers in the sixteenth century there hardly existed a conscious unity in the German language. In the next century such a goal was clearly before the mind of scholars, but the deviations from a direct course toward it were still sufficiently evident. It was not until the latter half of the eighteenth century that unification was really an accomplished fact.

Upon the border between the old and the new era the most prominent figure is Haller. In the two first editions of his poems there are marked traces of the Alemanian dialect; for as he himself says, "I am a Swiss. The German language is a foreign one to me and I have little practice in the selection of words," where he evidently means that he has been in the habit of using the words that he had learned in childhood. But in the third edition the traces of his maternal dialect have almost disappeared. Eleven editions of his poems were issued during his life, or between the years 1732–77, though nearly all were written before 1735. His long residence in Germany dating from 1736 had doubtless much to do with this change in his language.

Complete uniformity does not even yet prevail and will probably never be attained. Provincial variations in language still occur, especially in the borderlands, as would be expected. In most cases when a writer is an Austrian or a Swiss one can discover his nationality in his writings. It is, for example, a characteristic of the latter to use the word *rufen* in the sense of *hervorrufen*, *verlangen*, as *der Antrag rief einer längeren Discussion*, for *der Antrag rief eine längere Discussion hervor*. Here both the verb and its object are not in accord with good German usage. Or, *man hatte schon lange einer Verbesserung dieser Strasze gerufen*, for *man hatte schon lange eine V. deiser Strasze verlangt*. This phraseology is found even in Godfrey Keller one of the leading poets of the present century. Another Swiss peculiarity is the word *jeweilen* for *bisweilen*; *bemühend* in the sense of *peinlich*, *an einer Sache beitragen* for *zu einer Sache beitragen*.

The Shibboleth of the Austrian is the construction *vergessen auf etwas* for *etwas vergessen*, as "*auf die Erweiterung des Wahlrechts hatte er vergessen*" for *die Erweiterung des W.;* and further, *über* instead of *auf*, *gemäsz*, as, *über Beschlusz*, *über Auftrag;* likewise the word

Gepflogenheit (Sitte, Gewohnheit)—which has, however, come to be something more than an Austrian peculiarity. *Ueberall* is not unfrequently found in North German writers in the sense of *überhaupt*, as, "*es wäre die Pflicht des Herausgebers gewesen, wenn er den Aufsatz überall accéptierte*" (Rundschau VII., 317). The use of *erinnern* for *sich erinnern* is likewise characteristic of North Germany, as, "*von der Melodie erinnere ich nur einen Theil* instead of *erinnere ich mich*, etc. It is not improbable, now that the political metropolis of Germany is on L. G. territory and is likewise gaining more and more prominence in art and literature, that we shall find an increasing number of L. G. provincialisms finding their way into books and periodicals. The number of variations from a uniform standard becomes much larger when we take into account those that are not local in character but the result of individual initiative. And while it is conceivable, though not probable, that local peculiarities might in time disappear, those that have a personal stamp will from their very nature never cease to find utterance, owing to causes that lie in the nature of language.

There is not a moment, as we shall see farther on, when the development of a language is at a standstill. By virtue of a law of inherent necessity new word-forms, new combinations of old words, and even wholly new words are called into existence without cessation. And so there goes on an endless struggle between the old and the new; there is a prevailing uncertainty, a vascillation in the use of language that can never be removed from a living tongue. We may call the product excrescences and corruptions, blossoms of style or weeds of style, neologisms or barbarisms, or what not, but we know that the thing exists and will continue to spring into existence. It was the observation of these phenomena that led the poet Horace to write, "It is a license that has been granted and ever will be, to put forth a new word stamped with the current die. At each year's fall the forests change their leaves, those green in spring then drop to earth; even so the old race of words passes away, while new-born words, like youths, flourish in vigorous life."

These observations are true not only of German and Latin, but of every language, so long as it is in constant use. The same forces are everywhere at work and the products similar. It is plainly evident in our day that the birth of new words, like the birth of human beings, largely exceeds in number the death of old ones, as may be seen from a comparison of a recently compiled dictionary with one of older date. In fact there seems to be a concerted effort on the part of lexicographers to secure from entire oblivion any word that has ever found its way into print.

In what may be designated as morphology, the German exhibits a comparatively small number of variations. It is equally correct to say *der Friede* and *der Frieden*, *des Bauers* and *des Bauern*, *die Lumpe* and *die Lumpen;* and so of other doublets. *Er kommt* and *er kömmt* are both permissible though the former is doubtless to be preferred; *er schwor* and *er schwur*, *er fragte* and *er frug* are all in use though perhaps in all cases the weight of authority is in favor of one or the other of the two forms. In the following examples the second is preferable to the first, *die Bröte-die Brote*, *die Spornen-die Sporen*, *hand gehabt-gehandhabt*. Variations in the usage and mistakes in the collocations of words are of frequent occurrence. Persons who have not sufficient education to write grammatically have nevertheless something to say in which the public is often interested, or which the writers believe will be of interest to others besides themselves. We accordingly find such errors as, *trotz des Regens* for *trotz dem Regen; während des Tages* and *während dem Tage; der Gehalt* and *das Gehalt; ich habe gestanden* and *ich bin gestanden*. But *trotz* as a preposition properly takes the genitive case like *während*, Gehalt is of the masculine gender, and *stehen* is conjugated with *sein*. Not unfrequently *ich anerkenne* is used for *ich erkenne an*; *der mich betroffene Unfall* instead of *der Unfall, der mich betroffen*. We read of *einer reitenden Artillerie-Kaserne* or of *einer ländlichen Arbeiterfrage*, though the barracks are not mounted nor is the question agrarian. A large number of erroneous collocations of words arise from the circumstance that during the act of writing or speaking two equally authorized expressions occur to the mind at the same time and a part only of each is used. This will explain such phrases as *sich befindlich*, which is evidently a mixture of *sich befindend* and *befindlich*. Reuter often uses the formula, *wat gelt mi dat an*, plainly a combination of a part of *was gilt mir das?* and of *was geht mich das an?* In Emilia Galotti, when Claudia tells how furious Emilia's father had been on learning that the prince had lately seen her "*nicht ohne Miszfallen*" (not without displeasure), she really meant *nicht ohne Wohlgefallen*, the exact opposite of what her words taken literally, signify.

Mistakes in the use of words are usually of two kinds. On the one hand, old words are used with new meanings which do not properly belong to them; as for example when *verdanken* is employed in the sense of *Dank sagen* while it can properly be used only in the sense of the French 'devoir.' It is correct to say *ich verdanke ihm dieses* (I am indebted to him for this, je lui dois ceci), but *ich sage ihm Dank für dieses* (I thank him for this) has a somewhat different meaning. Again, *beiläufig* (incidentally) is used as if it were *ungefähr* instead of *nebenbei bemerkt;* or *bereits* in the sense of *beinahe* (almost) instead of *schon* (already). On the other hand—and the number of errors of this sort is legion—new words are formed, generally new derivatives or new compounds. As the German lends itself so readily to combinations of this kind there is a great temptation for those who have occasion to use a new word to coin one to suit their real or imagined purpose. But it requires an adequate knowledge of the language to coin new words in conformity to its principles. Some of the most offensive of these neologisms are *diesbezüglich, Lebendgeburten, Nebensätzlichkeiten (Nebensätze), daherig, demnächstig, mittlerweilig, verbescheiden,* and so on. A mere glance at the mode of composition employed in these words will enable the reader to see its illegitimacy. The largest contingent of neologisms is furnished by the newspaper press. Newspaper German and bad German are pretty nearly synonymous terms, a statement that is true of other modern languages also. And the complaints are growing in frequency over the degeneracy of this current ephemeral literature. Almost all who write are so eager to come before the public that it does not seem to make much difference to them in what garb. The illegitimate offspring of the faculty of speech to which attention has been briefly called above, together with other divergences from the normal type are chiefly those of construction and word-formation. They are not as noticeable to foreigners or to persons of limited culture as the variations in pronunciation to which attention has already been called. The same vowels and diphthongs as well as the same consonants and combination of consonants are very differently pronounced in different parts of Germany. This is mystifying not only to the foreigner who has learned his German chiefly from books, but a stumbling-block to the Germans themselves who are often at a loss to understand the language of a district lying at some distance from their own. In view of the facts in the case, it is a question how the efforts toward the unification of the N. H. G. can be most judiciously directed toward the accomplishment of the desired end. If, as I hope to show later, all these divergences and errors have a psychological justification; if all progress in language is closely related to them, are we not in duty bound to let them have free course? Shall not we make a practical application of the words of Goethe, "What we understand we can not find fault with"? It is doubtful whether such a conclusion naturally follows. In morals, in social life, many things are done to which we can not justly take exception, but which may nevertheless be prohibited by ethical or statute laws because they are incompatible with the objects for which society exists. The unconditioned liberty of one person interferes with that of others. He is a rare man who can do as he pleases without coming in conflict with his fellow men. The ends at which society aims in the use of language may also require an interference against a license that is proper enough in itself. The mere fact of the existence of a written language is in contravention of the hereditary rights of dialects. Errors of speech and disregard of the laws of language are contrary to the ends for which languages exist, and to a greater or less extent defeat those ends. These are the accurate communication of thoughts and feelings to others. In order that communication may be adequate and exact, language must possess two characteristics: perfect comprehensibility and perfect beauty of form. Offenses against beauty of form are harmful in two ways. The attention of the reader or listener is withdrawn from the contents of a communication to mere externals and therefore to non-essentials. Generally when our æsthetic sense is offended by an inartistic form in language we unconsciously get an aversion to the content. An educated person is rarely impressed by the words of a speaker who uses bad grammar, as he would be if he spoke correctly. Most errors of speech are not only a bar to perfect intelligibility but are also sins against the canons of style. An unusual expression or a word to which we are unaccustomed does not call up in the mind with the same rapidity the designed representation that an old and familiar one does. A keen sense of beauty and propriety is painfully wounded when words having an entirely modern stamp are used side by side with obsolete ones. There is no doubt then, it would seem, that we are perfectly right when we demand of each individual that for the benefit of all he shall refrain from the employment of all incorrect forms of speech. And though the variations in German may have a certain justification for their existence, we do right in demanding the avoidance of everything that may lead to uncertainty, and in setting up a norm of correct speech. The simplest style,—a mode of expression that is easily understood by the most unlettered rustic—may nevertheless be just as correct in grammar and as careful in the choice of words as the most ornate. There can be no possible advantage in fostering dialectic diversity and there is considerable disadvantage, while the tendency of advancing civilization is clearly toward uniformity. Almost everything that can be said in favor of diversity is that it is easier for everybody to express himself in his native dialect than to accustom himself to a style with which he is more or less unfamiliar. But if we attach any weight to such a *laissez-faire* doctrine we may as well go further and object to learning everything that is difficult.

But the serious question is this: How shall we decide in each particular instance whether a word or a mode of speech is to be regarded as correct, or at least admissible, or incorrect. At the first blush we should be inclined to demand that language shall conform to the laws of logic. For there is no doubt that the logical contradictions and vague expressions that we meet with in language obstruct a clear comprehension of the meaning and disagreeably affect the artistic sense. On this ground then much that is spoken and written must at once be discarded as illogical. But our faith in the competency of the rules of logic to decide questions in language is rudely shaken when we discover that in many cases language and logic are not on friendly terms with each other, and that the concepts frequently combined in words do not comport with the rules of logic. The term *Maulwurf*—which in old English was 'mold-warp' because the animal so named casts up the mold—ought to mean a throw that is made with the mouth or snout, but not a little creature that casts up the earth with its feet. In this case the English designation is more nearly correct than the German. We hear of a *Vaterbrust*, of a *Gänsebrust* as designating the breast of a father or of a goose, and a bodice is called a *Schnürbrust* because it is used to lace the breast. In all these compounds there is not much deviation from the meaning of the simple words that enter into them. But who by taking these as a guide could divine the signification of *Armbrust* (crossbow)? The Germans say *eine Ansicht teilen* just as we say in English ' to share an opinion ' or 'a view,' in spite of the fact that when an opinion is shared with one or more persons it does not for that reason become the less, as if it were a material substance. It is sometimes said of a person that his coat or his home or his native land got too small for him; and yet it was the man alone who changed. Logically then we could only say that he became too large for his coat after the manner of the homely proverb "he got too big for his boots." It is illogical and objectionable to speak of one who has drunk as *einen getrunkenen*; nevertheless *ein Trunkener* is exactly equivalent in meaning to *ein Getrunkener*. Similarly we say in English, the man was drunk, when in fact it was an intoxicating liquid that was drunk. It would be logical to say, the man has drunk, but not that he was drunk. The word *Bedienter* (literally, one who is served) does not designate the recipient of a service at the hands of another, but one whose business it is to render service to another. A biting dog is a dog that bites just as a kicking mule is one that kicks, but a riding-saddle or a riding-horse is a saddle or a horse to be rode on, while a drinking-cup or a drinking-fountain are neither to be drunk nor things that drink, but they are objects to be used for drinking purposes. We thus find that the English participle in -ing is used in two exactly opposite senses, and its particular meaning in any given instance must always be determined by the context. The same is true of other languages. The German *entblöden* is formed just like *entkleiden* and *entfärben*, and might rationally be supposed to signify, to lay off one's modesty, shamefacedness, or in other words to be equivalent to *sich nicht scheuen*. In fact, however "*er entblödete sich nicht*" is used like "*er scheute sich nicht*," where the negative in the first sentence is plainly illogical. The terms *Fastnacht*, *Weihnacht* refer not only to the hours of the night, but much more to those of the day. The English fortnight is similarly used. It would be an unendurable contradiction to speak of a piece of wooden iron or of a quadrangular circle; yet *Wachsstreichhölzchen* is in common use as well as *viereckige Fensterscheibe*, notwithstanding the fact that *Scheibe* means disk. It will thus be seen that there are illogical forms of expression that are linguistically incorrect and others that are universally regarded as correct. In some cases we notice the logical inconsistency, in others we do not. The rules of logic will not therefore enable us to decide whether a given word or phrase is grammatically correct or incorrect. Questions of this sort must be brought before another tribunal for decision. This will be further evident from some additional considerations. Of a given number of words formed exactly alike, some will stand the test of logic and some will not. The German vocabulary contains the word *Mannesalter;* logically then it ought also to contain the word *Frauenalter*, or at least such a compound would be in accordance with the principles of word-composition. Yet it does not occur. Conversely we find *Frauenzimmer* but not *Manneszimmer*. From *Tag* are formed *tagen* and *Tagung* to designate the meeting of a congress, diet, etc., by day. It would be logical then to speak of the same occurence if it took place at night as *nachten* and *Nachtung*. But these words are not a part of the German vocabulary, and if one were to coin them they would be scarcely intelligible in spite of their familiar analogues. It is correct to say *ganz und gar nicht* and even *gar nicht*, but the people of Basel are clearly in the wrong when they say, as they often do, *ganz nicht*. From the few examples above given, which might be increased almost indefinitely, it is easy to see that grammatical analogy affords little or no aid in determining what is correct in language and what is not.

But perhaps the æsthetic feelings will furnish us with a more trustworthy guide than anything else; for it is universally admitted that in order to fulfill the objects for which speech exists, beauty of form is of paramount importance. We might make a test by allowing the intelligent public to decide between two forms of expression, in order to ascertain which is the more nearly perfect. Here too, as is usually the case where the beauty of an object is the matter under consideration, the question to be determined is how far the passage under consideration combines harmony of form and content. But since, in language as we find it to-day, with only the rarest exceptions, no relation exists between the form of a word and its meaning the whole discussion falls to the ground at once. If we were to assume that the beauty of a word or of a collocation of words consisted solely in their power to furnish gratification to the sense of hearing we should find ourselves in the domain of music and of pure subjectivity, when, in effect, we are doing what we can to curb the tendency to resort to individual judgment. And as there are all degrees of capacity among men to appreciate the beauty of musical sounds, the same is true when applied to language. Here then as in music there are a number of generally recognized and well established laws that can be broken with impunity only by the privileged few. Men equally competent judges and equally masters of a language may differ as to which of two words or two expressions is the more harmonious. It is well to remember too that what is familiar is generally more or less agreeable. We listen with pleasure to the language or the melodies to which we have been long accustomed though to others they may sound harsh and inharmonious. In like manner long usage may blind us to blemishes of style and bad grammar, a fact of which daily observation furnishes us with numerous examples. The question is easier answered if we put it thus: which of two words harmonizes better with its environment in a given sentence? The chief beauty of discourse consists in unity of style. No attempt should be made to place antique ornamentation on modern furniture, nor should venturesome innovations be mingled with well established art-forms of the past. In this respect, then, the competence of the æsthetic judgment is beyond dispute. Unfortunately the æsthetic sense of the Germans is not at all sensitive. We have sufficient evidence of this in the obvious tendency to use foreign words. Many persons who attach great importance to style and to being "in the style," in many things and who would regard it as little short of sacrilege to put modern furniture in an old German chamber do not hesitate to employ a motley intermixture of German, Latin and French words in discourse without the faintest conception of the sins against style they are committing. How much more difficult then will it be for this feebly developed feeling for style to discriminate justly among pure German words? The only remedy lies in the cultivation and development of a higher sense of propriety in matters of literary form before it can be relied on for guidance. It is however always easy to determine by direct perception whether a word or an expression is perfectly clear without calling in the adventitious aid of logic and æsthetics. Words, whether simple or compound, and sentences are intelligible in proportion to our familiarity with their use either by ourselves or by others. Usage alone decides what is correct and what incorrect. That which is in common use is linguistically right and what is unusual is wrong. Careful observation of usage alone will cultivate the sense of harmony in speech whether written or spoken, and it is only by this means that absolute perfection can be more and more nearly reached. The sense of style is nothing more than knowledge that has become unconscious, a reminiscence of the collocation of words often observed before, and a recognition of others that have an unfamiliar look. This is the rule of Horace, or rather a statement of facts observed by him, nearly two thousand years ago, when he says that new words come into existence and others die

  si volet usus, quem penes arbitriumst et jus et
   norma loquendi:

Every Grammar and every Rhetoric that has ever been written, beginning with Aristotle, is nothing more than an attempt to formulate into rules the usage followed by the best writers. Language precedes grammar, and not grammar, language. But how shall we proceed to ascertain the laws of linguistic usage? The German as well as the Englishman is not so fortunately situated in this regard as the members of several other nations. For him there is no legislative body, no Academy like the French, always prepared to render a decision upon doubtful points. Many have regretted this; in spite of the fact that it is doubtful whether such a corporation has much influence in directing the development of language. The comprehensive mind of Leibniz concerned itself more than two hundred years ago with the formation of a German Academy, and in quite recent times the demand for such an institution has again found expression in public prints and elsewhere. It is very doubtful, however, whether the results likely to be attained are worth the effort. In the first place, where could a dozen, or even half a dozen German scholars be found who would be able to come to an agreement as to what is the usage of their language, and competent to lay down a set of rules in the matter? When the question of regulating German orthography was discussed at a conference recently called to meet in Berlin for that purpose, it was found that even upon such a subordinate and apparently unimportant matter no agreement could be reached. The English advocates of a spelling reform are likewise meeting with but little encouragement. But aside from such practical difficulties it lies in the nature of the case that a set of printed rules can not keep pace with the growth of a living language. The writing public pays little attention to such rules. If a new word aptly designates a new thing it will be generally adopted, no matter how illogically it may be constructed. In like manner, a happily turned phrase rapidly gains currency no matter how repugnant it may be to a cultivated taste, provided it be expressive. The experience of the French shows very plainly the difficulties that such a code has to encounter. The more persistently the *Dictionnaire de l'Académie* adhered to its elegant classicism the stronger grew the sentiment against it, and the more rampant did unbridled license in language become as the Romantic school began to grow in popular favor. As a result the French are to-day not much better off in this respect than the Germans; their periodicals are about as much as the German the arena on which carelessness in the use of words and expressions have full play, and where neologisms abound.

Fewer drawbacks, doubtless, attach to the labors and suggestions of private individuals than to dicta of official bodies. Rules are not so likely to become obsolete, for the reason that with a constant efflux of fresh writings the new takes its place alongside of the old. Books of rules no doubt have their uses, but it is neither convenient nor profitable to turn to their pages when writing or speaking in order to ascertain how that which we have to say may be most fitly expressed. Such a proceeding would be very much as if one were in a company and the question happening to turn upon some difficult point of etiquette we should have recourse to Knigge's *Umgang mit Menschen*, or to some similar manual that we might happen to have with us. Usage in language must not be a mere external matter; it needs to be a part of one's self. This it can never become if we do not drink for ourselves from the same fountains from which the compilers of lexicons and dictionaries have drawn. How to express our thoughts intelligibly and intelligently as well as with grace, is a power that can only be acquired through a familiarity with the way others have habitually given utterance to their thoughts. We must make our own the highly developed sense of form in language acquired by others. Generally speaking, the more one reads the more acute will his sense of the beauty of diction become. But it should be carefully noted that it is not the quantity of the matter read that makes the well-read man. The votes must not be merely counted; they must also be weighed. We can not learn what constitutes good breeding from those who are indifferent to good breeding. The literature of the passing day—most of which is entitled to be called literature solely because it is expressed in the letters of the alphabet—that is produced so hurriedly as to exclude every consideration of style, can not exercise a formative influence on the mode of expression of those who read it. Its tendency is deformative, rather. This is true not only of the average newspaper, but of the writings of many authors who are the favorites of the multitude, and who consider themselves under obligations to bless the world every year with a fresh novel. Yet it is true, on the other hand, that one of the most prolific living authors, Paul Heyse, is likewise an incomparable master of German style. But there is one other practice besides the reading of newspapers and other periodicals that blunts the keen sense of style: this is translating from foreign languages. Translators rarely succeed in eliminating all the peculiarities of the foreign tongue. Latinisms and Gallicisms have almost become an integral part of German, or are in a fair way to become so. But the German itself may be the means of defiling its own purity. How this is liable to happen can be seen in the writings of Jacob Grimm. It is with genuine enjoyment that the appreciative reader observes his wonderful mastery over his native German. With what warmth and enthusiasm does he enter into its life and spirit! How thoroughly he has at command all the resources of the language! But his familiarity with its earlier stages seems not unfrequently to have blunted a comprehension of the legitimate claims of current speech; old German words and combinations of words are not uncommon in his works. There are doubtless intentional deviations from modern usage for the purpose of expressing thoughts and things belonging to the past. A like proneness to resort to the use of archaisms is often noticeable in the writings of clergymen and others who are habitual readers of the English Bible.

Language, as has been said above, is in perpetual growth and movement. As new words come into vogue with new things, old ones pass into oblivion with the disuse of the objects to which they are affixed. There will thus often occur cases where the exigency of the occasion compels a writer, when dealing with the past, to sacrifice either the accuracy of his designation of an object or the justness of the conception he wishes to express, or to introduce antiquated words and formulas. It may be assumed to be altogether impossible to write in a strictly modern style upon subjects that pertain chiefly or wholly to the past. There is a class of writers who of set purpose deviate from the current fashion of language. They are the humorists. Errors readily noticed often serve to heighten the comic effects they wish to produce, and the design of portraying the petty concerns of life frequently leads to the use of new and unheard of compounds. Richter has incidentally touched upon the value to him, of any newly coined word that he can press into his service for the portrayal of half and quarter tints. To the same class belongs also the large guild of popular writers whose aim is either to describe the life of the people or to exercise some influence upon them for a purpose. In order to make themselves easily understood they designedly ignore the laws of cultivated or even of correct speech. It would be wholly out of place to cite as models of good German such authors as Hebel, Gotthelf or Rosegger. The first of these, a writer of remarkable merit, employed almost exclusively as the vehicle of expression, the Alemanian dialect; the second made use of several Austrian dialects; while the third, whose real name was Bitzius wrote for the most part in the German of the Bernese Swiss. In the writings of scholars we often find an intentional neglect of style. There was a time when it was regarded as somewhat of a reproach among the learned to write well. He who attached much importance to elegance of diction was liable to the charge of superficiality, though it needs to be said that this state of affairs prevailed hardly anywhere except in Germany. Fortunately, this opinion is losing ground more and more, so that the modern historians are scarcely less careful of their manner of writing than of the matter they use. It has come to be regarded as an essential qualification of the historian that he shall combine artistic skill in the use of language with thoroughness of research. Accordingly the prose of writers like Ranke, Gregorovius, Hausrath and Treitschke is almost a model of excellence.

It may surprise the reader that the works of the classical German writers—Lessing, Schiller and Goethe—are not placed in the front rank in point of style. The reason is plain: it is inadmissible to set up as models for contemporaries, the works of writers who belonged to a past age. A careful examination will make it clear that the process of development in language has carried us a considerable distance beyond the literary form they employed for the expression of their thoughts. This is more particularly true of Lessing, but it must also be said of Schiller and Goethe that we can hardly open a page of their writings without finding words and phrases that have a somewhat foreign look. It may seem a little discouraging to find that the clearness after which we are told to strive in writing will soon count for little or nothing. Nevertheless this changing fashion in language will no more justify us in neglecting the proprieties of form than the mutability of social observances excuses us from paying any attention to them. There is however a large element of permanence in literary work that fulfills the highest requirements of literary art. It is not probable that the time will ever come when any nation will permit its masterpieces to sink into neglect. On the contrary, it is the excellence of its style that keeps alive many a work of which the contents have ceased to be of general interest. Not unfrequently it is possible for us to anticipate the course of development that a language will take. The most careful observer even when possessed of the keenest sense of the beauties of style will not always be able to determine infallibly which of two or more verbal forms or phrases is entitled to the preference. In the struggle between the old and the new there must always be times when two forces are in equilibrium; when for two different modes of expression, two equally weighty authorities may be cited. Under such circumstances, what is one to do? Regard for clearness will not solve the difficulty, and so we must project the present into the future. In this case as in many others, the historian of the past may become the prophet of the future. One who has carefully studied the development of a language in the past.is often able to predict which of two forms equally correct at the present time will ultimately displace the other. If the question were asked, for instance, whether one ought to say *des Bauers* or *des Bauern*, the thorough student of German might with confidence predict that the former will in the not distant future be regarded as the only correct termination. Half a century and more ago a number of English words were accented on the penult or antepenult; but the tendency of the accent is regressive so that it now rests one or even two syllables nearer the beginning of the word. It is therefore safe to assume that others will follow the same law. Of course, these are criteria that not many persons are able to use and there are comparatively few instances in which a safe prediction is possible. It only remains then for us to recognize with philosophical resignation the uncertainty of the situation. It is folly to make demands upon language to which in the nature of things it can not respond; we must allow to it the freedom of development which we grant to every living organism and deny to no other product of the human soul.

UNIFORMITY IN THE SPOKEN LANGUAGE.

It has been shown that there are a number of points upon which the N. H. G. has not yet reached the stage of complete uniformity and regularity. It is now proposed to call attention to some additional facts that point in the same direction. The uniformity thus far spoken of, exists in reality only on paper and has to do only with reading matter. The advance that has been made toward securing unity in the spoken language is still in its inception. But the movement in this direction, though only fairly begun, is destined to continue with accelerating speed and the dialects are doomed to extinction. Whether this is to be looked upon with regret or with satisfaction is not a matter to be here considered; the result is inevitable and to contend against it, useless. The objects for which language exists imperatively demand the removal of this obstacle to facility of communication. Under existing conditions the peasants of Westphalia and the herdsmen of Switzerland, when each uses his vernacular, comprehend each other as little as the French understand the Chinese, though both the former speak the same language.

The most potent agency in this mission of civilization is the school. Here the attention of both eye and ear is persistently directed to the language as it is written and printed. The living word as it is heard in the pulpit likewise exercises an influence, though not a powerful one, because its chief object is comprehensibility, and it accordingly conforms to local conditions. There are, however, localities where the sway of dialect is still comparatively unbroken. In the Canton of Bern a few years ago, ministers still preached in the local vernacular. Still weaker is the influence of the stage, because only a small part of the population comes within its sphere. Of great importance is the habit of reading which is simply an intensifying and continuing of the work begun in the school, a habit that is greatly encouraged by the issue of numerous periodicals. The facilities for easy intercourse between different parts of the country do a good deal toward obliterating dialectic differences. In the not distant past, persons could easily be found who had never passed a day beyond the sound of their local vernacular. At the present time it would be hard to find a school-boy whose travels have not extended farther. The same causes likewise make a change of residence comparatively easy. Removals from one place to another are, accordingly, more frequent than formerly and are often to a greater distance. The slight divergences between the language spoken in the different parts of the United States are largely due to the easy means of intercommunication. Here too, one may see to what extent the least visited sections have the most marked peculiarities of speech and to what extent they are persistent.

The relation existing between written and spoken language may be of various kinds. The majority of persons employ their native folk-speech in conversation. Many who are able to understand the language of books are unable to use it. There is, besides, a tolerably large contingent that can understand only their local vernacular. Those persons are rare who use only the written language; and they are for the most part such as have acquired the German later in life. Among native Germans this can only be the case where there is below them no numerous and comparatively uneducated populace. This is the situation of the Germans in the Baltic provinces of Russia. Among persons who use both the spoken and the written language, there are many gradations. Comparatively few speak in pure dialect, and the number of those who are wholly free from any trace of dialect is equally small. Usually there is a mixture of both, with the preponderance in favor of the one or the other. The unconscious oscillation between one and the other frequently produces a comic effect and has even been represented in literature. Fritz Reuter is perhaps the best known writer who has made use of it. The mixture is often different in the same individual; or it may vary in the same class of persons, or in the different provinces of the German empire. In conversation with a stranger, a German is likely to discard local peculiarities as much as possible; in familiar intercourse with an acquaintance he will probably use the vernacular most freely. The more serious the subject of discussion the nearer is he likely to approach the language of books. On the platform, in public lectures, in the professor's chair the hearers do not readily tolerate the use of dialect. In addressing a superior, the language of books is more likely to be employed than to an inferior. The language of deliberation will usually be more correct than that of passion or exhaustion. The educated man is less apt to use a dialect than the illiterate; the man who has traveled extensively, than he who has spent most of his life at home; the dweller in the city, than the inhabitant of a rural district; the courtier, than the plain citizen.

Within the territory of the L. G. pure H. G. is much more frequently heard than in other portions of the Empire. Dialectic peculiarities are most common and most noticeable in the higher classes of Swabia, Bavaria, Austria and Switzerland. In fact, it is rare to find a person whose language is not more or less tainted. In some parts of Switzerland even the proceedings of the courts are conducted in the local speech of the district. The spirit of republican independence makes the people of this country loth to conform, even in language, to the rules prescribed by those who live under a monarchial government. The feeling of local importance that one may find in all parts of Germany, but more especially in the south, is here intensified by the difference in the form of government. While the speech of wider areas has certain general characteristics in common, there are other characteristics that pertain to narrower circles within these. In Basel and Bern, to speak now only of Switzerland, the use of local dialects is more common than in other parts. This is doubtless owing to certain native peculiarities of the inhabitants. It may be that in one locality more importance is attached to external form than in another; in another, the people may incline to local isolation; while in still another, the language may be tenaciously adhered to because it is an inheritance that has descended to them from their ancestors and which they feel ought to be transmitted to posterity as little impaired as possible. The fact that the people of North Germany generally speak the language with greater purity than those of the

South is to be attributed in part to the greater conservatism of the latter and in part to the wider gap that exists between the northern vernacular and the N. H. G.

Wherever the written German is understood the High or South German dialects are, in a measure at least, intelligible; this can not be said of the Low German dialects. There is, accordingly, a stronger motive for the native of North Germany to learn the literary language, than there is for the native of other parts. He must conform as far as possible to the language of books in order to be understood even by his own countrymen who have not learned his particular dialect. Again, it is easier to learn an entirely new language and to use it in its purity, if it is sharply distinct from that to which we have been accustomed, than it is to learn one that deviates but slightly. This statement is subject to some exceptions, but is true in the main.

The relative ease with which we pass from the use of one language to another will receive some additional elucidation if we look somewhat more closely at the way in which the literary German and folk-speech are intermingled. Single H. G. words find earliest and readiest entrance into the dialects, because in such cases the difference between *meum* and *tuum* is clearly marked. Much later and rarer is the introduction of H. G. phrases and expressions. There exists, however, another consideration. H. G. words even in dialectic guise are more easily understood than phrases or sentences when used in the place of dialect-words. But not all H. G. word-forms find equally ready admission into folk-speech; the more frequently a dialect word is used the greater the difficulty of displacing it. It happens quite frequently that persons who attach much importance to purity of speech inadvertently let slip the dialectic forms of *ist* and *nicht*. These words being among the most frequently used in all languages, their pronunciation acquired in childhood becomes so confirmed by habit that it is almost the last to be exchanged for another.

But most difficult of all is to observe carefully the rules for the pronunciation of particular sounds. This is so because, in the first place, that utterance which has been acquired in connection with the printed page is not clearly indicated by the characters to which it is attached. Whether *st* is to be pronounced as it is written, or as *scht;* whether *ch* is to be sounded as in *Bach* or as in *Bäche*, can not be learned by the eye alone. A second obstacle is often interposed by the dialect when it makes no difference in pronunciation where one exists in the literary language: the latter has two distinct sounds where the former has but one. Persons who are in the habit of using a dialect observe that those who speak the H. G. employ two different sounds, of which one accords with their vernacular while the other does not. But the memory often fails to keep them distinct and an uncertainty arises as to when the one is to be used and when the other. The result is that the dialect sound is frequently carried into the H. G., where it does not belong. Few things are more difficult to acquire and to remember accurately for any considerable length of time than a sound or a tone. This failure of memory often produces curious linguistic effects. The Alemannian, for instance, knows that he should sometimes use an *ei* in the H. G. where his vernacular has *i*, as *Weile* for *Wil*, or *schleiche* for *schliche*. But by following the analogy of the case too far he is apt to say *veil* when he should say *viel*, or *ich versetchere sie* when he means *ich versichere sie;* and so on. The Swabian pronounces the H. G. *sind, Wind* as if printed *send* and *Wend;* and misled like his Alemannian brother by a false analogy he utters *Mensch* as if it were written *Minsch*. Or, again, because the H. G. *gehabt, geholt* are pronounced in his native dialect like *g'habt* and *kabt*, or *gholt* and *kolt*; he in like manner introduces an *e* after the initial *g*, thus making *Gehockeler* out of *Gockler* (cock). The Austrian utters final *-er* almost as if written *-a*, saying, for example, *Winda*, when he means Winter. In like manner then he is apt to say *in Sommer* when he means *in Summa*. In the dialect of Leipzig and vicinity *au* is pronounced like *o*, so that *laufen*, for example, becomes *lofen*. Accordingly when the natives want to say *Ofen* they are apt to call it *Aufen*, and because *Knopfloch* (button-hole) and *Knoblauch* (garlic) are pronounced substantially alike in their vernacular, they confound the sounds where the result is ridiculous: instead of saying *Knopflochseide* they may say, when trying to speak H. G., *Knoblauchseide*. The same uncertainty and confusion appears when a native Low German tries to use the H. G. *mir* and *mich*, *dir* and *dich*; for in a large portion of L. G. territory the dative and accusative of these two words is simply *mi* and *di*. It is only those that have been well educated who are in all cases able to decide quickly which of the two terminations is to be employed. Mistakes of this kind are likely to occur whenever and wherever there is considerable difference between the speech of the educated and the uneducated; that is, where a language of books exists along with one that is only spoken. We find persons who having learned that it is incorrect to say "talkin'," "plantin'," and the like will carry the analogy too far and say "chicking" or "planting" when they mean chicken and plantain. Sometimes these incorrect forms finally make their way into the literary language, as, for example, chickens, which is a double plural. The singular is chick, and the plural should end in -en like that of ox. Compare also the plurals housen, children, brethren and even "sistern." There is hardly any doubt that a similar mental process has unconsciously been an important factor in giving forms to many German words that it would be difficult to account for in any other way. We have here simply a process that is of frequent occurrence in all languages, because the human mind acts in much the same way. It is certain that a number of pure H. G. words are the result of earlier false analogies. *Löffel, ergötzen, löschen* were in the M. H. G. *leffel, ergetzen* and *leschen;* but because in many dialects the H. G. *e* and *ö* stood for the same sound they became confounded in the course of time, and usage finally settled upon the wrong one. Since the mistake has become known efforts are being made to correct the error and restore the correct orthography. The proverb *sein Schäfchen ins Trockene bringen* has arisen from the L. G. *sein Schepken*, etc. In this dialect *Schepken* corresponds to the H. G. *Schäfchen* and *Schiffchen;* but the wrong word was transferred because the proverb has reference to putting the ship not the sheep into a dry place. In those parts of Germany where little is known of ships and much of sheep, the mistake was almost certain to be made.

In many instances when wrong forms, judged by the H. G. standard, are used they are not the result of an attempt to reproduce the correct one, because the speaker is incapable of recognizing the difference between the two; or if he recognizes the difference when made by the vocal organs of another he makes none when he attempts to pronounce the words himself. The Saxons and Swabians are to a considerable extent afflicted with a sort of deafness which prevents them from distinguishing between p and b or t and d. It may thus occur that *ein typischer character* becomes *ein diebischer character*. A lexicon of the Swabian has no words beginning with t and p, their places being occupied by d and b. So far as the p as related to t is concerned the Gothic prototype is preserved, as there are few, if any pure Gothic words beginning with this letter. In the case of the initial t as related to d the latter in most cases preserves the Gothic sound; which is also retained in English. The Gothic *dauhtar, dags, daigs* are the English 'daughter,' 'day' and 'dough,' and the Swabian

Dochter, Dag and *Deig* or even *Doag* are represented in the N. H. G. by *Tochter, Tag* and *Teig*. How tenaciously the dialects resist the displacement of some sounds is evident from the fact that for several letters and combinations of letters there is no recognized pronunciation to this day. It is perhaps admissible to say that the L. G. pronunciation of sp and st, which is in accord with the English, is incorrect, and that these letters should be sounded as if written schp and scht. On the other hand the pronunciation of g varies considerably. Sometimes it is sounded like j (Eng. y), sometimes like ch, sometimes like the English letter of the same name before a, o and u. None is universally recognized as correct. A similar state of affairs exists in regard to final ng. In some localities it is sounded as if written nk, so that *Gang, Sang* become *Gank, Sank;* in others, it has the same sound when final that it has elsewhere in a word. The sound represented by the letter r is produced in some districts with the tip of the tongue; in others, with the palate. Sometimes it is made to resemble closely the sound of eh, or even a. Professor Vischer recently published a humorous article in " Gegenwart " under the caption " Sufferings of the wretched letter r during its travels through Germany." In South Germany s is pronounced sharp like the English initial s; but in North Germany like s in ' houses.' Some of the differences that prevail in the pronunciation of the vowels and diphthongs have already been pointed out. The divergence in the pronunciation of *s* is perhaps of little importance and is doubtless not generally observed. The others are of greater consequence and are liable to lead to a misconception of the meaning of the speaker. They ought therefore as far as possible to be removed. So far as the *r* is concerned there are physical obstacles in the way; but none in the case of *g*. It is well therefore to follow the example of the German stage which is almost a unit in pronouncing it, at least initial and medial, like the English g in such words as game, go and gun.

SOME DISADVANTAGES OF UNIFORMITY.

Uniformity in spoken and written German, so far as it exists at present is the result of a conscious effort and the outgrowth of internal necessity. It has nevertheless brought with it some disadvantages. So long as a dialect was the mode of speech employed by everybody, each writer was at liberty to use that particular name to designate an object or an idea which it had in the vernacular. All newly coined words could forthwith be transferred to paper or book. As soon however as a literary language came into existence this could no longer be done because such a language sought general currency wherever German was used. The needs of a larger constituency had thenceforth to be kept in view; and only such words and forms of expression were likely to be understood as had already come into use in one way and another. The vocabulary of a speaker or writer is confined within somewhat circumscribed limits. The more abstract and colorless the signification of a word the larger is the number of dialects in which it occurs; the more sensuous and concrete its meaning the wider the divergences in the various dialects. It is for concepts of this class that it is very difficult to find designations that will obtain universal acceptance wherever the language is spoken. But there is another obstacle in the way. The nature of the subjects discussed in print necessarily limits, to some extent, the vocabulary that can be used, and the entire body of words is drawn upon somewhat unevenly. The portion, therefore, that most fully represents local diversity is the least used in literature. Given a language in common use among the educated only, and it follows as a matter of course that objects have a less general interest for this class if they supply purely physical needs or if they are closely identified with the trivial concerns of the every day life of those living at the other end of the social scale. This statement applies with particular force to the German literature of the seventeenth and eighteenth centuries. In fact, the literature of Germany can hardly be called German literature. As has already been pointed out scholars wrote chiefly in Latin, and later in French; and when they condescended to use their vernacular they expressed themselves very clumsily. Where a uniform language is employed over a wide extent of territory there are many words that can not be used because they have only a local existence and many things that can not be spoken of because they have no name that is universally understood. This is true of a number of plants and animals; of articles of food; of utensils for domestic use and in agriculture; as well as of many acts that are essential to the preparation and use of these objects. It needs but the cursory examination of a dictionary intended for general use to convince one that it lacks a considerable number of words in actual or daily use among the people whose language it aims to embody. Much of what is known in English as *slang*, but for which the German language has no exact equivalent, is excluded. One may be familiar with the language used at times by almost all Germans and yet find in every section of their country many new words that he will be unable to comprehend or old ones used in a sense unfamiliar to him.

It may be stated here because it affords a familiar example of a similar fact that nearly all our so-called Americanisms are not words newly coined here, but English words used in a different sense from that which they have in the mother-country.

It is also to be noted that the literary language has, strictly speaking, no sympathy with, and therefore no designations for, the small and trivial mental processes that belong to the daily experiences of the average man,— for the words that express anger and vexation, for curses and terms of reproach, for exclamations of joy and pain, or for the thousand utterances of flattery or kindly approval.

While it is still true that there are classes of concepts that are not without general interest yet the stock of words is nevertheless inadequate for their accurate designation. This state of things is however passing away gradually. The great interest manifested in our day for the scientific investigation of the most trivial phenomena of nature,— and I use the word trivial in a relative sense—is not without its influence upon the study of the speech of the most ignorant and uncultivated. This interest not only has a tendency to elevate those who stand at the bottom of the social scale; but since there will always remain those who can not be raised, it descends of set purpose to their level in order to study social life in its lowest forms. The great increase in the size of our modern dictionaries is the outgrowth of a desire to embody in them every visible sign that has ever been used to give utterance to a thought or an impression, no matter when or by whom. It is in this way that the vocabulary of each is made the common property of all, at least to examine and study, if not to use. There is a realm in which the living folk-speech gives evidence of a creative power: it is in the invention of onomatopoetic words intended to designate insignificant actions and sounds. These however find their way into literature but slowly, or not at all, for the reason that there is an absence of sympathy between those who use the language of books and those who do not. The progress of intelligence as manifested in the creation and development of a uniform literary language has however done a good deal to curtail the linguistic material at its disposal by removing its modes of expression from the hearts and sympathies of the common people. Nor has a reaction been wanting. This protest against a language having general currency has found expression in the creation of a dialect literature. This is not a mere play and pastime, the amusement of such vacant hours as a writer can not otherwise fill up. It has a deeper significance. And for the reason that it fills a want felt by the human heart it will probably never cease to exist. When literary form is given to discourse in dialect there is not seldom exhibited the phenomenon which has been characterized above as hyper-High German. Just as the user of a dialect often expresses himself incorrectly when he attempts the H. G., so he may also wrongly transfer his H. G. into his dialect. A very common L. G. error of this kind is affixing the ending -et to neuter adjectives—*en grotet Hus*, *en levet Kind* for *ein groszes Haus, ein liebes Kind*. The pure dialect has no adjectives terminating in -et.

CHARACTERISTICS OF THE NEW HIGH GERMAN.

Having now concluded our observations upon the tendencies toward uniformity in the German, and their results, it is proper, finally, to glance at the constituent elements of the unified language and at those special characteristics that mark the N. H. G. as temporally and topographically distinct from other speech-unities. The reader should, however, keep constantly in mind that what is habitually designated as N. H. G. is not a homogeneous whole. Not only do the different periods of the N. H. G. show different stages in the process of unification, but the language apart from these gradations, has, during the entire N. H. G. period advanced step by step. The language of Luther was no longer that of the German classics; that of the classic writers is not the German of to-day. But the character of the tongue as a whole has remained substantially the same: it is a mixture of various dialects of which the chief ingredients are those of Middle Germany. Its vowel system is mainly that of the middle region, but its consonants are for the most part Bavaro-Austrian. Neither in the forms of the individual words nor in their combinations is there much difference among the dialects represented in the N. H. G.: the gender of the nouns is M. G., not Upper G. In the dialects belonging to the latter region we find *der Backen, der Butter, der Trauben;* but in M. G. and also in the N. H. G. these words appear as *die Backe, die Butter, die Traube.* A number of other words do not have the same gender in Switzerland and South Germany that they have farther north. The different dialects have contributed very unequally to the vocabulary of the N. H. G., though here again Central Germany predominates. The purely U. G. contingent is very small. Almost the only words from this region that have become an integral part of the written tongue are the names of objects that are found here exclusively, and pertain to mountainous districts. Among these are *Alp, Fluh, Gletscher* (from the French glacier), *Lawine* (from late Latin labina and related to labi), *Matte* and *Senn.* Most of these words can not be translated into English. The verbs *lugen* (perhaps related to Eng. look) and *staunen* are of Swiss origin though in common use in South Germany. The contribution of North Germany to the written language is quite large. There is a long list of words relating to navigation, to life along and on the ocean. Among these are *Brise, Bucht, Düne, Hafen, lichten* (lift, make light the anchor), *Steven, Tau, Wrack,* etc. The connection of some of these words with their English equivalents is evident at a glance. But there are other terms that come from the same quarter, such as *echt* from an older *ehaft,* that which pertains to *ē* (Ehe), that is, law, right. The change from *ft* to *cht* is a characteristic of the L. G. as may be seen in *Schluft* for *Schlucht, sanft* for *Sacht,* etc. Further *Fracht, Harke, Kneipen, Knicken,* and many more. In some cases both the H. G. and L. G. words have gained currency, as *Brunnen* and *Born, feist* and *fett, sanft* and *sachte, sühnen* and *(ver) söhnen, Waffen* and *Wappen.* The points of difference between the pronunciation of the N. H. G. and the M. G. will be discussed further on. It may be stated here, however, that it relates chiefly to the long vowels. In place of the older *zīt, wīt, hūs, mūs, hiute, lute* the modern German has *Zeit, weit, Haus, Maus, heute, Leute*. The differences between the etymology and syntax of the two periods are less regular and consistent. Some examples will be given later in the book.

It has already been remarked that the material which constitutes what we call language is a traditional inheritance received by each generation which it in turn transmits to posterity with very slight changes. We learn our vernacular from hearing it spoken and not from the printed character. When speaking of language it is important to keep in mind its two-fold nature: as a series of vocal utterances that impress themselves on the mind through the sense of hearing, or as a number of characters that reach it through the sense of sight. It is the gradual changes through which the words that constitute a spoken language passes that it is proposed to consider here. The first part of this book has shown that a great many differences exist within what is called the German language. It changes with times and places, but differs also according to the social position of those who use it. We have now to examine somewhat more closely into the nature and character of these variations. The attempt has been made to represent graphically these varieties by comparing words to stones which a brook or a river carries along with it and which thus gradually become more and more abraded and less and like their original form. In this metaphor the flowing stream is intended to represent current usage; but the comparison is radically erroneous. A word is not a thing which after it is once coined continues to exist forever afterward. It is an activity, an event. And this event consists in the simultaneous occurrence of a movement of the soul and a sound produced by a move-

ment of the organs of speech, so that, briefly expressed, a
mental concept and a vocal sound are combined. This
combination is not under all circumstances of the same
kind. The number of intuitions inhering in the consciousness is dependent upon the number of impressions
made upon the mind of the speaker and upon those with
whom he comes into conversation. The narrower the
social circle to which a person belongs, the lower his grade
of culture, the more circumscribed will be the range of his
intuitions. The factory hand and the peasant need a comparatively small number of words to satisfy their linguistic
wants, while on the other hand the scholar and the poet
find several thousand barely sufficient. The more unusual
a man's occupation, the farther he is removed from the
ordinary affairs of the mass of mankind the more singular
is his vocabulary. The German language contains a long
list of art-terms that constitutes a kind of separate speech
for the use of artists and other persons interested in art.
The merchant, the fisherman, the beekeeper, the miner,
the sailor and the hunter, have each a vocabulary peculiar
to their craft. The novice who is in process of initiation
into the mysteries of these occupations is compelled to
acquire a new language to correspond to the new concepts
called into existence in his mind. The great body of concepts embodied in a language is different at different
times. When chivalry and the feudal system began to
decay; when old systems of jurisprudence fell into disuse; when the study of astrology was abandoned, many
words were irrevocably doomed to oblivion.

But the mere existence of objects in the external world
is not the only factor in the formation of concepts and
their corresponding words; the depth and therefore the
permanence of the impression made by such objects is also
of great importance. The character of this impression is
in turn dependent upon the relation of the external object
to man—whether detrimental or beneficial. Huge ani-

mals and large trees, those animals and plants that are serviceable to man for food and clothing, or that threaten his life by their voracity or by their poisonous qualities received names long before the tiny bug that burrows in the earth and the little flower that blooms in the depths of the forest. And so It comes that the names of the larger animals, the great trees of the forest, and the most important cereals are common to all the members of the Germanic family. Some of these, such as wolf, cow, ox, birch, beech, alder, barley and the like have radically the same designations in other branches of the Indo-European family of languages. On the other hand the names of flowers and insects are often different in the different dialects of the same tongue, so that at the present day the zoologist and botanist are still obliged to use Latin technical terms in order not to be misunderstood. We may cite as instances the primula elatior (oxlip primrose) for which the German has about sixty names and the colchium autumnale (meadow saffron) some fifty. These statements, though made with primary reference to the proto-historic period of the languages here under consideration are amply confirmed by the familiar facts of daily experience. Everybody knows the names of the larger trees, the common grasses and the useful animals, but hardly one person in ten thousand recognizes or takes any interest in the unimportant forms of animal and vegetable life that are about us wherever we may be.

The stock of representative images varies therefore according to different individuals and groups of individuals. The possible number is still further increased when there is a choice among several concepts: the same person may give vocal utterance to one percept in one way and to another in another; or he may express the same concept in different ways at different times. It may be that in one case the language with which he is familiar already contains in its vocabulary the word by means of which he may express his percept and this word or term may come into the consciousness of the speaker and suffice for his momentary needs. He then voices his percept in exactly the same way, that is, with precisely the same term as others before him; or he at least essays so to do. For the minute reproduction of a word that has become a part of the body of speech is rendered difficult by various circumstances, and is dependent upon divers conditions. The most important preliminary condition is that the word shall have been heard and perceived in all its minutiæ; it must have been perceived by the hearer exactly as it was uttered by the speaker. The accurate perception of a foreign or new word is rendered most easy when all its separate parts are pronounced slowly and distinctly. It is by such a method that the child will most readily and accurately learn to speak and to read. When some particular sound or combination of sounds uttered by the speaker finds a lodgment in the consciousness of the hearer and is accurately grasped by the intellect one would suppose that when the latter attempted to reproduce it by imitation the reproduction would correspond precisely to the original. It is perfectly natural for one man to believe that he can imitate any sound made by another when both use the same vocal organs. This however by no means follows as a matter of course; in fact experience proves the converse to be generally true,—for just as all imitation is imperfect so is imitation in language. The child in order to reproduce by imitation the words uttered in its hearing, proceeds to put its vocal organs into action, with but a faint comprehension of the methods by which its object is to be attained. Its first efforts produce very imperfect results, but it constantly compares its linguistic achievements with the vocal images, so to speak, inhering in its consciousness and is in this way constantly reminded of its shortcomings. It then brings into action other portions of its vocal organs, and finally by oft-repeated effort it succeeds in making its own words approximate very closely to those it hears spoken by others. Only persons with an abnormally acute sense of hearing are able to reproduce accurately any word they hear. But the human ear is a very untrustworthy instrument. Two sounds may seem to be exactly identical and yet be considerably different in the mode of their production. Then again different causes may produce similar effects; in order to produce the same acoustic effects the learner's organs of speech are likely to make movements and to get into positions that do not accord with those of the teacher. And this substitution of vocal effects produced in one way for those produced in another which produces the same sum of results is likely to be often necessary because the organs of speech of different persons are differently constructed and when two products, of which the one factor is unlike, are to have equal value, the remaining factors must also be dissimilar. To illustrate this proposition by a mathematical formula: if we multiply 5 by 9 the product is 45, but if we substitute some other digit for the 9 we must change the 5 also if we want to still get 45 as our product. By a somewhat similar process it happens that words when transmitted from father to son, from generation to generation, undergo a variation or a series of variations in pronunciation. It is a well established fact that languages undergo change in the course of time when there is no appreciable external influence affecting them. This gradual change is usually spoken of as decay, though there is no good reason for so designating a process of development that is perfectly normal and that in no way impairs the efficiency of a language as a medium of communication.

The deviation from any particular type is at first almost infinitesimally small, but the slight difference that in course of time comes to exist between the pronunciation of the son and the grandson continues to grow greater through several generations and in a century or two becomes quite marked. These differences are usually of two kinds: they are either qualitative or quantitative. In the first case other parts of the organs of speech are brought into action and other muscles used than before. An example is furnished by the transformation of the labial *m* into the dental *n* as when *Inbisz* becomes *Imbisz*. In the second case the same muscles are employed with greater or less vigor or force. For example, less muscular exertion in the organs of speech is required to pronounce *Ferd* and *Fund*, as the Westphalian does when speaking H. G. than the correct forms *Pferd* and *Pfund*. Those cases where greater muscular exertion is made in trying to imitate a particular sound are comparatively rare compared with those in which the result is sought to be effected with less. Laziness, as it is sometimes called; a disposition to ease of utterance, plays an important role in the development of language, less important however as a cause of variation than in giving a particular character to changes that are already in progress.

It is customary to designate the mutations in language we have described above as phonetic laws, or to speak of these as due to phonetic laws. The obstacles that hinder the accurate reproduction of a sound always appear whenever an attempt is made to utter it, no matter in what word or how often it may recur. In other words, a sound produced by the organs of speech always follows the same line of variation from any given type. By noting the circumstances under which the variations occur we are able to formulate the phonetic law of the case, law being here simply an order of sequence. It is a phonetic law, or to express the same fact in other words, it is in accordance with a phonetic law, that the long *i* of the M. H. G., which is still preserved in some modern dialects, becomes the diphthong *ei* in the N. H. G.: *gige* appears as *Geige*, *hirat Heirat, miden meiden, nit Neid, zit Zeit*, and so on. This statement is true not only of the German language within itself, that is of one dialect as related to another or of one period of the language as compared with another, but likewise of every other language. It is by the study of phonetic laws that the relationship of the most distant members of the same family of languages is determined. To these laws there are no exceptions, the apparent exceptions being due to the action of yet undiscovered laws.

This uniformity of development, however, holds good in the first instance of the individual only. In the case of a larger number of persons the circumstances that influence the development of a language may, and often do, vary greatly. The sense of hearing is not equally acute in all; or the organs of speech may not be formed precisely alike. From the nature of the conditions, then, it must follow that in course of time as many languages will be formed or developed as there are separate individuals. And it can not be denied that even within the narrowest circles slight differences of pronunciation may be recognized among those composing it. But it is true, furthermore, that the learner is not wholly or even chiefly under the influence of a single speaker, but under several; so that the speech of each person is in a certain sense an epitome or average of the speech used by the social circle to which he belongs. This is always true of every member of the rising generation. Where this is part of a circumscribed circle the language that serves as a model is relatively homogeneous, and the various averages represented by each individual differ but slightly from each other and from the more primitive type. It follows naturally that when two persons or two groups of persons cease to be in close relation and frequent intercourse, or when their intercourse ceases altogether the development of their language must bifurcate; one sound will gradually change in one direction; another will slowly vary in a different direction until in course of time dialects come to be formed that vary considerably from each other. The farther two contemporary social spheres lie apart, the less the intercourse between them, the greater will become the differences of speech peculiar to each, just as similarly differences increase with the lapse of time. It will thus be seen that there is no radical difference between the causes that produce variations in language whether we consider them in regard to place or in regard to time.

INNER HISTORY OF THE GERMAN LANGUAGE.
THE INFLUENCE OF ANALOGY, ETC.
(See also farther on the chapter entitled What is Analogy in Language?)

If a language underwent no changes except those that were due to phonetic laws its history would be very simple and transparent. It would be an easy matter to formulate these laws; and by a knowledge of them one could, by a simple mechanical process, turn verses from Goethe into the language of the Nibelungen Lay, or the poetry of Otfried into the language of Ulfilas. But the real state of the case is altogether different. A common form of variation from the normal type is due to abbreviation or abridgment. This may take place in the case of a single word, as when we say, a glass of soda, for a glass of soda-water; or a kilo for a kilogramme. This is particularly frequent in proper names that are shortened into pet-names or nicknames. Instances are so common that none need be given here, especially as this subject is taken up again in the last chapter. A different class of abbreviations are those in which only part of a familiar phrase or sentence is expressed, the hearer being left to infer the rest. We say, " Good morning," instead of, " I wish you a good morning," or " Wait a little," for " Wait a little time ; " and so on *ad infinitum*. Here we have what grammarians usually call ellipsis. The possibility of understanding such an incomplete series of sounds is easily understood when we take into careful consideration the psychic processes that underlie and control our comprehension of a spoken word or sentence. The case will be made plainer by a simple illustration from the material world. If two stringed instruments are in the same room and a string of one is set in vibration, the strings of the other instrument that have the same pitch or that stand in certain harmonic relations to it will vibrate of their own accord. A somewhat similar phenomenon takes place in speech. When a word or sentence is uttered in our hearing, it does not merely produce a mechanical effect upon the mind, but awakens like or similar concepts that exist in its mysterious depths. Latent images are brought under consciousness thro' the medium of the ear. This echo, as we may call it, is returned in the exact form of the original word or phrase, provided it is one that has been heard before. This is an important element in the comprehension of another's language. It would be a gross error to suppose that in ordinary conversation we stop to consider each individual word in a sentence as it enters our ears. Unless a word is very short, we rarely hear it entire. We take note only of the important parts of a word or sentence, and when we hear these the complete concept lying dormant in consciousness is awakened. We generally fail to observe how fragmentary is that which we can properly be said to hear. This will also explain why it is that we understand spoken words less readily than written words, especially when they belong to a language with which we are not very familiar. More or less time is often necessary until a word that we hear or see touches a responsive chord in our consciousness—until we understand it. Sometimes it may happen that we are obliged to carry a word in the memory for days until we can recall its meaning, that is, until we find the corresponding word and its definition that had been previously learned. But words may awaken concepts that are not identical though containing similar radical elements. Let us take, for example, the word 'stone' and suppose that a child after hearing it repeatedly has fixed it firmly in memory. If now it hears the word 'stony' without any clue to its signification, this word will be unconsciously associated with the former, though the child may not recognize clearly the relation existing between them. Or we may take the word 'horse' and we shall find the same mental process in regard to 'horses' together with such compounds as 'horse-whip,' 'horse-thief,' 'horse-play,' 'unhorse,' 'horse-back,' 'horse-radish,' 'horse-shoe,' 'horse-fly,' and many others. To express the same fact somewhat differently: words having the same vocal elements are unconsciously associated together. The feeling arises in the mind that in order to express any particular representation or concept a certain sum of vocal sounds must enter into it. Nor is a perfect coincidence necessary between the newly awakened concept and that already in the mind; a certain degree of resemblance is all that the mind requires in order to associate together words that are etymologically related. Not only is the resemblance between *nehmen*, *genehm*, and *Vernehmung* easily seen but *nimmt*, *nahmen*, and *genommen* are readily associated with them.

Evidently then, such word-groups, by the principle of mental association, afford important aid to the memory in retaining the individual members of the group, and they play an important part in transmitting an inherited language to posterity. On the other hand, words may be associated into groups though they have a merely external resemblance, while in signification they have no connection at all with each other. It is often the case that this mistaken grouping together of unrelated words has the effect of neutralizing phonetic laws. The law of association is more powerful than the tendency to ease of utterance and counteracts it. Take the series *nehm-*, *nimm-*, *nahm-*, *nomm-*, and how shall we know which of these forms is the bearer of the signification? When Luther says, *ich kreuche, er kreucht, wir kriechen, sie kriechen*, is *kreuch-* or *kriech-* the true representation, either vocal or ideographic, of the concept 'creep'? The illiterate user of the words has no means of determining this question. He only remembers that the present tense employs *nehm-* or *nimm-*, and the perfect *genommen;* that formerly the singular number was *kreuch* and the plural *kriech-*. If his concepts become confused owing to a momentary failure of memory he is just as likely to say *ich krieche, wir kreuchen,* as to use the correct forms. Viewed externally we may say that *krieche* has changed its form after the pattern or the analogy of *kriechen*. From many similar examples we take the following: in some of the German dialects we find *fahrt, schlagt, tragt* used for the correct forms *fährt, schlägt, trägt*. In this case the original *ä* has been modified after the analogy of *ich fahre, schlage, fahren, schlagen,* etc. In such instances it is often rather difficult to determine how the influence of analogy operated. We can only see that a given expression which we may represent by x has taken on so close a resemblance to another which we may represent by y that it must always remain doubtful which was the original and which the copy. Of this character are the expressions given on p. 106 ff., where we have the mixture of two locutions. The number of words and phrases that have undergone changes under the influence of analogy is very large—probably as large as those that have been regularly developed according to phonetic laws. To treat the subject fully would require a volume. Its importance is, however, such that it seems advisable to pursue it somewhat further.

The first results of the creation of new forms through the influence of analogy are doublets. Thus *krieche,* spoken of above, existed for a time alongside of *kreuche,* just as we have *gelehrt* and *gelahrt, gesendet* and *gesandt, gewendet* and *gewandt,* or 'proven' and 'proved,' 'digged' and 'dug,' 'lighted' and 'lit.' Doublets or double forms of the same word are found in all civilized languages.

The two words do not however generally long exist side by side with equal rank. The genius of language is opposed to the maintenance of two words or two expressions that mean precisely the same thing; in the course of time one of the two forms becomes obsolete. If both are preserved they become synonyms. Both the English and the German languages contain a number of words, the one of Germanic, the other of Latin or Greek ancestry that are substantially or exactly equivalent. To this class belong *Telephon* and *Fernsprecher*, *Lichtbild* and *Photographie;* but the tendency of all languages is to seek to accomplish its ends with the least expenditure of effort. It is not improbable, therefore, that one of these will erelong cease to be in current use, and it will likely be the borrowed word. The struggle for existence between *ich krieche* and *ich kreuche* has been decided in favor of the former, while of the couples above cited, one word in each case may be regarded as obsolescent in the N. H. G. Usually that one of two forms survives which is the most firmly fixed in the memory; in other words that which is the most frequently used and therefore has the most support by analogy. *Kreuch* occurs only in the three persons of the present indicative, and in the singular number of the imperative, while *kriech* was regularly used in the plural of the present indicative, in the entire subjunctive, in the infinitive, in the present participle, and in the plural number of the imperative. If the forces contending for the mastery are about equally matched chance decides the victory in favor of one or the other party—and when we speak of chance, in this connection we mean no more than some hitherto undiscovered law. The users of a language that belong to the same class or circle naturally tend to uniformity of speech. Thus it happens that groups of persons who are separated and have no intercourse with each other do not retain the same verbal forms, but what persists in one group dies out in another. It is in this way that the force of analogy contributes to the formation of dialects. As an example of this we may cite the fact that in the M. H. G. period the first person plural corresponding to *ich fand* was *wir funden*. In the N. H. G. the vowel of the root is the same in both cases, the *u* of the plural having been changed by analogy into *a*, so that we now have *ich fand*, *wir fanden*. The L. G. has taken the opposite course so that Fritz Reuter has *hei funn, wi funnen*.

Again, uniformity may be attained in one district and not in another. The variation between *a* and *ä* as shown in *ich fahre, er fährt* or *ich trage, er trägt* of the M. H. G. as compared with the N. H. G. is not found in the Middle-Netherlandic, nor in many of the contemporary dialects that still have *er fahrt, er tragt*. Why uniformity is attained in one case and not in another is a question not easily answered. This much may, however, be asserted. Where original differences of sound are associated with differences of function the tendency toward uniformity is feeble and the opposite tendency strong. If we compare, for example, the forms, *ich nehme, wir nehmen*, on the one hand, with the widely different *ich nahm, wir nahmen*, on the other, we observe that diversity in form is associated with differences of function, the one form expressing present, the other past, time. These two forms have accordingly remained distinct in all German dialects. But in the M. H. G. the preterite of *ich hoere* was *ich hôrte*; in which case the distinction between the *oe* and the *ô* was needless, the *t* being sufficient to indicate the difference in time between the present and the past. The N. H. G. is accordingly *ich hörte*. This is in conformity with a trend everywhere manifest in language, to achieve the largest results with the smallest expenditure of means—the law of least effort. The difference of function between two cognate words may, in the course of time, become so great that they are no longer felt to be related. *Schon* and *fast* were originally the adverbial forms of *schön* and *fest*, and similar differences in pronunciation between adjective and noun are by no means uncommon in the M. H. G. They have, however, only been kept separate in cases where, owing to the meaning, an isolation of the forms of the words had taken place: in almost all other instances the influence of analogy has made the adjective and the adverb alike. In the M. H. G. the word *rauh* was inflected, Nom. *ruch*- Gen. *ruhes*. It is related to Eng. 'rough,' and in M. G. occurs only in the compounds *Rauch-werk*, *Rauch-handel*, etc., where, however, the primitive adjectival significance is no longer remembered. Innumerable examples of such isolated forms may be traced, and some additional ones will be given further on.

If the results of the influence of analogy are compared with those changes that took place according to well established phonetic laws, it becomes evident that the two processes stand in a certain contrast to each other. Phonetic changes, in the course of time made identical types unlike: the *hoere*, *hôrte*, before given, were at an earlier stage *hōriu*, *hōrte;* the *horiu* was gradually transformed into *hoere* through the influence of the *i*. In other words, *i* in any syllable of a word that had become familiar to the users, being slightly anticipated in pronunciation, in the course of time modified the vowel in the preceding syllable. But the tendency of analogy is to bring together again words that had been differentiated under the influence of phonetic laws acting in a contrary direction. In obedience to the laws of association the effect of a sound embodied in words extends beyond the limits hitherto considered and suggests others that have no related significance or etymology, when the mere external form is sufficiently similar to recall a former word—and by form we mean the word as pronounced, not as written. Or, to put the matter somewhat differently, a word which the speaker is in the habit of using exists in his mind as a latent concept. When now he hears another with which he is unfamiliar, but which bears some resemblance to the former, a connection is at once suggested. As spoken words are but sound, this process bears a good deal of resemblance to the harmonic overtones that are produced when certain fundamental notes are put in vibration. Usually the speaker is scarcely conscious of a possible relation when none really exists, or only becomes so when really related concepts do not appear. Often none exist, as is usually the case with foreign words; and sometimes the existence of an etymological relation has been forgotten. For example, *wahnwitzig* (*wahnsinnig*) is formed of an adjective *wān* (empty), which was lost at a very early period of the O. G.; and another adjective related to our word 'wit.' After it had dropped out of use as a separate word, another closely resembling it though unrelated, the substantive *Wahn*, took its place in popular belief. The same results may follow when etymologically related words exist, but in such a corrupted form that the relation is no longer perceived. Sometimes the formal resemblance between unrelated words is greater than between such as are really cognate. The word *Eiland* is a simplified form of *Einland*: after the loss of the *n* it looked more like a compound of *Ei* with *land* than of *Ein*, and was often so regarded. I may repeat here what I have before said that mere external similarity between words is hardly any more a sign of relationship than is resemblance in form or face, between persons. There is no visible connection between the cognate words *echt* and *Ehe* (see p. 114) though one might be suspected between the former and *achten*. It sometimes happens that the phonetic resemblance of a word to another that is unrelated is less close than to a related word, and yet the former will be taken as its congener. This happens when the proper word has become obsolete and the wrong one is in current use. An instance occurs in the word *Gallusthor*, a designation of one of the gates of the city of Frankfort, which was formerly *das*

Galgenthor. After the gallows, which gave the name, had been removed and forgotten, the inappropriateness of the older designation became evident to even those who did not know what the new compound meant. Its unpleasant associations may likewise have contributed to the disuse of the correct designation.

This process of mental suggestion and association which leads to the grouping of unrelated words as if they were cognate solely on the ground of external similarity is usually designated as popular etymology or folk-etymology. Word-groups brought together in this way are of great importance for the comprehension and memorizing of new words—perhaps hardly less so than those which are formed on true philological principles. In such cases words indistinctly heard are associated with those of which a part has been retained in the memory and called into consciousness by the principle of association. If then the words imperfectly grasped correspond at least partly with such as are already familiar to the hearer he generally completes them correctly and they are reproduced unchanged except in obedience to the proper phonetic laws applicable to the case. *Wahnwitz* and *Eiland*, given above, are examples of this process. But if no corresponding word exists in the mind of the hearer, he completes the new word as best he may with others that deviate more or less widely from the original. In popular speech, for example, *unguentum Neapolitanum* becomes *umgewendter Napoleon* and *Mautturm* is transformed into *Mäuseturm*.

Cases where foreign or obsolete words are perverted into native ones are as common in English as in German, and a few examples may be cited to show how frequently this mental process finds expression in sound. Ibrahim Pacha was known by the unlettered in England as "Abraham Parker," the name of the ship Hirondelle was called "Iron Devil" by the English sailors; and "chateauvert" has become "Shotover." The Indian name Swatara, which occurs in Pennsylvania, is frequently pronounced "Sweet-arrow," and libel is often taken to be a compound of the two words lie-bill.

The tenacity with which the elementary parts of word-groups formed by the influence of folk-etymology cohere is not equally great in all cases. Words may be thrown together because of a mere external similarity of sound without any reference to the sense. Some of the illustrations above given exhibit this. In the last century *Abenteuer* was written *Abendtheuer;* but it is doubtful whether any one who used it thought of it as designating an event that took place in the evening (*Abend*). If it occurs to the speaker that no relationship exists between words more or less alike he sometimes seeks to find a reason for the form before him. The designation *Sauerland*, originally *Suderland*, i. e., *Süderland* applied to the southern portion of Saxony, was justified in popular belief by the anecdote which represented Karl the Great as having exclaimed after its conquest "*das war mir ein sauer land,*" *sauer* being still used as an epithet of that which costs great labor. Similarly *Achalm*, the name of an old castle in Wurtemberg, is said to have come from the interrupted exclamation, "*Ach Allmächtiger,*" of a dying knight; and the story goes that the Wartburg in Saxony is so called because its builder cried out on looking from the eminence on which it stands, " *Wart nur Berg, du sollst mir eine Burg werden.*" Shotover Hill in Oxfordshire is popularly believed to get its name from the circumstance that an archer *shot* an arrow *over* it, and Quebec is often explained as being a contraction of "quel bec!" (what a peninsula!) the exclamation used by a delighted Frenchman upon a first view of the site of the town. It must be remembered, however, that in almost every case of this kind the occurrence was subsequently invented to explain the name, and that its real origin must be looked for elsewhere. This process takes place in what is sometimes designated as the myth-making stage of popular etymology.

In some cases the phonetic similarity between two or more words suggests to the hearer a relationship of signification. This may be favored by attending circumstances. The statement holds good, for instance, in *Sündflut*, transformed from the original *sin-fluot*, which means, the great flood, and not, as popularity imagined, a flood sent upon the earth on account of men's sins. Here the old meaning of *sin* has been displaced by a modern word having a somewhat similar form, but an entirely different meaning. There is reason to believe that the term "Mysteries" (Mysterien) as applied to the well known mediæval religious dramas was generally associated in the popular mind with the mystery of divine service (Cf. Luke VIII., 10. "Unto you it is given to know the mysteries of the kingdom of God." "Vobis datum est nosse mysterium regni Dei"), when in reality it is derived from the Latin 'ministerium' and has no connection with mystery. Examples of this kind are however comparatively rare.

The assumed relationship between a new word and a familiar one is generally based on slight grounds, sometimes on facts that are incompatible with each other. The word *Armbrust*, from the Latin *arcubalista*, easily suggests *arm* and *Brust*, but the connection between these parts of the human body and the weapon remains obscure. Few people would think that an *Eiland* ought, properly speaking, to designate a portion of land having the shape of an egg. To most persons doubtless the word *Maulwurf* suggests the thought that the animal was so named because it casts up the earth with its mouth; when in fact it does this with its hind feet. The word was originally *Moltwerf*, which is the nearer the Eng. 'mold-warp,' an animal that casts up the mold. The current term mole, which appears also in mole-hill, is a part of the original, somewhat modified. Nevertheless, however great the transformation a word has undergone owing to a popular misconception of its etymological relationship, its meaning generally undergoes no change. But there are exceptions. Sometimes resemblance of sound suggests a wrong meaning which may in the course of time entirely displace the correct one. *Das gelobte Land* meant originally 'the promised land,' the adjective coming from *geloben;* but it is now generally supposed to belong to *loben*, which is however a different word. *Sucht* can hardly be used in any other sense than to designate a blameworthy striving. This grows out of the fact that it has long been mentally associated with the verb *suchen*, when in reality it originally designated a disease and is etymologically related to *siech*. There is still a third kind of phonetic suggestion. This takes place when words as wholes are so unlike that a confusion of meaning is impossible, while yet there seems to be a certain remote connection between them. Hence it results that two words are brought into mental juxtaposition the significations of which in part overlap. There is a manifest tendency in the Germanic languages to place such words together and the effect has been to enrich them with a number of formulas containing two or more members that are associated because of the similarity of certain sounds which they embody. The initial syllables or letters may be the same and produce alliteration. The systematic employment of such initial sounds is a recognized principle in old Germanic metrical composition. The number of alliterative formulas in German is very large and they belong under several different heads. They may combine synonyms as *los und ledig, Lust und Liebe, Schimpf und Schande;* or antonyms, as *Lust und Leid, samt und sonders, Wohl und Wehe;* or parts of a whole as *Haus und Hof, Küche und Keller, Mann und Maus*. Phrases of this kind are not uncommon in English, as "neither praise nor pudding," "weal or woe," "chick and child," "watch and ward," "hale and hearty," "glory and gloom." They may be made up of words placed in a syntactical relation to each other, as *bitterböse*, *der wilde Wald* (cf. the wild-wood), *seine sieben Sachen, wenn die Maus satt ist, ist das Mehl bitter;* or the initial sounds may be different, but the principal words rime together, as *Lug und Trug, Saus und Braus, toll und voll, Dach und Fach, Freud oder Leid, Handel und Wandel, Sang und Klang, Wahl macht Qual, heute rot, morgen tot.*

When there is no word in the mind of the hearer to be recalled by a new one that is brought to his attention and by which it may be remembered, considerable mental effort is required to retain it even when clearly apprehended. When then this is not the case fancy has free play and there is no check to the mutilations it may produce. For this reason proper names usually fare the worst because they are of comparatively infrequent recurrence and do not afford much opportunity for revision and correction.

There is another principle of association leading to the formation of word-groups that is different from any so far considered. Owing to the habit of bringing together words that have the same or similar sounds, a certain one comes to be regarded as the bearer of the signification, as *stein* in *steinigen, versteinern*, etc., and this is the only important part of the words. It is this notion that often leads to the formation of popular etymologies.

But there is another mental process that goes hand in hand with the observation of the points of agreement between words, and that is the observation of their differences. Many words have what are apt to be regarded as superfluous syllables—syllables that seem to have little or nothing to do in determining the meaning, and which in fact have nothing to do with the radical signification. How wide-spread this notion may become is forcibly illustrated in the case of the French, which consists almost entirely of Latin words, less that part that follows the accented syllable. Many Anglo-Saxon words suffered a similar apocopation during their transition in the English. One German word may end in *-e*, another in *-igen*, and still another in *-ern*, as *Steine, steinigen, steinern*, and these endings add nothing to the root that is peculiar to it. Sometimes the radical meaning is embodied in one form; sometimes in another; sometimes it is contained in a single syllable; sometimes in two or even more syllables. In other cases it represents an action; in still others it merely designates the accompaniment of a different concept. When now a word differs in meaning from another having the same stem, the notion may easily arise that the difference is owing solely to the termination. On comparing *Stein, Steine, steinigen, steinern*, it is natural to suppose that the plural is represented by the final *-e*, the casting of stones by *-igen*, and something made of stones by *-ern*. But it should be carefully noted that we are concerned here with a definite, simple, concept only; it by no means follows necessarily that the *-e* is used to designate quantity. When now a person, who has come to the conclusion above noted as to the use of the *-e*, hears such a word as *Kreuze*, it will not only suggest *Kreuz*, or some similar word, but also the termination *-e* found in *Steine* and perhaps the word itself. The same may happen in the case of *Fische, Tage, Tische*, etc. Not only is the etymologically related word suggested, but two others that are unrelated, merely because of a certain similarity of sound. The suggestion is usually weak so long as there is nothing in common between two words except a similarity of sound. For example, *laste* and *Last, fange* and *Fang*, resemble *Steine* and *Stein* only in the added or subtracted *-e*. The case is different when the similarity includes intellectual elements also. If we compare *Kreuz* with *Kreuze*, or *Stein* with *Steine* it seems evident that the final *-e* serves the purpose of indicating the plural number. Groups of words are thus formed bearing all manner of relations to some radical or elementary signification. From *steinern, Stein* or *hölzern, Holz*, the natural inference is that the ending *-ern* is used to designate material, while from *höre, hörte* or *sage, sagte* it seems plain that the *t* indicates past time. It is evident that such word-groups are further important for the transmission of language from generation to generation, as they are of the greatest importance for every single act of speaking. It is neither necessary nor possible to remember whether in the case of each separate word, one has ever noticed how its plural is formed; it suffices to recall a few that can be taken as models. So long as the speaker follows correct models the new forms will be correct, but without a thorough knowledge of the materials he is using he will now and then be led unconsciously astray. If the preterit tense of *klagen* is *klagte* and of *sagen* is *sagte*, that of *schlagen* would naturally be supposed to be *schlagte*, though it is not. In like manner if *Apfel* and *Acker* make their plurals with *Aepfel* and *Aecker* respectively, the inference is natural though incorrect that the plural of *Adler* will be *Aedler*. And blunders of this sort are constantly made by learners of a language, whether children who are acquiring their vernacular or adults, a foreign language. A somewhat careful examination of the whole question will convince any one that all languages exhibit this tendency toward greater uniformity —a tendency that is however less marked in those that have acquired a more fixed character through the art of printing than in others. The inclination to form words into groups is directly opposed to the operation of phonetic laws properly so called. Like as *Stein* and *Kreuz* become plural by affixing an *-e*, so do *Blatt, Haus* and *Lamm* by the addition of *-er* and infixing an *e;* or *Graf, Bär* and *Herr* by adding *-en*. In *sagen* and *klagen*, *t* is employed as a sign of the preterit, while in *graben, tragen, schlagen* the same result is effected by a modification of the radical vowel. It will thus be seen that German like most other languages has more than one way of indicating phonetically grammatical and logical relations. When now the speaker remembers that one method is employed in one case and a different one in another it is a matter of some chance which of the two he will employ in a third. It is probable that the new form will be shaped according to the model with which he is most familiar that is the one which has been most firmly fixed in his memory. Under such circumstances it may happen that a word of frequent occurrence will have an equally strong influence with several others of a uniform type, but which are less common.

It will be seen from this brief statement of some of the most important principles of the life and growth of language that phonetic laws can be as little controlled by man as the laws of the physical universe. While each separate individual may modify his own speech and regulate it according to his own pleasure, his influence under the most favorable condition does not extend far. If he would speak and write for the purpose of being understood he must use words that can be easily understood. A language goes its own way and not much can be done toward intelligently directing its course. In the words of the poet Uhland

Indes Gelehrte walten, bestimmen und gestalten
der Sprache Form und Zier,
So schaffest du inwendig, thatkräftig und lebendig
gesamtes Volk an ihr.

INADEQUACY OF THE TRADITIONAL VOCABULARY.

Supposing a language to possess the proper terms for the accurate embodyment in speech of certain concepts, it may happen nevertheless that the right word or words do not report themselves to the consciousness of the speaker when they are wanted; or he may know them and be unwilling to make use of them. In order to express himself at all he will be obliged to have recourse to words not previously employed in the sense he attaches to them. He may use old words with a new meaning, or he may create new words. The result in the former case is, in a certain sense, the impoverishment of language; in the other its vocabulary is enlarged. The causes that lead to the use of new verbal designation, are many and various. Of course the memory can not recall that which was never entrusted to its keeping. Adults are frequently unable to give expression to thoughts and feelings new to them. On the other hand children often coin new words that the adult easily dispenses with. But the power to recall that which was once in the mind likewise differs with different persons. Words rarely used are more likely to be forgotten than those of common occurrence. The same is true of those that have but few cognates as compared with those having many. For this reason it is found to be a great help in the acquisition of a language to associate each new word with one in some way related to it with which the beginner is already familiar. Besides, persons of equal intelligence and culture do not recall words with the same facility. Much depends on the degree of attention and on time in recalling previous concepts. The ability to hold the attention steadily to what is before the mind is least in persons of meager education, and defective intellectual training. It is a matter of common observation that persons of this class are fond of using familiar formulas, and leaving the hearer or reader to infer the particular shade of meaning they are intended to convey. Widely diverse significations are attached to the same word or phrase. The word "make" like the German *machen* is used in many senses differing widely from the original. We hear, the train made (ran) forty miles an hour; he made (earned) a great deal of money; he made (gained) many friends; they made (elected) him president; to make the beds; to make love; to make one out a fool; and so on, almost *ad infinitum*. It is further to be observed that a certain mental inertia, oftener called laziness, is characteristic of certain classes of society, and exhibits itself in speech. There is in current use a large list of students' words and phrases, a sort of college slang, in which there is evident the desire to make the same word-forms do duty on a hundred different occasions and to express the most diverse ideas. The same tendency is observable in every occupation in which any considerable number of persons are engaged. It is not necessary to be very explicit to those who habitually share our thoughts and feelings: they will understand what we mean upon the merest hint. Such consciously or unconsciously formed guilds have generally certain characteristics of speech in common that constitute a kind of badge of membership in the same craft. Besides, it is not natural for human beings to exert themselves either mentally or physically beyond what is necessary; and where the interest is mainly turned in certain directions other interests are neglected.

Different mental states in the same person also exert an influence on the facility with which words are recalled, and on the vocabulary. Generally speaking, a much smaller number of new word-forms is likely to be coined in speaking than in writing, because the tone of voice which accompanies our utterances makes our words more readily intelligible and makes it less important that we confine ourselves to a well established vocabulary. In serious discourse we are apt to use a smaller number of words than in the familiar language of every-day life. When engaged in the calm interchange of thought with another we usually hold ourselves closer to the traditional forms of speech than when under excitement or in passionate argument. The degree of our attention is also influenced by the importance we attach to the thoughts we have to communicate. This factor has had no inconsiderable effect upon the language of law and diplomacy. Here the slightest inaccuracy of expression or statement may give rise to complications and disputes. Accordingly well established words and formulas are sought with painstaking accuracy, either by an effort of memory or by recourse to written or printed documents: and when these recur they are not avoided by the substitution of synonyms—a practice that is well nigh universal in discourse where artistic effect is aimed at.

But even when the speaker is in position to employ other than stereotyped modes of speech to express his thoughts he may have reasons for not doing so. Generally his main object is to be understood and his hearers may be less cultured than he; or he may be able to express what he has to say in several different ways, but his hearers to comprehend but one. In the M. H. G. there are three different words having the form *wern*. One of these is equivalent to *dauern*, which has Eng. cognates in 'dure,' 'endure,' and is the modern *währen*. Another of its meanings is 'hinder,' 'keep off.' The simple form is no longer common and occurs only as an archaism. The usual forms are *abwehren* and *verwehren*. Still another of its meanings was *zahlen*, *geben* (pay, give) and is etymologically related to the Eng. 'warrant;' it is preserved in *gewähren*. The identity in form of these three words gradually led to the disuse of two, in common speech, and the same fate has overtaken other words.

The danger of ambiguity is, however, generally less than might be supposed at first blush, because the context usually shows in what sense the speaker wishes his words to be understood; though in written or printed documents misapprehension is more likely to occur than in living speech. But the ends for which language exists are not subserved if it be understood after mature reflection. Frequently the object of the speaker is attained only in case his words are easily understood and as rapidly as they are uttered; often, too, a thing or a thought is of no interest to us in its relation to other things and thoughts; we are concerned about a single phase or quality of it only. We accordingly want it to be designated by such a term as will cause its concept to stand out prominently among its surroundings and secure for it a ready comprehension.

Ease of comprehension may be further facilitated by the addition of modifying elements to existing formulas of speech, and these elements may be either additions to individual words or to the phrase. At present prepositions are often used with cases where formerly the case was of itself sufficiently definite. If one compares a page of Anglo-Saxon, or Greek, or Latin with one of English or French it becomes evident almost at a glance that particles are of much more frequent occurrence in the modern than in the older languages. In the N. H. G. the number of connecting words is larger than in the M. H. G.; and we can trace step by step the substitution of compound for simple words. A few examples have already been given. Similarly *bedürfen, begehren, bewegen, erbarmen, erbleichen, erhitzen, gedeihen, gehören, genieszen*, are now used in precisely the same sense which these words formerly had without the inseparable prefix. *Einladen* has usurped the functions of an earlier *laden; abgesandter* that of *gesandter; loslösen* that of *lösen; mindern* was gradually displaced by *vermindern*, and this, in turn, is being supplanted by *herabmindern;* Sometimes words of like or closely related meanings are combined and the compound used in the sense of one or the other, when the fact of composition had been forgotten. Formerly *Maul, Saum* and *Elen* meant precisely what *Maultier, Saumtier* and *Elentier* mean now. The first part of the compound *Windhund*, Eng. 'greyhound,' has no more connection with 'wind' in the sense of air in motion than 'grey' in the above word has with 'gray' a color. Both compounds are in one respect curiously alike. In the M. H. G. *wint* was a sufficient designation of the animal, and some word now represented by 'grey' seems to have meant 'dog' in an early period of the Germanic languages. In the compound *Lindwurm* (dragon) the first syllable in the form *lint* was originally equivalent to *Wurm, Schlange*.

Of two expressions that one is always the clearest and most easily understood which is etymologically the most transparent,—in other words, that has one or more cognates in form and signification. The M. H. G. *mâc* has been displaced by the modern *Verwandter* which means the same thing; an older *maere*, by *berühmt*, and *magezöge* by *Erzieher*. *Minne* and *minnen*, so frequent in mediæval German, have been supplanted by *Liebe* and *lieben*, doubtless because these words have a strong support in the adjective *lieb*. In some instances it is not easy to understand why one word has gradually fallen into disuse and another meaning the same thing taken its place, when the object which it designates has remained unchanged. There is an evident disposition in common speech to avoid the solitary adverb *sehr* and to supply its place with such intensives as *fürchterlich, eklig, haarig, höllisch, mörderlich, ochsig*, and the like,—a tendency that is also quite marked in Eng. where we frequently hear such substitutes as ' awful,' " mighty,' 'devilish,' etc. Instead of the German *Maul* one frequently hears *Fresse, Gefräsz;* and the still coarser terms *Schnabel, Rüssel* are not uncommon among the lower classes for *Mund; Riecher* (smeller) is used for *Nase; verrecken*, properly said of the lower animals only, for *sterben; Deckel* (lid, cover) for *Hut*, etc.

An indirect or tropical manner of speech is more graphic and therefore more easily comprehended than a direct. By means of a trope the attention is drawn to that characteristic of a whole complex mental image in which lies the point of comparison of its two members. Figurative expressions are more frequent in poetry than in prose. That of the orient is usually filled with strongly metaphorical turns. Many examples may be found in the Book of Psalms, as witness numbers XXIII., XCI., CXIV.

The language of what would generally be regarded as a widely different sphere, that of common life, is interspersed with metaphors. Instead of·the direct *sich täuschen* (to be mistaken), one hears *sich schneiden* (to cut one's self), *sich stoszen* (to hit against, accidentally), *sich verhauen* (to hew over the line); in place of *vergessen, verschwitzen* (to spoil with sweat); instead of *studieren, ochsen* or *büffeln*. A rude fellow is designated as *klobig, klotzig* or *knotig* (cloddish, or gnarly—cf. the Eng. block-head, one whose head is like a block of wood); a bed (*Bett*) is called *Korb, Klappe, Nest;* for *Bauch, Ranzen* (paunch) or *Schwartenmagen* is used while the head (*Kopf*) is spoken of as *Kübel* (bucket), *Aepfel* or *Simri*. It will be seen that in cultivated languages there is a sort of double current of development, one of the direct mode of expression, the other of the indirect or figurative. In the last analysis all words used to describe mental acts and states are borrowed from such as once designated operations performed by the body: in some cases the same word still has both functions.

It yet remains to consider another factor that contributes to the perspicuity of language. The facility with which an expression is comprehended and therefore its force, depends in some measure upon the number of parts that enter into it: the fewer these are the stronger it is. A single word is more graphic than a combination of two or three or more. German poetry is full of compounds, made for the occasion, that would hardly be used in prose; and the same is true, though to a less extent, of English poetry. Translators from German or Greek into English are constantly tempted to transfer compounds, which the genius of the latter tongue, owing to French influence, scarcely admits. One of the chief elements of strength in the German is the facility with which compounds of almost any length can be formed. When carried to excess, as the Germans themselves not unfrequently do, it leads to heaviness of style, though it can not be said to produce obscurity.

In direct contrast to what has been said regarding

the preference of words on account of clearness and the rejection of such as would lead to obscurity, circumstances sometimes arise where an expressson is preferred for the sole reason that it is not likely to be understood. Talleyrand was right, in part, when he said language was given to man to enable him to conceal his thoughts. One person may have occasion to address another in the presence of a third person whom he does not wish to understand what he is communicating. When both have command of but a single language it must be so transformed as to make it unintelligible to those from whom it is deemed advisable to conceal its content. Children sometimes invent a kind of esoteric speech by prefixing a syllable to every word they use, while on the other hand older persons resort to similar jugglery to tell what they do not wish children to understand.

No class employs a mode of speech so widely different from that in ordinary use as do those who are associated together for the purpose of preying upon society. Such a class exists in every large city and it is greatly to their interest to be able so to express themselves as not to be understood by law-abiding people.

German rogue's slang is largely made up of corrupt Hebrew intermingled with words from the gypsy tongue, together with such terms as are not to be understood in their common acceptation. A goose may be called a flat-footer; the cheeks, gills; the hands, either fore-feet or paws. Sometimes this style of speech is highly figurative, as when a cunning fellow is called a fox, or when one who is hung is said to dance in the air; or when one who offers his opinion unasked is spoken of as putting in his oar. It is probable that such a mysterious language is in use in every large city, composed in the main on the same principles, though differing somewhat in its constituent elements. A kind of aristocratic desire to be different from ordinary mortals gives the language of sportsmen a somewhat unique cast. In effect, [sport is in most European countries the almost exclusive privilege of the rich, or at least of those who have money to spend freely, and is rarely indulged in by those who labor with their hands. Many of the terms here used are a part of the language of technology and have a peculiar and special signification. There is further exhibited in language a propensity under certain circumstances to the use of words which, though intelligible, are vague in signification. This remark is applicable to most euphemisms. Sometimes single words are substituted for others, as *unbekleidet* (unclad, nude) for *nakt*, or limbs for legs; a stupid person may be called innocent or unsophisticated; or a bore, quiet, uncommunicative, and the like. Sometimes circumlocutions are used: death is very often designated in this manner in all languages. This style of expression is the exact opposite of plainness and directness of speech. Many persons who would shudder to use oaths, nevertheless make use of words that are substantially the same thing, though in a form recognizable only to those who are familiar with their history. Darn, dickens, de'il, deuce, are examples of this sort. If we trace the history of certain words in all civilized languages we shall find that they exhibit a downward progress in the moral scale. This may be readily seen by an examination of such English terms as wretch, skeptic, miscreant, wench, and villain. The German *Dirne* was originally equivalent to maiden, and might with entire propriety be applied even to the Virgin Mary; now it means "harlot." *Frech* at one time meant spirited; now it signifies "froward" or "impertinent." *Geil* was equal to *fröhlich* (joyous); its present sense is "lascivious." *Wicht* was beforetime the designation of "thing" in general, and is still used in a slightly different sense in the Eng. "wight;" now its usual sense is "rogue." In all these instances a possible quality of the object gradually usurped the entire meaning of the word. An opposite propensity is exhibited in the names originally given in derision to sects and political parties.

There is in the nature of language and the objects for which it exists no justification for the adumbration of the meaning of words and phrases just discussed. It is in part, at least, explicable by the development of the ethical consciousness. Men have gradually become averse to taking in vain and to using on every occasion the name of that which is sacred, and seek to avoid, in refined society, the mention of what is disagreeable. The heroes of Homer do not hesitate to exhibit on every occasion their most intense feelings; the modern hero strives to conceal them. There is also a sort of superstitious fear in the minds of many persons lest to name the Evil One may cause him to appear. The supposed power of the words used in incantations is well known. There is, moreover, a disposition on the part of cultivated persons to avoid the manners and customs of the uncultured, which extends even to language. Not only the life and thought of the two classes are different, but also their modes of expression. Again, language that is adequate for the ordinary occasions is often too tame and commonplace under unusual circumstances—in solemn moments, in the sanctuary, under strong emotion. Hence has arisen the language of politeness, the phraseology of law and diplomacy, and the diction of poetry.

The same concept may thus find utterance in one of two or more possible words or phrases that differ widely in their social value. Compare, for example, *Schmutz* with *Dreck;* *Mund* with *Maul* and *Gosche;* *Ross* with *Pferd* and *Gaul;* *Haupt* with *Kopf* and *Schädel;* *abscheiden* with *sterben, hingehen, krepieren, verrecken;* and many more.

The language of jurisprudence and diplomacy is characterized by a certain rigidity and formalism, for reasons already set forth. Besides, as dignity is naturally associated in the minds of men with age, the solemnity and importance of an occasion is enhanced when the speakers employ a mode of speech that has the sanction of immemorial usage. A familiar illustration of this may be seen in the prayers in a language with which those using them are totally unacquainted. Age is supposed to give them an efficiency which would be wanting if they were translated into the language of every-day life. But comprehension is often rendered difficult when the language of former times is employed in speaking of the present; and the difficulty may inhere in the individual words, or in the structure of the sentences.

The valedictory address to the imperial diet of 1518 begins as follows: "We, by the grace of God, Roman emperor elect, at all times augmenter of his realm, etc., proclaim by this letter and make known to each and every one, after we as elect Roman emperor, governor and protector of christendom, with solicitude have noted and taken to heart the tumults and disorders, which do more and more, as time advances, manifest themselves in all parts of the empire, and the weighty and obligatory affairs of all christendom, of our holy faith and the German nation, with what annoyance the enemy of Christ our Lord and Savior, the Turk, strives daily to oppress and destroy our faith and the universal christian church and for this reason has caused our legates and those of all christian kings and potentates to come to his Holiness the Pope, to take counsel together and to determine how resistance may be successfully made to such nefarious schemes and projects and, further, from the same and other determining motives have decided upon an imperial diet in our city and that of the Holy Empire, Augsburg, purposing, together with the estates of the Holy Empire, in the same empire, to take counsel and adjudicate upon the seditions of our estates and of the German nation, the wants and disorders, unity and peace, in virtue of the written authority of our estates authorized at the last imperial diet held in Mainz and what further may be necessary in order that such sedition, wants and disorders may be put an end to; and that affairs may be placed in a permanent and commendable state, to the end that there may result efficient aid against the Turk, for the rescue of our Holy faith."

The object of the above translation has been to exhibit the lumbering style of the German just previous to the reforms instituted by Luther, rather than to put the extract into good English. For the benefit of those who are interested in the original it is also given :

"Wir Maximilian von Gottes Gnaden, erwählter Römischer Kayser, zu allen Zeiten Mehrer desz Reichs, etc., Bekennen offentlich mit diesem Brief, und thun kund allermänniglich, nachdem Wir, als erwählter Römischer Kayser, Vogt und Schirm-Herr der Christenheit, ausz Christlichem Gemüth betracht, und zu Herzen gefaszt, die Empörungen und Gebrechen, so sich allenthalben im Reich je länger je mehr erzeigen, auch die schwere und obliegende Sachen gemeiner Christenheit, unsers Heiligen Glaubens und Teutschen Nation, mit was Anfechtung der Feind Christi, unsers Herrn und Seligmachers, der Türk, unsern Glauben und gemeine Christliche Kirch zu benöthigen und unter zu drücken, sich täglich übet, und deszhalben hievor verfügt das Unser und aller christlichen konige und Potentaten Bottschaften, zu Päbstlicher Heiligkeit kommen sind, zu rathschlagen und zu beschlieszen, wie solchen erschrecklichen Obliegen und Fürnehmen, Rath und Widerstand beschehen mag, und ferner ausz denselben und anderer beweglichen Ursachen einen Reichstag in Unser und desz heiligen Reichs Stadt Augspurg fürgenommen, der Meynung mit desz Heil. Reichs Ständen, in desselben Reichs, seiner Ständ und Teutschen Nation Empörung, auch Mängel und Gebrechen Rechtens, Einigkeit und Friedens, laut der Stand Schrifft, auf nechstgehaltenen Reichs-Tag zu Mayntz ausgangen, und was ferner die Nothdurfft erfordert, zu rathschlagen und zu handeln, damit solche Empörung, Mängel und Gebrechen abgestellt, und in gut löblich beständig Wesen gebracht werden, und daraus eine auszträglich Hülff wider den Türken, zu Rettung unsers Heil. Glaubens, folgen mag."

The language of politeness like the arts of civility has for its object to promote the social intercourse between man and his fellow-man, and to make it as attractive and agreeable as possible. It originates in the desire to say what is pleasing, but has nevertheless a clearly marked sphere, and therefore a sort of technical character. It proceeds mainly upon the assumption that one person should always show to another the evidence of his esteem, either by enhancing the importance of him who is spoken to, or humbling one's self. This may be done either by expressions of good-will in general, or by demonstrations of joy at seeing another, or by expressing the hope of soon meeting him again. Society has, however, not left it to each individual to decide with what degree of esteem he shall regard his fellow-man. It has established a particular style of address for particular persons and for special circumstances. The language of politeness must, therefore, of necessity have a kind of fixed and formal character. It is a matter of little moment to the historian of language, nor has it any relevancy to the question of morals, whether the sentiments felt correspond with the words employed, or indeed whether the language used expresses any thought at all. The words employed in the language of courtesy may, of course, give utterance to the same concepts to which they give expression when the speaker uses them with perfect freedom; but it is often the case that these appear too commonplace on occasions when it is considered good form to employ them, and this statement is true not merely of the vocabulary but even of the syntax of common speech. Not only should the general mode of address be different, but one should speak in a different way of himself. The most characteristic divergence from the language of every day life is the tendency to make the difference in rank between the speaker and person addressed as great as possible, to the advantage of the latter. This may be done by the use of the plural number instead of the singular. The speaker minifies his own importance by using 'we' instead of 'I,' thus merging himself in the great mass of mankind; or magnifies that of the person addressed by using 'you' instead of 'thou,' as if he were in the presence of more than a single individual, or the speaker may omit all reference to himself by the omission of the personal pronoun altogether. This form of address is used in the familiar phrases, "thanks," "pray," "beg pardon" (*danke, bitte*), for, I thank you, accept my thanks, I beg your pardon. Generally, however, this style of speech is used because of its brevity and because the words not expressed are easily understood. Again, the person addressed may be spoken to, as one not present, that is, in the third person. It is customary to say *Euer Gnaden, Euer Hoheit* (your Grace, your Highness), when the meaning is 'thy Grace,' and petitions are usually presented, not in the name of the petitioner personally, but "your humble subscriber makes bold to pray," etc. The use of *er, sie*, was originally intended to mark politely the difference in social station which the speaker felt in the presence of the person spoken to; but now, conversely, these pronouns are used to make the latter realize this difference. The use of the third person in direct address is later than that of the plural, and belongs to the N. H. G. period; but ir (*ye*) instead of *du* (thou) is a trait of the mediæval period.

With these facts the reader may compare the frequent use of "thy servant," meaning I in the Bible, and the closing formulas still employed in epistolary correspondence and elsewhere, such as "your most obedient servant," and so on.

The latest, and in some respects the most curious, stage of development is one that has been reached by the German language alone in the assignment of equivalent values to the plural number and the third person—*Sie haben* for *du hast* of the ordinary style of address. *Wie befehlen der Herr Oberst?* means *Oberst, was befiehlst du?* This *Sie haben* is often mistakenly employed for *er hat, sie hat* in speaking of one who is present and who would be directly addressed with *Sie haben*.

In the category of professional etiquette belong also the epithets "honorable," "his honor," "reverend," etc. All these are to be regarded as titles accompanying the office, but having no necessary relation to the office-holder; though it is natural to expect that a man who has been honored by election or appointment to an honorable office shall himself be honorable. This is by no means always the case, as abundant experience proves. The editorial " we " gives a fictitious importance to the person using it, as if the writer spoke for a number of persons besides himself. It has been frequently remarked that this "we" carries with it in the eyes of many, much more weight than the simple "I," though both usually mean exactly the same thing. The English " thou " is now rarely used except in addressing the Deity; and by an apparently strange anomaly the German *du* is used in the same way, but likewise in conversation with familiar friends.

The English is perhaps the most democratic of modern languages just as the English-speaking people have everywhere made the nearest approach to a pure democracy in government, and there are but few occasions where the use of 'you' is inadmissible. The ancients were, at least in point of language more modest than the modern. Two well-known instances are furnished by the personal narratives of Xenophon and Cæsar; both of whom uniformly speak of themselves in the third person.

Some interesting facts in the history and use of pronouns may be found in Schele De Vere's Studies in English under the appropriate caption.

But it is in poetic composition that æsthetic considerations produce the most conspicuous peculiarities of speech : it is here that the far-fetched, the affected and unusual in expression are most frequently to be met with. Not only is the vocabulary often uncommon, but the composition and the order of words differ from ordinary prose. It is true that no hard and fast line separates prose from poetry, but a certain class of objects is most frequently represented in one than in the other. So in prose we find *du lebst*, *er lebt;* in poetry the writer is allowed to choose between these forms and *du lebest, er lebet* (thou livest, he liveth). Prose prefers *hob, gerächt, schwor, webte, wurde;* poetry, *hub, gerochen, schwur, wob* and *ward.* Such plurals as *Bänder, Denkmäler, Länder* belong to the former; *Bande, Denkmale, Lande,* to the latter. Abbreviations like *mächt 'ge, wen'ge, Reu', klagt'* are admissible only in poetry. To it alone belong such forms as *Herze, Genosz, zurücke, mein, dein,* for *meiner, deiner, desz* and *wesz* instead of *dessen, wessen;* likewise *inniglich, wonniglich* for the shorter prose forms *innig, wonnig.* The poets give us *welch Getümmel, ein glücklich Land, Röslein rot, gebraucht der Zeit, tönt die Glocke Grabgesang,* and they generally avoid the insertion of clauses between the article and the noun. The vocabulary of poetry contains comparatively few loan-words, and to it alone belong such words as *frevel* for *frevelhaft, frommen, gülden, Hain, Hindin, Mähr, Odem, lind, schwank, siech, zag,* while such as *Erlebnisz, Gesichtskreis, deswegen, derjenige, Seelenruhe* pertain exclusively to the province of prose. *Gemeine* is more poetic than *Gemeinde, Fittich* than *Flügel, Ross* than *Pferd, nahen* than *sich nähern, mehren, zeugen, zwingen* than *vermehren, erzeugen, bezwingen.*

Generally speaking, poetry represents the conservative elements of language; prose its progressive and growing force. English poets like their German brethren are fond of employing archaic words in preference to those in every day use; pure Teutonic in preference to engrafted words. Tennyson exhibits a marked predilection for the older words and word-forms. William Barnes, the Dorsetshire poet advocates the restoration of the homely Saxon compounds in many cases where they have been displaced by borrowed equivalents. He proposes "fore-elders" for ancestors; "forewit" for prudence; "inwit" for conscience; "wort-lore" for botany; and many more. In some cases it is difficult to give a reason for assigning a word to the vocabulary of poetry rather than prose, or vice versa; yet few persons will deny that such a distinction exists in all languages. But it is well to remember that much the largest portion of verse-composition can not with any propriety be ranked as poetry. The gap between the language of prose and that of poetry is not equally wide at all periods in the history of any literature. There are times in the annals of every nation when it places little value on works of the imagination. Then, too, there are intrinsic differences in national tastes. The Romans produced hardly any genuine national poetry at any time; the Greeks comparatively little of genuine merit after the loss of their independence. During the greater part of the seventeenth century poetry of a high order was held in comparatively little esteem in England, and during this period German poetry had sunk almost to the level of prose. For about two centuries beginning with the middle of the sixteenth, Germany produced hardly any literature worthy of the name. Brokes (born 1680) uses such expressions as "*das Gehör bezaubernden Gesang, von solchem nach der Kunst gekräuselten Geschwirre.*"

Contemporary poets often differ widely as regards the interval which separates their writings from prose. The court-romances of the M. H. G. period are much more nearly related to the spoken language of their time than the popular epics of the same era. The same statement may be made of Otfried's Harmony of the Gospel when compared with the old Saxon Heliand, which was probably composed but little earlier. An important factor is likewise the social condition of the poet. If he belongs to the class of bards or professional minstrels, or is in familiar intercourse with it, the influence of tradition will be much more marked in his compositions than when this is not the case. This fact will account for the divergence in style between the authors of the Heliand, the Nibelungen Lay and Gudrun, on the one hand, and Godfrey of Strasburg on the other.

Purely external considerations often have great weight in determining the language of poetic composition. What is not designed to be read either publicly or in private, but to be recited, generally contains a large number of stereotyped formulas to which the rhapsodist may have recourse when his memory is at fault, or when there is need of a pause as a sort of preparation for what is to follow. The poetry of the old German gleemen is full of such standing epithets. The *epitheton ornans* is a prominent characteristic of the Homeric poems. The ships are designated as "hollow," the storm as "sweeping," and the sea as "barren" or "dark blue" or "swarming." We have "light-haired" Menelaos, the "discreet" Telemachos, and the "white-armed" Nausikäa; Mykenae is the "golden," Pylos the "sandy" and Thebes the "seven-gated." Voss a contemporary of Goethe mechanically imitates Homeric usage in this respect in Luise, although his poem was composed for a wholly different purpose; and while his skill as a translator, especially of Homer, has never been surpassed, he failed to achieve permanent fame as an original poet. Goethe with true poetic instinct does not employ standing epithets to describe the characters of his Hermann and Dorothea, but judiciously varies them to suit the different situations.

As the old Germanic poetry was alliterative the need of words having the same initial sound no doubt contributed much to the development of frequently occurring epithets. The number of words of this class required was much larger than is necessary to satisfy the demands of modern rime. This becomes easily evident upon a glance at the specimen already given. On the other hand the construction of modern German poetry is rendered much more difficult by reason of the large number of words having more than two syllables, but of which two successive syllables are equally accented. For example, *Leuchtwürmchen*, *Maikäfer*, *Mondscheibe*, and many others, can rarely, if at all, be employed in poetic diction, and when needed their place must be supplied by substitutes. Such

English compounds as death-dealing, way-faring, bloodthirsty offer a similar difficulty. Sometimes dignity and congruence; or in other words æsthetic appositeness is intentionally eschewed by writers and speakers. A coarse and vulgar expression may now and then be used for its own sake. This trait is characteristic of students' slang of which we have already spoken. With a designed disregard of the rules and traditions of language we find here *Maul* used for *Mund*, *fressen* and *saufen* instead of *essen* and *trinken*. Euphemisms are rare. When vulgar or trivial words are used in close connection with those that express emotions of sublimity; or when words that are almost void of meaning are placed alongside of such as are weighty and significant a comic effect is produced. Moritz Busch, a popular contemporary writer, is in the habit of employing such combinations to excite the risibilities of his readers. Sustained efforts of this sort give rise to what is usually called the mock-heroic, examples of which are the Battle of the Frogs and Mice by Pigres, in Greek; the Hudibras of Butler; the Rape of the Lock by Pope, and the Jobsiade of Kortum. An intentional deviation from linguistic tradition, or, in other words, a violation of grammatical rules, sometimes produces a comic effect. Such expressions as "bif of ditterance," "we thunk," "many a smile he smole and many a wink he wunk," etc., will illustrate this usage from the English standpoint. Irony, or the employment of words in a sense nearly or quite the contrary of their usual meaning, also deserves to be mentioned as one of the forms of language.

It has been shown in a former section that the laws of logic have but little influence on the formation and development of language, and that the chief object sought to be attained are beauty of diction and ease of comprehension. Still, it can not be denied that a species of applied logic, what may be called the theory of grammar, has had some effect on the N. H. G. as well as upon all cultivated languages. So far as the German is concerned the labors of Gottsched and Adelung, the former of whom belonged to the earlier part of the eighteenth century, the latter to its later years, have not been altogether fruitless.

AMPLIFICATION OF THE MATERIALS OF SPEECH.

What has been said thus far has had special reference to the causes that were mainly instrumental in producing changes in language and have been an answer to the question why the new is unceasingly displacing the old. It has become evident from the study of particular examples that for various reasons the same word can not be perpetually employed in one and the same sense. It behooves us then to examine the relation existing between vocables used with a certain signification now with that which they had in the earlier periods of the language, and how it is possible by means of the same word to awaken one concept at one time and a different one at another time, or, to express the thought otherwise, how can a word undergo a change of meaning during the period of its existence as an integral part of spoken language? And again, how shall we find words to express a concept of which we are conscious for the first time? The answer is to be found in the study of any cultivated language; for it will show that old words have undergone a gradual transformation of meaning, and that new ones have been coined to designate new objects.

CHANGE OF MEANING.

When an existing word is employed in a new signification it is generally the case that no formal connection exists between the old and the new word. The speaker then employs one with which the hearer is already familiar, but in a different sense. If however he expects to be understood some relation must exist between the thought to be communicated and the word to be used. This relation between the two words may be their greater or less similarity to each other. We have no difficulty in recognizing a person whose portrait we have seen. The delineation may be rude, a mere outline sketch; yet the imagination easily supplies the missing traits. In like manner any concept may be awakened in the mind by another concept that bears a general resemblance to it. This concept may indicate no more than the general type of a class or of individuals, provided it be used in such a way that the missing parts may be readily called to mind. For example, Luther says, "*das Wort sie sollen lassen stan*," in speaking of the Word of the Holy Scriptures. This " Word " is employed in precisely the same way in English. In like manner *Schrift* or " Scriptures " is used for the contents of the Bible though it simply means writings. In such expressions as "*er gehört der Gesellschaft an*," "*er ist von Familie*," the mind readily supplies the adjective *gut*, as the speaker intended it should. *Sitzen, brummen, spinnen* are frequently used in the sense of *gefangen sein; machen* as we have seen may be applied to a great number of acts. If there no longer exists alongside of this unliteral and indirect meaning one that is literal and direct,—in other words, if a term has become obsolete in one or more senses we say that its signification has been narrowed or particularized. It may be said of civilized languages as a whole that they exhibit a tendency toward greater definiteness in the meaning of their words. If we compare Latin, for example, with English or German, it is often impossible to find a modern equivalent for the ancient term. Even in the same language the difficulty is often insurmountable. *Ecke* was formerly applied to anything sharp or pointed, and might be applied to the edge of a sword; now it means " corner." *Gerben* (tan) meant simply *bereiten* and had no reference to any particular object. The Greek σύνταξις originally meant an arrangement of any sort, a body of troops, or of laws, a constitution, and it was not till later that it was applied to the arrangement of the words in a sentence, as its derivative is still used in both German and English. We say of a child that it knows its letters, and of an adult that he is a man of letters; yet nobody is at a loss for a moment as to the meaning in each case.

If we wish to call up in the mind of a child the concept of a dog or a horse we can do so by showing him the picture of either of these animals. The apprehension of their essential traits is not rendered defective by the sight of some that are unessential; nor is the mental picture of the animal made less vivid by the rudeness of the picture before the eye. So in language, the naming of a particular characteristic may call to mind the concept of an entire class or species. The German word *holzen* (handle wood) is used of any kind of a fight even when no weapons of wood are used, just as *bechern* (use cups, or goblets) is said of a drinking bout from mugs as well. We frequently say of a man that he drinks too much, or that he likes drink, or that he is too fond of his cups, when we have in mind only drink that intoxicates.

We are sometimes reminded of one person by the sight of another; but there must be some point of resemblance, however slight, between the two, though they may be unlike in every other particular. What is true of objects presented to the eye is equally true of sounds that enter the ear. A single individual may awaken the reminiscence of an entire class. But in such cases the word class must be understood in its most comprehensive sense, for, strictly speaking, a class or genus is created whenever we discover any similarity between two wholly different things. A white horse, a snow-drop, Parian marble, linen, snow, a taper, and other white objects form a class or genus, of which the common characteristic is the color, just as much as do horse, ox, and hare in the genus mammalia, or snow-drop, lily and rose, under the general class phenogams. The same object may generally be ranged under several categories at the same time. But we may likewise be aware that divergences exist between different classes or genera. The more conspicuous the qualities are upon which the similarity of two concepts rests the more readily they are observed and the more easily the subordinate elements are ranged under those that are of a more general character. In this way the mind forms categories of objects that are evident to all and become a matter of continuous tradition. When the connection between two objects is close and their relation intimate one may be easily and unconsciously exchanged for the other, as when the idea of time is common to both. In some of the current German dialects the word *Mittag* is also used in the sense of *Nachmittag;* in others *Abend* is employed, where still others regard *Nachmittag* as the proper term. In the South German dialects the perfect tense has entirely displaced the older imperfect, *er ist gegangen, er ist gekommen* mean *er ging, er kam.* In French there is an evident tendency in the same direction. The Latin perfect of historic times is both a perfect and an aorist, the result of a failure to distinguish between two different forms of the earlier language.

Again, in contemplating an action we may fail to notice whether it originated at a certain point or took place there; for this reason the notions of active and passive are sometimes confounded or interchanged. Thus, *heiszen* was originally equivalent to *einen Namen geben*, later, to *einen Namen besitzen, haben.* Hence, we must translate *Ich heisze Peter*, my name is, or I am called, Peter. *Kehren, treiben, wenden* in the older language meant no more than to put an object in motion; now they are used in a number of different senses. It is correct to say *einen fahren*, but formerly the verb could take no object and was used like the English 'fare' which is virtually the same word. The participial adjectives in *ein besonnener, ein überlegter Mensch* are both passive in form, but active in signification. *Ein Bedienter*, literally, one served, is one who serves, a servant, *ein Studierter* is one who has studied, though in strict grammar it should mean one who has been studied. Similarly, we say in English the lesson is learned and the man is learned, where the word "learned" has two widely different meanings. If we wish to render these two phrases in German we shall have to translate the first learned by *gelernt* and the second by *gelehrt*. Attention has already been called to the fact that the German as well as the English dialects make no distinction between *lehren* (teach) and *lernen* (learn).

It seems to be natural to recognize a close affinity between impressions produced on the sensorium through its different organs. Sensations received through the eye are transferred to those perceived by the ear. We speak of a round tone or the dull sound, of the tones of color as loud or soft. *Grell* and *hell*, now referred to the organ of sight or hearing, related originally to the ear alone, *Grille* (cricket) and *Hall* (clang, resonance) being connected with these words. *Süsz*, at first used of the taste, is now used of the taste or smell or sound. Its derivative *Geschmack* like our "taste" is even used of perceptions by the æsthetic sense. Impressions received through the sense of touch are sometimes applied to those coming originally through that of hearing, seeing or smelling: bitter means that which bites, *stinken* at first meant that which pricks or stings, while both the German and the Englishman speak of tones or words as warm, sharp, pointed, cutting, soft, harsh, rough, and so on.

Another kind of interchange between different categories of concepts takes place when objects primarily designed for one use are spoken of as if intended for another. The original purpose embodied in the radical form of the word is lost sight of, in the transferred meaning. For instance the name *Streichhölzchen* is still applied to matches made, not of wood, but of wax, just as *Fensterscheibe* is used of panes of glass that are not round but of some other shape. So in English we speak of an ovation or of an inauguration to designate ceremonies that have nothing to do with either sheep or augurs. A vivid impression and a painful one are nearly related. Accordingly many intensive adverbs are derived from words that in their earlier history designated feelings of pain. "*Es ist grausam kalt,*" "*es ist schrecklich heisz,*" are the counterpart of the English "it is outrageously cold," "it is fearfully hot;" *es dauert furchtbar lang* is our "it lasts dreadfully long." We even hear of a thing being "awfully pretty," "awfully good" or "awfully nice." The word *sehr*, Eng. sore, originally meant painful. The Scotch "sair" still preserves in sound its connection with the German while such expressions as "sore need," "sorely in need" show clearly the original signification. In many of the Middle German dialects *oder* is used in the sense of *aber*, the notion of contrast or opposition in both leading to their interchange.

In cases where the close connection between two or more concepts is not made evident by striking points of similarity alongside of which minor divergences are lost sight of, in other words where resemblances are chiefly external, they give rise to what are called metaphors, or metaphoric language. The result is the same where class distinctions are merely casual or superficial marks, but where nevertheless the relations between objects and their mental concepts are not entirely hidden. It is not possible, however, to draw a fine line of demarcation between the examples given above and those here had in view, as the mental processes are closely akin. Examples are endless. The same designations are applied to lifeless and living objects. The human form suggests many comparisons with inanimate things. We speak of the head of a valley, of a stream, of a nail (*Nagelkopf*); of a neck or of a tongue of land (*Landzunge*); of an arm of the sea

(*Meeresarm*); of the leg of a chair (*Stuhlbein*), and so on. The process is reversed when the head is called a pumpkin, a gourd, a calabash and other names taken from inanimate objects. The German word *Kopf* (head) is etymologically related to Eng. 'cup' and had originally very nearly its meaning. The Latin word 'testa,' a vessel of burned or baked clay, has in part furnished the Romance languages with their word for 'head,' 'caput,' the proper word having been supplanted by it. Other familiar German words of this class are *Brustkorb*, *Herzkammer*, *Kniescheibe*, *Becken*, etc.

Designations of time are generally named from concepts of space. Corresponding to the English 'point of time,' 'portion of time,' 'piece of a day,' the German uses *Zeitpunkt*, *Zeitraum*, *eine Spanne Zeit*, *Zeitabschnitt*; *um*, *nach* and *vor* originally had reference only to space. The notion of space or of time is plainly seen in expressions embodying the relation of cause and effect, "to do a thing out of hatred or envy," "to die from fright," "to fall from grace" are examples under this head. *Wegen* is an old dative plural of the substantive *Weg*, whence the older phrase *von—wegen*; *des Geldes wegen* accordingly means, *auf den Wegen des Geldes*. The English 'way' has a great variety of similar uses in both the singular and plural number, as "by way of making amends," "this is nothing out of the way," "in a business way," "always," and so on. *Weil* originally had a temporal signification, but is now chiefly causal, as may be seen in the Eng. "while;" and is a sort of adverbial case of *Weile*. The Eng. word is still used as a noun and a verb in addition to its function as an adverbial conjunction, as may be seen in 'a long while,' 'to while away the time.'

The largest number of metaphorical expressions belong to the class in which mental phenomena are described in terms that were originally used to designate purely sensuous acts or experiences. Such words are *einsehen* (see into), *erfassen* (grasp), *begreifen* (comprehend), *vernehmen, Fassung, Zustand, Verhalten,* and many others of this character. In English the etymology is not always so transparent because Latin derivatives have taken the place of many Germanic words; but these when carefully examined show precisely the same origin. Returning again to the German, *erinnern* means bring into; *lehren* is to bring into or upon the way; goth. 'laisjan,' related to *Geleise; lernen,* to be brought into the way, and the primitive signification of *befehlen* was to give over. *Vernunft* is almost equivalent to *Vernehmen* and is from the same root, —compare with it the Eng. under-stand-ing. *Angst* like the Eng. 'anxious,' 'anxiety,' and *Bangigkeit* are based on the idea of pressing or bending. *List* (artifice), which in the M. H. G., still had the general sense of 'insight,' is connected with *lehren, lernen, Geleise.* The Germans say of insane persons that they are *Verrückt,* that is moved out of their proper or natural state. Our word 'insane' means simply 'unsound,' and might logically be applied to those who are sick in body as well as to those who are sick in mind, if usage had so determined. Persons are said to be beside themselves when they do not clearly apprehend what they are doing. "There is a screw loose" is a thought as common among the Germans as among the English. 'Whim' is probably a veiled expression for a buzzing or stirring in the head, and we say even more undisguisedly "he has a bee in his bonnet," to designate about the same cerebral condition. Comparatively few proverbial expressions can be literally translated from one language into another, but the similarity of concepts underlying them is remarkable.

It is a well established fact in the life and growth of all languages that mental processes are without exception designated from acts of the physical body or from occurrences in the material universe. In the case of many metaphorical expressions transmitted to us from former times it is not always easy to recognize their origin.

Words undergo changes in form, as we have seen, in obedience to phonetic laws; but a word or an expression may remain unchanged and the custom out of which it grew pass away. The Germans still say *Wir haben einen Span wider jemand*, because in olden times a chip or flat piece of wood was used to cite persons before a judicial tribunal. In German as in English we may speak of throwing down or taking up the gauntlet, when we wish to challenge an opponent or take up a challenge from him. In order to understand the etymological meaning of *Angebinde*, something bound on or to, we need to remember that it was once customary to bind a birth-day present to the arm or around the neck of a child. At present it may be used of any gift. The Germans say *einen Korb geben* (give a basket) just as we say to "give the mitten," because formerly the maiden let fall the basket in which an unacceptable lover wished to be drawn up to her window, or prepared it so that the bottom broke out. *Sündenregister* is explained by the mediæval belief that the devil kept a record of the sins of each person, which was to be presented for adjudication after death. In the metaphorical expressions above cited the quality in which the correspondence rests is not always the most salient, but is at least one that is not irrelevant. But there is another group of concepts in which certain characteristics appearing only occasionally form the basis of the metaphor. It is thus that *Mütterchen, mein Sohn, mein Kind* are used as expressions of endearment, very much like the Eng. "mammy," "sonny," "sissy," etc. In some dialects a garrulous woman is called a *Schwätzfrabase* and *basen*, to act the aunt, cousin, means simply to gossip. In Basel, *Tochter* is used as the exact equivalent of girl, notwithstanding the fact that there are many aunts who know when to hold their tongues and that there are many daughters who are no longer maidens. Sometimes proper names are pressed into service to designate certain quali-

-ties: *Hans, Grete, Peter, Stoffel* and *Töffel*, both abbreviations of *Christophel*, are terms for expressing stupidity, just as we call an Irishman "Pat," a servant girl "Bridget," a Scotchman "Sandy" or a sailor "Jack." "Simple Simon," "Smart Aleck," "country Jake," "Jack-of-all-trades," are familiar phrases among us. A *Prahlhans* or a *Schmalhans* is a boaster, though there are many persons who boast, bearing other names than Jack or John. In Berlin persons who are better known on account of their many words than their profound thoughts are called *Quaselfritze, Quaselliese, Quaselpeter;* in each of these appellations there is a proper name. There too, a dealer in cigars is called *Cigarrenfritze*. In Basel a good-natured, stupid fellow is known as *Baschi* (Sebastian); Johann is the common designation of man-servant, while in Paris a certain class of women and girls is called grisettes, though they often wear garments of other colors than gray. In Lower Austria *Leahnl* means about the same that *Kerl* does in other parts of Germany,—it is an abbreviation of *Leonhardt*. Similarly, we speak of a Bohemian, a Philistine, an outlandish fellow, or an outlandish act. In documents of the fifteenth century occurs the term *Lazarusmensch* to designate a leper. In the seventeenth century "to dissect" was called in Leipzig *rolfingen*, because a well known professor, Rolfing, practiced this art in that city. Artificially cut and trimmed gardens were said to be lenotrized from the name of the French architect Lenôtre. A mischievious trick is still called *eine Eulenspiegelei*, from the name of a noted practical joker who is reputed to have lived in the thirteenth century and an incredible story is often designated as a Munchausen tale.

In order to call up in the mind the complete image or representation of an object is not necessary that it should be designated in its entirety. Any small portion, any object that bears the least relation to it, may by the principle of association, awaken a long train of concepts. A myrtle flower may call up in the mind of the aged woman her bridal wreath in which it was entwined; the marriage festivities; the table-talk that occurred; and the parting words of her parents, all of which may come vividly before her mind's eye. Words and phrases may be interchanged when the substituted concepts bear any relation to the original either by proximity in space or time, or cause and effect. Here, too, as in the permutation of similar images the closeness of the connection is not always the same. Owing to the presence of one concept the recollection of another may in all cases and almost of necessity be present also; or the association may be occasional and accidental. When we hear or read Schiller's "*er zählt die Häupter seiner Lieben,*" we know that he means not only the heads of his dear ones, but the beloved persons; the hospitable roof, the hospitable threshold, are often used for the entire hospitable dwelling. *Dickkopf* (thick-head), *Gelbschnabel* (yellow-beak), *Langfinger,* designate beings possessing these attributes. *Kutte* (cowl) and *Schürze* (apron) are sometimes used as synonymous with monk and housewife. Bench and bar often mean judges and lawyers. In the peculiar language of German students *Hausbesen* or *Zimmerbesen* designates the maid who takes care of their rooms. We often use the name of a place when we are thinking of the persons who assemble there, as the House (of Representatives), the Senate chamber, the church, the court. The curious word *Frauenzimmer* originally meant just what the separate parts of the compound would make it to mean, a chamber for women; and even in the last century it was used to designate a number of persons of the female sex. *Bursche* the popular appellation of a university-student comes from the Latin 'bursa,' the place where the students dwelt together. Concepts of things and persons and acts and circumstances reciprocally condition each other. Sometimes an object suggests a quality, then in time comes to be substituted for it. "Heart" is thus used to signify "courage," and "to take heart" means "to take courage." The keen eye and the strong hand of a man are sometimes extolled to express in another way the thought that he can see far and hit hard. A reenforcement means not merely the act of reenforcing, but a body of men sent to reenforce others. The government, as often used, is synonymous with those who govern. *Gefängnisz* in the older German is the same as *Gefangenschaft*, i. e. prison, is the same as imprisonment. Juvenile frivolity and youthful recklessness are but other terms for frivolous or reckless youths. Says Hebel, "*schon mancher Rausch ist seitdem auf den Bergen gewachsen*," but he is thinking of the grapes from which the wine was made that produced the intoxication. *Holen* (fetch) designated in the earlier time an act which frequently preceded the bringing of an object, the act of calling, and is etymologically the same word as the Greek καλεῖν; *lauschen* in its primitive sense means *verborgen sein;* and *verwegen* (rash) is related to *wägen*, this epithet being applicable to a person who has mistakenly weighed his powers and as a result exhibits over-confidence in himself. *Erschrecken* radically signifies to 'start up,' as may be seen in *Heuschrecke* (grasshopper, hayhopper). The cause is named from the effect, like the Homeric φοβός, the flight produced by fear. The phrase *in Harnisch geraten* (get into, put on one's armor) was in former times the frequent result of getting angry; it is still used in the latter sense, though the use of armor has been totally discarded. The Americanism "to put on the war paint" is simply a metaphorical expression for preparing to attack an opponent, and has its origin in the custom of the Indians when making ready to attack an enemy. Uprightness, honesty, simplicity as opposed to duplicity, may sometimes be the result of dullness: hence a stupid person may be called a simpleton. Occasionally the lack of moral qualities is designated by a term that indicates mental weakness; thus *schlecht* primarily means *schlicht* (plain, straightforward), as may be seen in *schlechthin, schlechtweg, schlecht und recht*.

In examining the development of words and the metamorphoses which their meanings have undergone we are confronted with a variegated and sometimes a confused picture. The science of language must confine itself wholly to what is past, and can not, like some of the physical sciences, predict what will happen in the future. If we know what a certain word signified five hundred or a thousand years ago, it will give us no more than a clue to its present signification. The various possible meanings not only run parallel to each other, but continually cross each other. The same word may be used in a number of different senses at the same time, or in different periods of its history. Every language has a tolerably long list of words which when used alone, that is, with no context, are likely to call into existence a number of different concepts. ' Head ' is a word of this class. We have already spoken of *Kopf* and its primitive meaning. Its modern signification as the equivalent of *Haupt* is the result of a two-fold transfer. At first the skull, because of its resemblance to a cup, was called *Kopf;* next this part of the head came to be used for the whole. The metaphors originating in the word *Kopf* as the equivalent of *Haupt* are very numerous, such as *Kehlkopf, Krautkopf, Balkenkopf, Bergkopf, Säulenkopf,* and so on, almost *ad infinitum*. Further, the head alone is often mentioned when the entire body is meant, a herd of cattle is said to consist of so many head; a tax is generally so much per head, and the proverb "*so viel Köpfe, so viel Sinne*" is familiar to all, though not all stop to consider that there is needed a good deal more than heads, if there are to be minds or opinions. *Kopf*, like head, is often used to designate certain mental qualities, just as the heart is the synonym for others. We say of a man that he has a good head, or a poor head; that he is hard-headed or head-strong, or that he has a head of his own. Parallel to these phrases are the German, *er hat einen eignen, einen guten, einen harten Kopf*, and akin to them are such compounds as *Hohlkopf, Querkopf, Schwachkopf* (numskull, blockhead). The Germans even go so far as to say *er hat Kopf*, or *er ist ein guter Kopf* when they are speaking of a person of talents. In the last instance we have a triple transfer of meanings,—first, from a cup to the human skull, then from the skull to the whole head, then from the head to the entire person. When we compare the changes in meaning with the mutations in the form and pronunciations of words that take place under the influence of analogy we find that in both cases the relation between form and content has shifted, and from the same cause. When any external impression upon our senses makes itself felt in consciousness, it awakens earlier impressions, already therein, provided some kind of relation exists between them. Changes in pronunciation are the effect of the reminiscence of former impressions or word-symbols; while changes in meaning result from a sort of confusion between concepts reciprocally awakened. It has been remarked in a former paragraph that in the transformation of words resulting from analogy, its influence does not extend to all the senses in which a word may be used. We may here call attention to a closely allied phenomenon, that the meaning of a word does not always change *in toto*, but only in certain cases; in others not. In some cases the form of a word may remain virtually the same through a long period of years, while its meaning undergoes more or less important modifications; in others, the meaning may remain unchanged, in spite of a change of form. In the former of the two processes of development above referred to, the original, or at least earlier, pronunciation of a word is preserved in isolated examples, and in the latter, a kind of isolation of meaning takes place in which certain words preserve a more primitive signification than pertains to them in their general sense. It is usually in compounds, rhyming couplets, proverbial expressions, and the like that the old meanings survive. In *Feuersbrunst* (conflagration) the purely sensuous signification of *Brunst* is preserved, while *Brunst* alone is now used in a much more restricted sense. *Ding* originally meant a judicial procedure. The Norwegian supreme legislative body is still called storthing, "the great court." From its earlier meaning it is easy to see how *bedingen* came to mean " make terms or conditions," notwithstanding the fact that the German *Ding* and the Eng. 'thing,' now have a widely different sense. *Fahren* could formerly be used of a going on foot: this signification is still preserved in *Wallfahrt.* The older meaning of *klein* (fine, elegant) is retained in *Kleinod*, to which that of 'costly' was afterward added. The termination *-od* is also found in different forms in *Einöde, Armut, Monat, Heimat*, and corresponds to the Latin *-atus* found in such words as 'magistratus,' 'senatus.' *Leib* formerly was the equivalent of the modern *Leben*, so that *Leibrente* means a life-rent, and *Leibzucht* a livelihood. *Leiche* at one time meant the same as *Körper*, whence *Leichdorn* (corn). The Eng. 'sweetmeats' has preserved the earlier meaning of meat as the equivalent of food. The "meat offering" of the ancient Hebrews contained no flesh.

This word *Körper* readily suggests the Latin corpus, corporis, from which it is derived and of which it still conserves the meaning. Its history in English exhibits to some extent the process above illustrated by means of several examples. There are a number of technical phrases in which the original signification is retained, such as "habeas corpus," "corpus juris," etc. But the derivative corps and corpse show both a metamorphosis of form and a restriction of meaning as compared with the Latin original. In Spenser's time 'corpse' meant a living body; consequently it underwent a change of meaning almost exactly similar to that of *Leiche* touched upon above.

We have already seen that sometimes the same verbal or vocal concept may have several meanings, or indeed. a large number, while it is equally true that the same thing may be said, the same concept expressed, in two or more ways. In one case several radii proceed from the same point, in the others they converge at the same point. As there often exist alongside of the metaphorical or figurative designation of concepts, one or more literal designations; or there may be several metaphorical designations for the same thing, it follows that, by a transfer of meanings, several words may develop alongside of each other, or rather parallel to each other in sense, that however differ more widely from one another than the double forms resulting from analogy. In other words, the so-called synonyms arise. The number of synonyms in existence for the various concepts that may be called into existence varies greatly. The simpler any phenomenon, the smaller the number of variations under which it appears, the less the interest it has for mankind, the fewer the synonyms by which it may be designated. *Luft* and *Wasser* as names of elements have, strictly speaking, no synonyms. But phenomena that appear in a great variety of forms; objects that excite humor or provoke mirth present an almost endless variety of points of view from which they may be regarded, and therefore furnish a fertile field for the growth of synonymous expressions. Words and phrases to designate beating or fighting, being in love, and cheating are particularly numerous. But perhaps the longest list of all would be the various ways to designate drinking and being drunk; it is probable that some hundreds could be collected from the different German dialects.

But even synonyms that designate virtually the same concept may vary in what may be called the degree of their application: that is, the occasion, the mood of the speaker, his culture and education determine to some extent the exact meaning he attaches to words and phrases. One person may, when employing such a word as cheat or deceive, wish to convey the additional idea of moral condemnation; another may use it with approval because it indicates to him the subsidiary notion of shrewdness. The same word may be used under precisely similar circumstances with a slight difference of meaning, or two words may be used in exactly the same sense, merely for the sake of euphony. Generally, however, this state of a language does not continue long, and of two words so related to each other one soon becomes obsolete.

The English language, owing to the double origin of its vocabulary, is somewhat different from other cultivated tongues. During the period of its formation it seems to have been necessary to use "yokes of words," one Saxon, the other Norman-French in order that the one might make the other intelligible. Chaucer's poems are full of such pairs; and even in Hooker we find "cecity and blindness," "nocive and hurtful," "sense and meaning," etc. But in such cases as may be readily seen, one of the two words has become obsolete, or nearly so, and is only found in writers like Carlyle, who purposely affect a style having an archaic flavor.

Whenever new material is added to the existing verbal stock of a language, as is constantly the case, by a transfer of the signification of existing words, an earlier concept or group of concepts, is employed in a slightly different sense, and the desired representation is called up in the mind of the reader or hearer through the relation existing between the sensuous concept and that in which the new word stands to it. But the converse of this may also take place: it may happen that the connection between the two meanings is not at once evident but may create an idea of a different sort. This mode of calling up representations is frequently employed in jests, the point of which depends on the double sense (*double entendre*) in which the word or phrase may be understood. When the German says, "*Er hat mehr Glück als Ferdinand,*" *Fer* in the proper name serves to call up in the mind of the hearer, the reminiscence of the word *Verstand*, and the expression is a little milder than if the words were used which the speaker really has in mind. Similar to this is the English, "You tell a li-kely story." It is sometimes said of an avaricious person, "*Er ist von Habsburg*," where the point of the remark lies in the similarity between the first syllable of *Habsburg*, and the verb *haben*. It is by a similar mental process that Swift connects Jupiter and Jew Peter, Andromache with Andrew Mackey, and Peloponnesus with Pail-up-and-ease-us. German jest books contain many names of places etymologically connected with the qualities from which their inhabitants are supposed to be chiefly known. On the whole, however, this mode of substituting one word for another is comparatively rare in comparison with that growing out of a real change of meaning. We shall see further on how words often come to be substituted for others on account of resemblance or similarity of sound, and thus lead to the coinage of entirely new ones.

A Glossary of Old English Bible Words, by Eastwood and Wright, is a volume of several hundred pages, devoted to a discussion of words that have gone entirely out of current use, or are now employed in a sense different from that of three or four centuries ago. As most English-speaking people are accustomed to the phraseology of the Bible from childhood, the changes are less noticeable here than elsewhere. A modern history, for instance, written in the language of the sixteenth century, would strike any one as a singular piece of composition. It should be remembered, too, that in both English and German we often do not have the continuous history of a word, and are not, therefore, in position to follow the gradual transformation of meaning it underwent. The careful observer of the speech of old people, especially of native Englishmen, or of those who are comparatively uneducated, may often notice words and forms of expression that are no longer used in the written language. Nearly all these, however, still flourish in the dialects of the different districts of England. The same statement is true of all the countries of Europe, whose language has had a continuous literary culture for several centuries.

THE COINAGE OF NEW WORDS.

Daily experience and frequent observation teach us that new words may be formed by the combination of existing ones. Two words are united to form a third in which the separate percepts or concepts are each embodied in the new compound. This method of compounding words may be of two kinds. By the one, both concepts are recognized as co-ordinate, and when placed alongside of each other hold about the same relation to one another that they would have if united by means of a conjunction. We have here accordingly a case of simple addition. This earliest and simplest method of forming compounds has in historical times become rare in the German language. In the oldest Teutonic one could say *sunvader*, meaning "son and father." At present such combinations exist only in the numerals from *dreizehn* to *neunzehn* and such adjectives as *bittersüsz*, *blaugrün*, *helldunkel*, etc. By the other, the two ideas are marked as unequal in rank, one being regarded as essential, the other as unessential or qualificative; the essential word designates the class or genus to which the whole belongs, the qualifying word the sub-class. The proper order is to place the less important term first, and the more important last. *Gartenbaum* means a tree that grows in a garden. So steamboat is a boat propelled by steam. In such cases the task of the hearer is not as simple as in the former sort of compounds where the mode of composition of two equally plain representations easily furnished the key to the intended unity. It is necessary to consider to what extent the areas, so to speak, indicated by the two separate words overlap each other, or what the relation existing between them. There is a wide difference between *Gartenbaum* and *Baumgarten;* that is, between a tree growing in a garden, and a garden full of trees, an orchard. The relation between the two parts of *Goldmensch* and *Goldgräber* is not the same; neither is it in *Königstiger* as compared with *Königssohn* and *Königsmörder;* between *Feuerwasser*, on the one hand, and *Feuertaufe* or *Feuerschein* on the other; nor between *Höllenstrafe* and *Höllenlärm*. Still we may say that there is addition even in such examples. *Butterbrod* is made of bread and butter; an *Altmeister* is not only old but he is also a master; and a *Mannweib* unites the qualities of a man and a woman— we might even say she was man and woman in one and the same individual. But the addition is of a different sort and leads to a real unity, a perfect fusion. *Werwolf* means a wolf that could assume a human form, or a man that had been temporarily transformed into a wolf, *Wer* being the Latin 'vir,' but such a being would be quite different from a wolf and a man. In the course of time the sense of unity produced by a word often grows stronger. So long as the two parts of a word can also be used separately, a compound into which they enter will produce the impression that the amalgamation is not entirely complete. Examples, however, occur where two words have so completely coalesced that their separate existence has ceased. When the first part of a compound has reached such a state it is generally called a prefix, as *un-*, *be-*, *ent-*, *ge-*, *ver-*, etc. Though these prefixes no longer exist by themselves they can be employed in the formation of new compounds, or at least, of new combinations, for it is not strictly correct to speak of composition in such cases. The German does not add together *un-* and *orthographisch* to form *unorthographisch*, or *er-* and *kapern* to make *erkapern*, but because such words as *unschön* and *unhold* exist alongside of *schön* and *hold*, or because the language already contains *erjagen* and *erstreben* as well as *streben* and *jagen*, analogy sanctions *unorthographisch* no less than *orthographisch*, or *erkapern* as a sort of derivative of *kapern*. It can be readily seen that the English furnishes a large number of parallel examples.

When the second part of a compound word ceases to exist as a separate entity it is usually called a suffix. The syllable -*heit*, Eng. -hood, and -head was originally an independent word meaning form, figure, condition, so that *Schönheit* was the equivalent of *schöne Gestalt* (beautiful form). The adjectives ending in -*lich* were probably substantives in prehistoric times since this suffix is the old substantive -*lich* (body) and is still extant in *Leiche* and *Leichnam*. The original meaning of *feindlich, freundlich* was accordingly *Feindesleib, Freundesleib*. This suffix, which is common to all the Teutonic tongues, appears in Eng. as -like and -ly, either being sometimes admissible as courtlike or courtly, saintlike or saintly, Godlike or godly, though the shorter form seems to be gradually displacing the longer. 'Like' is substantially the A.-S. *lic*, dative or instrumental, *lice*, so that saintly means etymologically, with or in the form or body of a saint. 'Like' has a separate existence in Eng.; not so the Ger. -*lich*, which in its modern form is *gleich*. We know further that -*haft*, -*schaft* and -*tum* were likewise independent words at an early stage of the language, and there is little doubt that the same is true of all words used in the formation of derivatives. This -*schaft* is A.-S. *scipe*, and -*tum* is the Eng. -dom found in such words as 'friendship' and 'christendom.' If, then, syllables like the foregoing, that no longer exist independently continue to be used in the formation of new words, these can hardly in strict justice be called mere derivative appendages, but the words into which they enter are in a certain sense compounds formed according to existing models. There is then, in reality, no radical difference between composites with prefixes and such derivatives as have just been considered: in both cases a self-existent word, at least in external appearance, is combined with part or parts of another. But it is not necessary to the formation of new words that they be composed of such as already exist, although there is no doubt that the coinage of entirely new vocables destined to general recognition is comparatively rare. Children not unfrequently invent names for objects with which they come in contact. Besides the words thus purposely coined there are others produced almost unwittingly in the effort to imitate the speech of older persons, and these often continue to be used by them after they have learned to use their mother-tongue with a considerable degree of correctness. If a group of children were isolated for several years there is no doubt that they would invent a language of their own. But words, in order to make them worthy of permanent preservation, must supply a felt want, in which case they will secure a more or less general recognition. Many a word coined in the spirit of innovation on the spur of the moment to suit the occasion is soon forgotten even by its author, because he hears no one else repeat it. There is an exceedingly slight demand for new words, simply because the stock on hand is amply sufficient for almost every actual and imaginary use. We have apparently in the English word "dude," that has gained remarkable currency within the last half dozen years, an example of spontaneous coinage, as it has no discoverable origin or traceable ancestry. "Highfalutin" is a somewhat similar instance, though here the model was probably at least in part the compound 'highflying,' to which it is allied in signification. "Boom" came into prominence several years ago, and seems to have gained a permanent place in the English vocabulary. The history of these words is similar to that of many in the German and in all other civilized languages.

It is probable that within the historic period of the German new words have been coined in imitation of existing ones and endowed with related significations. Such a vocable as *trippeln* probably gets its initial sound from *traben, trappen, treten*, with which it is also connected in meaning. The termination was most likely patterned after such a word as *zippeln*. *Zupfen* suggests both *ziehen* and *rupfen*, and is related in meaning to both; *schwirren* and *klirren* seem to have been influenced by *girren*, and *knarren* by *schnarren*. *Randal* is modeled after *Skandal*. It is not necessary that we be able to account for each separate sound and syllable in a new word that may occur, or that it has been previously used in a word having a like meaning. A large number of words are still formed, as they have been continuously throughout the past, in the same manner and in obedience to the same impulse that called words into existence thousands of years ago; it is the voluntary imitation of sounds occurring in nature, the so-called onomatopoiesis. For example, *bammeln, bimmeln, patschen, plumpsen, klatschen* and many more, are quite recent creations. Often, however, it is difficult to determine in any given case whether a word is an intentional specimen of fresh coinage or merely the modification of existing materials. Eng. 'clap,' 'clash;' French 'claquer, claque,' the Teutonic root of which is also represented in *klatschen* above, are doubtless entirely onomatopoetic, plus the various terminations, while such a word as "highfalutin" is only in part original. In the case of new words that have no relation of form to others in use the hearer has generally no difficulty in divining their meaning, for the reason that they are a sort of word-painting. But if new material is added or used that has no evident connection with or relation to that already in existence and there is no similarity of sound to suggest the meaning to the speaker or hearer it is not easy to discover it; the new word must be learned as a child learns a language from the beginning. The German, like the English, has received a very large increment of this sort in the shape of borrowed and adopted words from other languages. But new life and vigor have been imparted to the classic language from pure German sources. This has been brought about in part by the introduction of words from the dialects: Haller, Lessing and Goethe, of set purpose, transferred many vocables from this source into their writings. In some cases, too, these and other writers reintroduced into the language words that had become obsolete. Romanticism—the recurrence to the study of mediæval times—and the historical study of German have also had considerable influence. The stories of knight-errantry written toward the close of the last century and the historical novels of our day, particularly those of Scheffel and Freytag, have contributed their part. Sir Walter Scott's writings likewise exercised an important though indirect influence toward the same end. In this way such antiquated terms as *Fehde* (feud), *Gau* (district), *Ger* (javelin), *Hain* (copse), *Halle*, *Hort* (hoard), *Kampe* (champion), and *Minne*, came into use again as a part of current speech. The boldest innovator was Richard Wagner (died in '83), whose style is otherwise often difficult on account of the extent of his vocabulary, and is made still more obscure by the introduction of such words as *freislich* (*schrecklich*), *Friedel* (husband, lover), *glau* (bright, stirring, joyous), *neidlich* (*neidisch*), *Nicker* ("Old Nick") and more of the same sort.

This genesis and decay of words; the gradual changes in their signification and the various modes of word-formation by composition, together with the transformation in sound and appearance that words undergo in the course of their history exhibit to us the different aspects which the German language presented in the different periods of its existence. But the transitions from phase to phase are very gradual, so that it can never be said, one period ends here and another era begins with this date. Every absolutely new word is from the nature of the case, an instantaneous creation. There are a number of words and phrases to the genesis of which a tolerably definite date can be assigned. Yet this only means that certain expressions are used for the first time in the writings of a

given author; but these may have been in oral use long
before it occurred to any one to write them down. The
number of periodicals and the multifarious interests and
tastes represented by them is so great in our day that almost all words and expressions orally used soon find their
way into print. Strictly speaking, a definite birth-year
can be assigned to a word only when it is given to a new
discovery or invention by the discoverer or inventor, and
such words are generally adaptations from some other
language, as telephone, phonograph, cablegram, etc. The
modern word 'gas,' is a good example of new coinage in
the true sense. Its discoverer, Van Helmont, says he will
call the newly discovered compound 'gas,' though he has
furnished no clue to the name. It is probable, however,
that he had in mind some form of the word Geist, ghost,
or geest. With the introduction of the thing into the different countries of the civilized world the name also made
its way. Luther designates *beherzigen, erspriesslich* and
tugendreich as new words in his day. *Gehen wir, nehmen
wir* in the sense of *wir wollen gehen, wir wollen nehmen* came
into use in the last century. Lessing seems to have first
employed *empfindsam* and *weinerlich;* Jahn, *turnen, volkstum*
and *volkstümlich; abrüsten* is of still more recent origin.
Durchblühen was coined by Uhland. But the decay and
ultimate extinction of words is a gradual process, just as
new words gain currency step by step. In some cases not
all the parts of a compound word pass out of use at the
same time. The English auxiliaries are now more or less
defective, yet it is almost certain that at an early period of
the language they were as complete as any other verb.
Most of the missing parts can still be supplied from the
A.-S. In German the participles of a number of verbs
still exist as adjectives, though the verbs themselves have
become obsolete: among these are *aufgedunsen, abgefeimt*
and *entrückt*. Sometimes substantives live on in certain
combinations with prepositions, as *in die Irre, in der Irre*

gehen, zu Rüste gehen. In the second part of *Bräutigam,* the Eng. 'bridegroom' where the r is sporadic, we have the Gothic 'guma,' later 'gomo,' Latin 'homo;' in *Karfreitag,* there is preserved an old 'kara,' complaint, pain; and *durchbläuen* (drub) has no connection with *blau,* but has as its verbal part an obsolete *bleuen* (beat).

But again, there is no uniformity in the manner and rapidity with which the changes in the different departments of a language take place. Words and meanings that in one locality or in one class of society have long fallen into desuetude continue in current use in others. Sailors, for example, still use the term *Wanten* to designate knit gloves, an old German word preserved in 'gant,' 'guanto,' the modern French and Italian designation for gloves. Many archaic words are also found in the language of the chase; as, for instance, *abprossen,* means to bite off buds. Here we have a reminiscence of the M. H. G., *broz* (bud). *Rahmen* means *überholen,* and is from the M. H. G. *rämen* (strive after), while *wölfen* is the same as *gebären* and is related to M. H. G., *welf,* Eng. 'whelp.'

THE INFLUENCE OF FOREIGN LANGUAGES ON THE GERMAN.

The language of a people mirrors not only its intellectual and spiritual development, but also, in a large measure, its civilization and political history. By using language as a guiding thread we may find what intercourse a nation has had with other nations; what influence it has exerted on them, and to what influences it has in turn been subject; for there is probably no language in existence that has not taken up and assimilated foreign elements to a greater or less extent. It was not the privilege of the German people to work out their own destiny free from foreign interference, and their language bears abundant traces along the course of its entire history of the influence exerted upon it by the various nations with whom they came in contact. Notwithstanding this fact there is reason to believe that no language of Western Europe contains so large a proportion of words of native stock as the German. Still the question is one to which it is at present impossible to give a definite answer. Two languages may come into contact with each other in one or more different ways. There may be a direct intercourse between two nations speaking different languages but living in territorial contiguity; or one nation may conquer the lands of another and settle upon them, or a country may be invaded by a foreign army but which comes with no intention of remaining permanently. Instances of the first are common; the conquest of Gaul by the Romans and of England by the Normans are familiar instances of the second, while the various military expeditions of the French into Germany and Italy furnish examples of the third case. Under such circumstances the number of foreign words introduced will be few and generally of a kind that designate thoughts and things with which the borrowers were hitherto unacquainted. They belong for the most part to the class of substantives; borrowed verbs and adjectives are comparatively rare. It lies in the nature of the case that almost every portion of the earth possesses objects not found elsewhere and that the name of these objects will spread hence to the surrounding nations. But new qualities and new modes of action will rarely be met with.

The contact of one language with another is not necessarily the result of intercourse between individuals and through the medium of the ear; it may be purely intellectual resulting from the perusal of the printed page. When contact takes place in the way first indicated only a few persons are generally participants and the number of languages is necessarily limited to two or at most to three. But their reciprocal influence will be much greater than in the second case. Here the appropriation of foreign words is conscious and intentional, usually the result of a fair knowledge of the language from which the appropriation is made. It may therefore happen that persons will introduce into their native speech along with some foreign words that are a real gain others that are entirely superfluous. As a foreign language is always of later acquisition than the mother tongue and is, moreover, the result of an effort of will, some of its words and phrases enter so readily into one's consciousness as to take the place of native words that are adequate and equally expressive. Then too, a pride of knowledge often leads to the use of foreign words. Not only are occasional substantives introduced but even verbs and adjectives. Now and then the mode of inflection shows traces of a foreign model; the interior life of the language has been affected. This is more likely to be the case when words of native stock have for some time been exposed to the corrupting influence of a foreign tongue and retain in their form the traces of that influence. In both English and German there are a number of pure Teutonic words that have been reintroduced from the French but which still bear the marks of their sojourn among foreigners. A word may be coined in a more or less close imitation of a foreign word to express a concept for which no native word exists, or at least is known; or a native word may undergo a gradual change of meaning under foreign influences; or compounds may be constructed according to foreign models of sentence-composition. The various ways here spoken of, in which the language of a people has been instrumental in modifying that of another are for the most part impersonal and confined to the higher classes. Words acquired from foreigners through direct personal intercourse are not usually the result of conscious effort or intelligent adaptation. In this case the influence of the individual counts for less than in the former. In the one case foreign words are introduced by the educated and in the other, appropriated by the illiterate in the spirit of imitation. The earliest borrowings are those that result from the contiguity of settlements of two nations speaking different languages and the later acquisitions—that is, those that grow out of the systematic study of a foreign tongue, are made after a higher degree of civilization and a more advanced stage of culture has been attained.

The German language has taken up foreign elements from the earliest period of its existence — or at least from the earliest period accessible to historical research. But, of course, the nearer we approach its origin, the less the confidence with which we can assert the extraneous origin of words that have an un-German appearance; and the difficulty is the greater because in many cases it is impossible to discover, in regard to certain words, who were the borrowers and who the lenders; or to express the fact otherwise, when the essential parts of a word are common to two languages, it is often difficult to decide which is the older when we have no other means of determining the relative age of the languages.

The oldest words adopted by the German are names of metals and cultivated plants. We are in position to assert with reasonable confidence that silver and hemp do not bear native German designations, but from what people they were borrowed it is as yet impossible to say. We can form only more or less plausible conjectures. Their adoption must have taken place long before the division of the primitive German into the later Germanic dialects. Somewhat subsequently, but nevertheless still in the prehistoric period, the Germans came in contact with Finns and Kelts. That there must have been considerable intercourse between Finns and Germans is evident from the unmistakable traces of their language in that of the former. Some of these adopted words have undergone such modifications that their original form can be inferred only from the application of the phonetic laws of the Teutonic. The influence of the Finnish upon the German has left but faint traces; from which we may safely assume that their civilization during the period of contact was of a lower type. The relations between the Kelts and Germans were more intimate and of longer continuance; in fact, it was Keltish territory upon which the Southern and Western Germanic tribes planted their settlements. The Keltic background is plainly seen in proper names. Rhine, Main, Danube, Melibocus, Vosges, Mainz, Worms, of which the Latin forms are Rhenus, Maenus, Danubius, Maguntia, Vogesus, Borbetomagus, are names that have a clearly discernable Keltic ancestry. Keltic names are likewise of frequent occurrence in England, almost every river bearing an appellative that still retains traces of the nomenclators in spite of subsequent Roman and Teutonic invaders. Isaac Taylor, in his "Words and Places," says: "Over the greater part of Europe — in Germany, France, Italy, Spain — we find villages which bear Teutonic or Romance names, standing on the banks of streams which still retain their ancient Celtic appellations. Throughout the whole of England there is hardly a single river-name which is not Celtic."

One of the most remarkable items of evidence testifying to Keltic influence is the German word *reich*. Its present meaning is 'rich,' but it originally meant 'mighty' or powerful; a trace of this signification is still present in the noun *Reich*, meaning 'realm' or 'empire.' The word is related to the Latin *rex*, *reg-num*, but phonetic laws prove that it can have come only from the Keltic into the German. Its root is found in such proper names as Dumnorix, Vercingetorix, from which it would appear that even in political matters the ancient Germans were not entirely outside the pale of Keltic influence. The words *Düne*, *Falke*, *Habicht* and *Pferch* are likewise supposed to be of Keltic ancestry, and have their living English representatives in 'down' (a plateau), 'falcon,' 'hawk' and 'park.' The influence of the Latin upon the

13

German may likewise be traced to prehistoric times. It can be noticed as early as the beginning of the Christian era and continues still. But it differed greatly at different times, and it is not always possible to determine whether a given word was transferred into the German directly from the Latin, or indirectly, by way of a Romance language. The earliest loan-words are popular in form, and have come in partly through the early intercourse between Germany and Italy, and partly by way of the Roman settlements in the Southern and Western portions of Germany. It was through the Romans that the Germans first made the acquaintance of a number of animals and plants. Among these were the elephant, the pea-cock (*Pfau*), the fabulous dragon (*Drachen*), the pear (*Birne*), the fig (*Feige*), the cherry (*Kirsche*), the cole or caul (*Kohl*), the gourd (*Kürbis*), the lily (*Lilie*), the almond (*Mandel*), the mulberry (*Maulbeere*), pepper (*Pfeffer*), the radish (*Rettich*), the rose (*Rose*), etc. *Pflanze*, *Frucht* and *Marmor* are also from the Latin.

NOTE.—It may be well to remind the reader that in placing together several words because they are related it is not intended to indicate anything as to the nearness of their relationship. For example, dragon and *Drachen* mean the same thing and were originally the same word, though the former is only indirectly derived from the latter through the medium of the French. A direct descendant of *Drachen* is found in the obsolete drake-fly. In like manner Latin *calx*, Ger. *kalk* and Eng. 'chalk' are the same word, but chalk and *calx* do not mean the same thing. The resemblance of chalk to lime evidently led to the confusion of terms. The study of etymology reveals many similar mistakes. Nothing can be affirmed with certainty about the etymology of a word until it has been carefully studied by the light of established phonetic laws. Mere external resemblances are entirely misleading. Of the above words it may be well to trace briefly a few through some of the changes through which they have passed. The original of *Kürbis* is *cucurbita*, the French forms of it being *coourde*, *gohourde* and others with initial c and g. In the early English it is likewise spelled several different ways but they all have the initial g showing that in the dialect which was its prototype this letter prevailed. Whether the Germans themselves shortened the Latin form or received it after it had already been so changed is not yet established. *Kürbis* and 'gourd' are not, however, exactly equivalent in meaning. The Latin *marmor*, which is also the German form though the gender is different, appears in the Romance languages as *marme, marmo, marmore, marmel, marbre*, etc., and in English as 'marbre,' 'marbel,' marble,' usage finally settling upon the last as the normal form. *Mandel* and almond were originally the same word. Its earliest Latin prototype is *amendela*. In the Romance tongues it appears as *almendela, alemandle* and *alemandre*. The O. H. G. form is *mandala*, corresponding to the Italian *mandala*, but other languages, among them the English, have retained the initial syllable. The interchangeable l and r in the final syllable is the same phenomenon that we see in the final syllable of marble.

The higher civilization of the Romans made its impress upon the German language in three different directions: in architecture, in viticulture and horticulture, and in the culinary art. Under the first head belong such words as *Kalk, Pflaster* (Lat. plastrum, Eng. plaster, later, a paved way), *Strasze* (Lat. strata, Eng. street), *Platz* (platea), *Mauer* (murus), *Pfosten* (postem), *Pforte* (porta), *Kerker* (carcer, retained in the Eng. incarcerate), *Keller* (cellarium), *Turm* (turrem), *Pfalz* (palatium), *tünchen* (related to tunica) *Ziegel* (tigillum), *Schindel* (scandula and scindula). Under the second head we have to place *Wein* (vinum), *Most* (mustum), *Winzer* (vinitorem), *keltern* (calcitrare), *propfen* (propago), *impfen* and *pelzen*. To cookery and the art of preparing food in general belong *Kochen* (coquere), *Speise* (spesa and expensa), *Butter* (butyrum), the pure German name of which is *Schmer* or *Anke*, *Essig* (acetum), *Käse* (caseus), *Oel* (oleum), *Pfeffer* (piperem), *Semmel* (semola) and *Senf* (sinapem). *Weiher* comes from the Latin *vivarium*, a fish-pond. The names of many utensils are likewise derived from the Latin, among which are *Anker* (ancoria) and *Kette* (catena), *Kopf* (cuppa). (See ante p.). *Schüssel* (scutula), *Kiste* (cista) and *Sack* (saccus), *Tisch* (table) the English 'dish' is etymologically related to the Latin *discus;* the pure German word which designates this article of furniture being *biut*. The borrowed names for objects of personal adornment are noticeably few; among them are *Purpur*, *Krone* (corona) and *Spiegel* (speculum). The word *Kaiser* (Cæsar) is the only word belonging to the sphere of political life. As would be inferred, the number of loan-words relating to fighting is small, the Germans being in early times much given to war. Almost the only ones are *Kampf* (campum, the place of muster or combat) and *Pfeil* (pilum). On the other hand the words relating to peaceful occupations borrowed by the Germans from the Romans are tolerably numerous; among them are *Markt* (mercatus), *Münze* (moneta), *Pfund* (pondo), *Zins* (census) and *Zoll* (telonium). Some of these words the Romans in their turn had borrowed from the Greeks.

Writing, as a practical art, came to the Germans through the Romans, and the chief word (*schreiben*) is a modified form of the Latin *scribere*. The pure German word *writan* is preserved in the English 'write.' *Brief* (an epistle) is from *brevis libellus*, 'a little book,' and is preserved in our law-term 'brief.' *Siegel*, a seal, is from the Latin *sigillum*. It may be inferred from the nature of the case that the arts and sciences of the Romans would not, during the earlier period of their contact with the Germans, make much impression on them. They were regarded as encouraging effeminacy. A few terms relating to the healing art are borrowed, such as *Arzt* (archiator), *Büchse* (pyxem) and *Pflaster* (plastrum). The meaning of the last named word as here given is the earliest, while that above noted is a subsequent development; their relation to each other is, however, plainly evident.

A mightier power than that wielded by the Roman empire was necessary to make a permanent impression on the intellectual and spiritual life of the Germans. This was found in Christianity. The new faith came to them from three different directions: on their east it was preached by the Greeks; Irish and Roman apostles brought the Gospel to the western and interior tribes.

But Irish Christianity seems to have made no impression upon the German language, owing, perhaps, to the fact that the Latin had so thoroughly permeated this form of it as to leave but faint traces of the native language upon it when it was brought by Irish missionaries into Germany. Of the German tribes, the Goths were the only ones who had much intercourse with the Greek empire, or more definitely, with its capital, Constantinople, and they disappear early from history, having been in part exterminated, and in part merged with other tribes. Nevertheless, it was through them that one of the most important ecclesiastical terms was introduced into the German, and indeed into all the languages belonging to the Germanic stock; this is the word *Kirche*, the Scotch 'kirk,' Icelandic *kirkja*, English 'church.' *Pfaffe* (παπᾶς), *Pfingsten* (πεντεκοστή), and *Teufel* (διάβολος) also came in by way of the Gothic, but it is probable that *Papst*, (Pope, Latin papa) was not introduced till a later period. In fact, with the exception of these and possibly a few other words, all the ecclesiastical terms in the German come from the Latin directly, though the originals are generally Greek. In the nature of the case, the influence of the Roman heirarchy was powerful, a condition of things that becomes more plainly evident as we come into the historical period of the German language—or, more accurately, to the O. H. G. Most of the names used to designate buildings and utensils for religious worship are directly from the Latin. To this class of words belong *Klause* (clausa, Eng. close, an enclosed space), *Kloster* (cloister), *Münster* (minster, west-minster), related to the Latin 'monasterium' and the English 'monastery,' *Schule* (schola), *Altar*, *Kanzel* (chancel), *Kreuze* (cruc-em), *Oblate* (oblata) and *Orgel;* likewise the names of ecclesiastical officers and offices, such as *Abt* (abbot), *Küster* (custor, custorius), *Messner* (mansionarius), *Mönch* (monachus), *Nonne*, *Priester* (presbyter, prester), *Probst* (Praepositus) and *Siegrist* (sacristanus). The same may be said of ecclesiastical ceremonies and customs, among which are *Ferien* (feriae), *Mette* (matutina), *Vesper, Messe* (missa), *Segen* (signum), *almosen* (Greek ἐλεημοσύνη), and *Spende* (from Latin spendere, expendere). Of like origin are *opfern* and *predigen* (Latin offere and praedicare), *Engel, Marter, Pein* (poena), *Plage* and *verdammen.* Many of these words do not occur in classical Latin, and have the exact signification in German that they have in the Latin of the same period. Many of them, too, are popular in origin and meaning and came into the German with the introduction of Christianity; but besides these a large number were brought in through literary channels and are found only in translations from the Latin.

In the M. H. G. period we are face to face with entirely new linguistic materials. The crusades drew the Germans out of their isolation into the current of European life. Most important of all, these expeditions brought them into communication with their Western neighbors, whose higher civilization, the result of a longer and more direct subjection to the power of the Roman empire, made a deep and lasting impression on them. The French language and French literature became the chief intellectual food of the higher classes. M. H. G. lyric poetry received a new and strong impulse from the French and was for a long time patterned after French models. Nearly all the epic court-poetry of this period consists of more or less free translations from the works of French authors. Godfrey of Strasburg and others of his kind go so far in the spirit of imitation as to insert entire verses from French originals into their poems. Toward the latter part of the twelfth century a broad stream of French words begins to flow in upon the German language. The technical terms relating to the tournament and the chase, to play and dance, to music and poetry are borrowed from the West. A large number of articles of luxury was introduced from the same country into Germany and with them their designations. The same is true of words relating to the ceremonial of court-life and to courtly manners. Many of these were but short-lived and disappeared with the death of chivalry. A like fate befell those that passed into the English and other European languages. Some however have continued to the present day and are become an integral part of many European tongues. Among these are *Abenteuer* (adventure), *Banner, blond, fehlen* (Fr. faillir ; Eng. fail). *Fei, fein, Komtur, Palast, Plan, Preis, turnieren.* That French influence penetrated to the very blood and life of the German is evident from the fact that not a few words of pure stock were modified after the manner of French derivatives. Words like *vilanie, partie* were taken as a pattern for M. H. G. *jegerie, rouberie, vischerie,* of which the N. H. G. equivalents are *Jägerei, Räuberei* and *Fischerei.* The ending *-ieren* in words like *halbieren, marschieren, stolzieren* is derived from the French infinitives in *-ier,* which in the M. H. G. was pronounced with the accent on the i; and finally *-lei* in *mancherlei, vielerlei, einerlei* and their like is the French word *loi* which in this earlier time was pronounced *lei,* and signified also mode or manner. The influence of the Latin continues alongside the French throughout the M. H. G. period, without however equalling in force that of the French. The nearer we approach the Renaissance and the age of Humanism the more does the Latin come into prominence again. Beginning with the second half of the fifteenth century a great deal of attention is given to translating from the Latin, and to some extent from other languages. In the sixteenth century scholars speak the language of ancient Rome in preference to their own, a statement that is true not only of the Germans, but to a greater or less extent of all Europe. The mother-tongue has become an object of contempt to such an extent that the head of the Holy Roman Empire was willing to speak German to his horse only. The force of Humanism is not yet wholly spent and scholars, especially philologists, are continually introducing into their native language words taken from the Latin. The Greek has likewise been brought into pretty intimate relation with the German.

In the seventeenth and in the eighteenth century the Latin gradually loses its prestige as the language of cultivated society—Professor Thomasius began to deliver lectures in German at Leipzig in 1688 which were the first in this language given at a German university—and its place is in a measure taken by the French. This was in part owing to the spirit of Humanism the prevalence of which had accustomed the Germans to look upon their own language with contempt. To French influence upon the German now beginning to revive that of the Italian is also joined; it furnishing a number of terms relating to music and commerce. The words coming from this source are however comparatively few and the influence of the Italian is much less potent than that of the French. Finally, there has been in progress during the present century a considerable influx of words from the English, chiefly such as relate to politics, to social life generally, and especially to field-sports. The Germans have also borrowed a small number of words from their eastern neighbors, the Slavs, among which are *Dolch* (dagger), *Droschke* (cab), *Hallunke* (scoundrel), *Knute* (knout), *Kutsche* (coach, a word that probably has a singular history), *Peitsche* (whip), etc. There are likewise a few words in the Middle and Low German dialects that are traceable to the same source. Besides these, there are still a few others borrowed from the Dutch, Danish and Swedish. The Thirty Years War brought many Swedish soldiers and camp-followers into Germany of whom a considerable number did not return at its close, but settled in different parts of the country. Most of the Swedish words were probably introduced in this way and at this time.

All the influences exerted upon the language of the German nation as above described were external; in marked contrast thereto has been that of a single people dwelling in their midst, the Jews. The Romance nations, the English, the Greeks, the Slavs have always been and still are foreigners, from the standpoint of the German; their influence was extraneous and readily discernible. The case is different with the people who dwell in all parts of the land and who can not properly be called foreigners. Not many are the words which the Jews have unintentionally added to the German vocabulary, but a few of them have become an integral part of it. To this source we may trace *Gauner* (a cheat, trickster), *Kümmelblättchen* (three-card monte), *Schächer*, *schächten*, and others. But in the dialects the Jewish contingent is much larger. We find *acheln* for *essen;* *beduch* for *niedergedrückt;* *ganfen* for *stehlen;* *kapores* for *caput;* *koscher* for *recht;* *Makkes* for *Schläge;* *Moos* for *Geld;* and many more.

The above enumeration embraces all the nations who have directly contributed to increase the German vocabulary from their own; but the number of languages represented in the German is much greater, because many have not only given their own linguistic material, but also a portion of that which they themselves had borrowed from foreign sources. A considerable list of Arabic words came into the German through the medium of the Romance languages, as for example *Alchymie*, *Almanach*, *Algebra*, *Alcohol*, *Admiral*, *Diwan*, all of which belong likewise to the English language and have in it substantially the same form they have in German.

To this list is also to be added the names of new plants and new fabrics brought into Germany from all parts of the earth, chiefly through the medium of commerce. Beside those contributions made directly by foreign languages, others were made indirectly, that is, through intermediary languages, as when Greek words which had first been naturalized in the Latin were thence transferred into the German, or Romance words introduced by way of the English.

An examination of the history of quite a number of German words reveals the curious fact that they were at one period borrowed from the Germans by the Romance nations and subsequently reclaimed and reintroduced into the language to which they had originally belonged.

It thus happens that the German now has in a few words two different forms, one the original word, the other as it appears after undergoing the phonetic changes incident to its pilgrimage in foreign lands. As might be expected these last are greatly changed by their sojourn abroad, invariably as to form and in some cases in both form and meaning. For example, *Balkon* (balcony), and *Balken* were originally the same word; so were *Fauteuil* and *Feldstuhl*, formed through a popular misconception of derivation from *Faltstuhl*. *Gage* and *Wette*, *Garde* and *Warte*, *Liste* and *Leiste*, *Rang* and *Ring* are the same words. *Biwak* (bivouac) is derived from the old German *biwaht* (by-watch); *equipieren* is related to *schiff*, this verb like the English 'equip' meaning originally 'to provide a ship with necessary articles.' *Garniren* is connected with *warnen* of which the primitive meaning is to 'prepare' or 'equip,' and *Loge* (lodge) with *Laube*. Foreign influence is much more subtle and difficult to discover in cases where the genius of a foreign language has made its impress on words that have remained purely German in form. At different periods in the history of the High German, words were formed, partly with the object of attaining greater definiteness of meaning, and partly, in recent times at least, with the conscious purpose of opposing foreign influence and of supplying the place of foreign with native German words meaning etymologically the same thing. In some instances the new word is an accurate translation of the foreign word it is intended to supplant; in others it is designed to give only the spirit of the foreign word. In the O. H. G. period a compound *gomaheit* was coined after the pattern of the Latin *humanitas* (see *Bräutigam* ante); similarly *misericors* was rendered by *armherzi*, a term that is connected with *barmherzig* although the b is not yet fully accounted for. *Missa* (mass) that which is sent, was translated *santa*, and *propheta, forasago; apostolus* called into existence *zwelfbota*, one of the twelve messengers, while *bibliotheca* became *buohfasz*, and *jungiro* is probably a free rendering of *discipulus*. The O. H. G. translators used *wahrlich* and *gewisz* for the Latin particles *autem, ergo, igitur, itaque, profecto* and *vero*, a use of these words which, however, did not become popular. Again, the Latin words *emanatio, objectum, subjectum* and their like were rendered *uzfluz, gegenwurf* or *widerwurf* and *understôz*. More recently *alumnus* became *Pflegling; Volkherrschaft* and *Freistaat* are pure German for *Demokratie* and *Republik*. *Telegram* becomes *Drahtbericht, reconnaissant, erkenntlich, Karrikatur, Zerrbild*, and *incident, Zwischenfall*. On the other hand many German words, while not newly coined, have assumed new meanings under foreign influence, or even lost their original signification entirely. It is probable that *Heide*, derived from *Heide*, a heath, used to designate a person who lives in the country, gets its present meaning under the influence of the Latin *paganus;* in like manner *taufen* may have meant *untertauchen*, and *Jünger*, a younger person, then a disciple, a follower. In the sixteenth century the word *bürgerlich* has the meaning of *höflich, anständig*, and there is little doubt that this meaning had originally some relation to 'civiliter' or 'civilement.' *Zerstreut* got its present signification (distracted) in the time of Lessing, without doubt as an equivalent of *distrait; einem den Hof machen* is a literal translation of *faire la cour; antworten* sometimes used by scholars in the sense of *entsprechen*, shows the influence of the Latin *respondere.* The English word 'answer' is often similarly used. In cases where a foreign language becomes the model for the structure of the German sentence it is generally the Latin, but sometimes the French. The Accusative with the Infinitive is a construction that is often imitated, occurring to some extent in the O. H. G. translations, rarely in the M. H. G. period, but very frequently both in original writings and translations, since the second half of the fifteenth century. For example in Theuerdank—a historical allegory in verse written during the fore-part of the sixteenth century—we find, "*nym zu dir den Gesellen dein, den du weist verschwiegen zu sein,*" and "*der Held antwort, ich red on spot, mich gewesen sein in groszer Not.*" This form of expression is found far along in the eighteenth century. It is met with occasionally even in Lessing, as when he says, "*die Theaterstücke, die er so vollkommen nach dem Geschmacke seines Parterres zu sein urteilte,*" literally, 'the dramas which he so thoroughly believed to be' etc. In the German of to-day this construction has entirely disappeared. *Ich sehe ihn kommen*, was originally perfectly correct. But there is faintly visible the desire to represent literally a foreign construction in such expressions as, "*dein Bruder, von dem ich urteile, dasz er sehr reich ist.*" A very convenient construction is the so-called Ablative Absolute. The German originally had something similar but lost it early, and for this reason we find throughout the entire H. G. period an effort to restore it. The O. H. G. translators often make use of it. In the N. H. G. period the Latin prototype is reinforced by the example of the French. The language shows an evident effort in two directions to attain this exotic form of expression. One is to employ a sort of Accusative Absolute, as when Schiller says, "*dieses Geschäft berichtigt, eilen alle Stadthalter nach ihren Provinzen,*" and Dahlmann, "*das geschehen, hänge die Entscheidung von dem Könige ab.*" The other is the use of the preposition *nach*, which however generally produces a very disagreeable stylistic effect, as when Goethe says, "*nach aufgehobenem Kloster,*" and Schiller, "*nach genommenem Abschiede von seinem Freunde,*" or Grimm, "*nach dem abgeschüttelten Joch der Römer.*" All these constructions ought to be avoided. Two other vicious collocations of words found in modern German are to be traced to the Latin use of the relative pronoun: the first is the use of a relative clause introduced by *welcher* followed by a substantive, as "*auf die bayrischen Lande richtete er sein Hauptaugenmerk, welche Lande bisher vom Könige nicht gelitten hatten.*" ("Erant omnino itinera duo, quibus itineribus domo exire possent."—-Cæsar). The second is the joining of a relative to a principal clause when the former does not limit or explain the latter, but adds a new thought, as, "*der Redner schloss mit einem Hoch auf seine Majestät, welchem der Gesang der Nationalhymne folgte, worauf dann eine grosze Anzahl patriotische Toaste sich anschlasz.*"

It is safe to say that the influence of the Latin has been in general detrimental to the grammar of the German. The strong tendency of the N. H. G. toward the use of subordinate clauses and toward involved constructions is attributable to the influence of the Latin. The German of diplomacy and the German of scholars, both a highly artificial mode of speech—the language of persons who understood Latin better than their mother tongue—were the channels through which the various un-German and semi-German constructions found their way into the language of the people. Many peculiarities of the Latin have at different times been imitated by German writers which did not however take deep root. So late as the beginning of the present century a professor, in the preface to a book which he had written in his vernacular, felt called upon to apologize to his readers for employing a language that was less familiar to him than Latin. It is evident that under a system of education that aimed mainly at securing proficiency in a foreign language, a correct and elegant use of the native tongue was almost impossible even for those who made this an object. There are a goodly number of minor peculiarities of the Latin which were at different times imitated by German writers without, however, taking deep and permanent root. This statement is probably more applicable to the last century when German began to be the language of science, than to any other period. It is not difficult to understand why the influence of the French was less marked than that of the Latin; its genius is much more nearly akin to German than either is to the older language. The French does not contain much that the German could appropriate and be manifestly the gainer. It is to the influence of this language, however, that it owes a mode of expression with *sein*, as, "*von hier aus ist es dass man den weitesten Blick über Paris hat.*" It is uncertain whether in imitation of the Latin or the French there arose the mode of expressing quality with *sein von*, as, "*Friedrich V. war von einem freien und aufgewecktem Geiste, vieler Herzensgüte, einer königlichen Freigebigkeit.*" Similarly we say in English, he was a man of, etc. French prototypes may often be recognized in the German of newspapers, but not much of this has become a recognized portion of the language, as *Gefahr laufen* (*courir risque*), *von langer Hand* (*de longue main*). In southwestern Germany one frequently hears *es macht schön Wetter* (*il fait beau temps*). A number of isolated French words are also used with slight modifications, such as *Budel* (bouteille), *Kurasche* (courage), *Schossee* (*chaussée*), *blessiren* (blesser). In Austria one not infrequently notices forms of speech that betray the proximity of the Slavic languages.

We may once more, in passing, call attention to the fact that the old language now and then exercises a disturbing influence on that of to-day, tho' this phenomenon is found chiefly in the writings of leading German-

ists among whom Jacob Grimm easily holds the first place.
These various points of contact with foreign languages enumerated above have been instrumental in drawing upon the German a veritable flood of foreign elements. The number of exotic words in it has been estimated by some at seventy thousand and by others much higher, or about one-eighth of the entire vocabulary.

This is the statement of Professor Behaghel. It does not seem to be in accord with what has been previously said regarding the comparative purity of the language. The question is one upon which it is not easy to obtain accurate data. According to the estimate here given the number of words in the German would considerably exceed half a million. To extend the list to such an enormous length it would be necessary to include many words that have little claim to be regarded as properly a part of the German vocabulary. No English dictionary, so far as I am aware, professes to embrace so many as one-third this number of words, yet the English language is nearly or quite as copious as the German. A large number of words used by German writers are known to be foreign and are not entitled to a place in a German dictionary. Their place is in an encyclopedia or polyglot lexicon.

There is no sphere of life that has kept itself free from them, though perhaps the higher culinary art, medicine and military affairs have fared the worst. All social classes and conditions have done their part in bringing about this speech-mixture, though the share of each is not equal. A slight difference is noticeable between the language used by men and that used by women, provided, of course, that their education is virtually on the same level. The employment of Greek and Latin words is confined chiefly to the male sex; while women have greater facility in the use of English and French words and phrases. The different classes of society regard the French with diverse sentiments. The aristocracy and the court-circles intermingle their German with a variety of French words which an educated person readily recognizes: such as *antichambre, menagieren, soignieren*. On the other hand there lives in the speech of the uneducated and partly educated a large number of foreign words that are obnoxious or unknown to the cultivated classes,—they are such as *Budêl* and *Bŭdel*, *Gilet*, *caressieren*, *Plaisir*, *caput*, *Kamin*. The first of these, from *bouteille*, illustrates a mode or rather a defect of pronunciation peculiar to South Germany, the failure to distinguish between the surd mutes p and t on the one hand and the sonant b and d on the other. So just as 'bouteille' becomes *Bŭdel*, *Pudel* is likewise pronounced *Bŭdel*. On the whole the educated middle classes speak a German that is least intermixed with foreign elements.

This remarkable condition of affairs is not hard to understand when we take into account the causes that lead to the frequent employment of foreign words. They are in part the same that have been laid before the reader in a former chapter as leading to the coinage of new words. It is well known that language is constantly calling into existence new vocables, so to speak, because those in use do not, for various reasons, supply all the needs of men. It is a familiar fact that the new objects, new discoveries and inventions, the new concepts that are introduced from foreign lands bring with them new names. Even in cases where objects and ideas are our own creations we are fond of using foreign designations because it is more easy and convenient to adopt words already in existence than to coin new ones. Occasionally we employ alongside of each other a native and a foreign word, as a convenient variation of style. Sometimes foreign words are called into requisition because they afford an easy means of concealing a poverty of ideas and obscurity of thought. Perhaps the hearer is good-natured enough to believe that it is his own ignorance which makes the words of the speaker enigmatic and unintelligible in their foreign garb. Formally at least foreign words admit of a greater variety in their use than native. How few people are disagreeably affected on hearing hybrid compounds of Greek and Latin, or the senseless mutilation of terms belonging to a language which they do not thoroughly comprehend.

Vanity is often associated with mental indolence. Half educated persons like to get credit for more knowledge than they possess, and one way of gaining this credit is by the use of such foreign words as they may have at command. Often this number is so limited and their use so injudicious as to miss entirely its object and only to awaken the feeling of the ludicrous in the mind of the hearer. The aristocrat is fond of showing his superiority to the common herd by the use of words that are not a part of every-day speech. It is evident then that the strong inclination to employ uncommon vocables is to be found in an unfortunate but very general and wholly ineradicable trait of human nature. Nevertheless, we are in duty bound, for reasons elsewhere given, not to yield without a struggle to this prevalent tendency. The frequent use of foreign words interferes seriously with the object for which speech exists, namely, the communication of thought. It is a hindrance to the easy intercourse between the different classes of society and leads to misunderstandings that are often ludicrous enough. Educated persons and scholars are sometimes at a loss, when brought face to face with an exotic word and are compelled to resort to the dictionary in the hope that it may not, as frequently happens, leave them no wiser than they were before. But even after foreign words have become fully naturalized among the educated they will not, in the main, be so thoroughly comprehended and be used with the same definiteness as those of pure native stock—in fact they can hardly attain the same definiteness of signification. They lack the firm hold upon the language that grows out of their etymological connection with other and well known words of whose meaning there can not easily be a doubt. This absence of supports for the memory is the more dis-

14

tinctly felt for the reason that in the living vernacular, words of foreign origin are more liable to mutilation than native ones, quite apart from the unavoidable uncertainty of their orthography. The educated man must always be more or less in doubt about the pronunciation of foreign words. Shall the German accent the penult or the antepenult in *Barometer*, and shall he give the second *t* in *Aristokratie* its German or French sound? The laws of French accent on the one hand and of English and German on the other tend in opposite directions; and until a word transplanted from one language into the other has secured full naturalization its accentuation is uncertain. Is *Cœlibat* masculine or neuter? Is the plural of *Thema*, *Themas*, *Themen*, *Themata*, or *Thematen*? Exactly the same thing is true of the English, and it can not be said that one is sure what is the plural of 'index,' or 'memorandum,' or 'cherub,' or 'bandit.' Our best lexicographers disagree about the plurals and the pronunciation of a long list of words; and they are probably all such as are not yet fully naturalized. In many cases, the coiners of new words, generally compounds, out of materials taken from foreign languages, do not themselves venture to indicate their pronunciation. It sometimes happens that words incorporated from one language into another receive a modification of meaning that makes them unintelligible to the people from whom they were originally taken. This may lead to vexatious misunderstandings. The German term *Eisenbahncoupé* is equivalent to the French *compartiment*. *Coupé* in this sense is thus bad German and worse French. *Gourmet* and *Gourmand* are often confounded by both English and Germans. The former means, a man of keen palate; the latter, a great eater. It will be readily understood that the difficulty of getting at the meaning of words is not equally great in every instance. Many loan-words have become so completely an integral part of the German that the casual observer does not distinguish them from home-grown product. With most words this is, however, not the case: they contain sounds that it is difficult or impossible for German vocal organs to produce, or their accent is not in harmony with that obtaining in the native tongue. The French, for example, uniformly place the accent on the final syllable, except in the case of the mute e; the Germans, on the radical part of the word, which is usually the first or second syllable from the beginning. These conflicting tendencies are constantly cropping out in the use of French words by English-speaking people. It may be observed in such familiar words as debut, depot, ennui, etc. Even when the accent is rightly placed it is not the French accent. The difficulties in the way of acquiring the correct pronunciation of foreign words are so great as to be well nigh insurmountable. There is evidently, then, a sort of stylistic antagonism between the purely native and the loan-words that enter into a sentence. On æsthetic grounds such a mixture is highly objectionable. There is perhaps no modern language that is so little in need of aid from external sources as the German. The readiness with which it forms compounds makes it an easy matter to express in this language nearly or quite every possible concept of the human mind. There is at present a marked tendency among the Germans to substitute words of native origin for those of foreign parentage that have acquired domicil among them. There is no excuse but the gratification of vanity for calling in foreign aid to assist in doing that which can in most cases be done just as well out of native resources. Where a language is largely composite, like the English, the case is somewhat different. Writers of equal ability differ considerably in the relative proportion of pure Saxon words and loan-words, chiefly Latin, that enter into their working vocabulary. A good rule to follow is never to use a word of foreign origin, if one of native ancestry equally appropriate and expressive exists. On the other hand, it is well to avoid carrying purism in language to a pedantic and ridiculous excess. The difficulty of keeping the German free from alien elements is not so great as it may seem at first sight. In a countless number of instances it possesses good native words alongside of those of foreign origin between which the speaker or writer has the privilege of choosing. When there is no existing word to express a new concept it is easy to coin one. Generally speaking the Germans have taken rather kindly to the formation of new words. Often the mere translation of words is not sufficient to make their meaning clear. This fact is illustrated in the cases where the same words have been introduced into the language at different periods, and which now have divergent meanings. *Theismus* literally translated would be rendered by the same word as *Deismus*, yet they do not mean the same thing any more than do the English 'theism' and 'deism.' *Spital* and *Hôtel* are both from the Latin 'hospitale,' yet they differ widely in signification. The former means 'hospital' and the significations of the latter are not very different in French, German and English. Many similar cases might be cited.

In other ways also purism may fail of its object and become ridiculous. It would be unwise, to say nothing of its utter impracticability, to attempt to banish from any language all those words that careful investigation has shown to be of alien origin, as, for instance those that came into the German from the Latin, during the earliest contact of these languages with each other. Not a few words of recent importation have become indispensably German and may therefore be justly regarded as fully naturalized. On the other hand, dogmatic assertion as to the permanence of words is equally unwise, for some fortunate stroke of genius or the happy inspiration of a moment may call into being a new term that will fitly take the place of an old one. In the year 1815 a newspaper declared that no word could ever take the place of *Madame* and *Demoiselle*, and every suggestion looking to such a consummation would be dealing with the impossible. What a determined purpose may yet accomplish is best judged by what has already been done. The strife that has been carried on since the beginning of the N. H. G. period, by patriotic Germans, against the mania for foreign words has not been in vain. The greatest zeal and activity in this respect was shown by J. H. Campe. He was the subject of frequent attacks and not a little ridicule, and in truth was not free from fanaticism; yet on the whole his influence was salutary. Campe was a clergyman, an educator in the true sense of the term, a lexicographer and a voluminous writer of books chiefly for youth some of which are still in demand. He died in 1818 at the age of seventy-two. It can be shown that he exerted more or less influence on Goethe, Richter, Schiller and others, while a number of the best German words in use to-day were coined by him to take the place of loan-words. Among these are *sich eignen* for *qualificieren*, *Kerbtier* for *Insekt*, *Gefallsucht* for *Koketterie*, *Fallbeil* for *Guillotine*, *Zerrbild* for *Karrikatur*. Subsequently Robert Schumann showed the Germans that the musical art has no need of Italian words, and that German terms may fitly take the place of the current *allegro, grazioso, moderato, poco più mosso, vivace*, etc. In our day the establishment of the new German empire, the extraordinary growth of national feeling among the Germans, has given an increased impetus to the movement against the introduction and use of foreign words. The German penal code, the postal department, the official report of the war of 1870–71 by the department of military affairs, and certain influential newspapers, notably in South Germany the Landeszeitung of Baden, have inspired the nation with a commendable zeal for purity of speech, and have coined apt, pure German words for foreign ones in current use.

The terminology of medicine has perhaps been least influenced in this respect. There is some excuse for this. Not unfrequently the physician finds it advisable to discuss with a brother physician the condition of the patient in his presence in a language that he does not understand. Systematic botany and zoölogy can not easily dispense with a terminology that is largely of foreign origin, not because appropriate German terms do not exist but for the opposite reason: the same object is designated by a number of different names, each peculiar to a particular district, but not understood elsewhere. Some examples have been previously given. Many of the so-called scientific terms are the common property of science. They are in large part formed of material existing in the ancient Greek and Latin, and can not be said to belong properly to any one modern tongue rather than to any other.

It remains for us to consider the fate of loan-words as individuals both directly after they have been introduced and when they have become in a measure a part of the German vocabulary. They have, in the course of time, fallen into two general classes. Into one may be put all those that have assumed a German garb and may therefore be said to have become fully Germanized; in the other belong all those that have retained very nearly their original form. In effect, however, no fixed line can be drawn between the two classes for the same word has in some instances undergone both kinds of treatment. The former proceeding is more common in the earlier history of the language, and the latter, in its subsequent development. The words that were naturalized in the O. H. G. period were so manipulated as to present in every respect the appearance of native words. It is now difficult to recognize these as exotics, and it would be neither possible nor advisable to extradite or outlaw them. The accretions that took place during the M. H. G. period are rarely much changed in form or appearance and still bear evident traces of their foreign origin. The explanation of this phenomenon is not to be found in the fact that the assimilating power of the German had become weaker, but rather in the circumstance that the borrowing in one case was done by scholars and in the other by the people. In the latter we have an example of the popular treatment of foreign words, while the former exhibits the method of the literary class.

When the literary class acquire the knowledge of a foreign word they learn it by sight rather than by hearing. Met with again and again as a part of the sentence its original form is frequently reimpressed upon the mind of the reader. On the other hand when an exotic becomes a part of the living and spoken language of a people they intuitively shape it into conformity with the phonetic laws of their own tongue. This modification takes place just as readily now as at any period in the past. These statements are not only true of the relation of German to foreign words, but the facts are in conformity with a universal law of speech. The Latin furnished a large number of words to the Romance languages that appear as doublets: one form representing the original word as modified by the natural action of the vocal organs of the unlettered populace; the other, the form given to it by the literary class.

The most striking contrast between pure German words and a large number of loan-words from the Greek, Latin and French, lies in the accent. The German generally places the chief stress on the first syllable of a word, while the Greek and Latin have no such rule of accentuation. In French the accent is on the ultima owing to the fact that when Latin words became fully Gallicised they lost all that part which followed the accented syllable.

In the O. H. G. age the native accent was transferred to the foreign loan-words, and the result was that such words as 'monastérium,' 'monéta' and 'palatium' became in

German *Münster*, *Münze* and *Pfalz*. The English accent corresponds in the main with the German; where such is not the case it is usually owing to the disturbing influence of the French, from which however the language is gradually emancipating itself. Thus, from the French *monastère*, *monnáie* and *palàce*, we get 'monastery,' 'money' and 'palace,' all accented on the first syllable. In the M. H. G. period we find both the German and French accent on the same syllable. The French *la banière* appears both as *bánier* and *baniér;* whence we get the N. H. G. doublets *Banner* and *Panier*. At the present day the foreign accent is generally retained on loan-words which results in producing a shifting accent, as, *Proféssor* and *Professóren*, *A'tlas* and *Atlánten*. It needs to be remarked, however, that many words did not come into the German directly from the language of which they originally formed a part, but through the medium of another in which their accent had undergone some modification. The names Menelaus. Themistokles and Oedipus are accented according to the Latin and not the Greek or we should have Menélaus, Themistoklés and Oedípus. In such terms as *Katholík*, *Musík*, *Protestánt* the accent remained where it is in the French. In some cases a word may be accented either according to the analogy of the French or the German and we may pronounce *Phaenómen* or *Phaenomén*, *Arithmétik* or *Arithmetík*, *Metaphy'sik* or *Metaphysík*, a fact to which, as far as it bears upon English pronunciation, we have already called attention. The Germans say *Antipathíe*, *Politík*, *Mathemathík*, but in the derivative adjectives the accent falls on the penult making *antipáthisch*, *politisch*, *mathemáthisch*. In cases of double accent such as we find on *Státue* and *Statúe*, *Physík* and *Phy'sik*, it is doubtful whether the accent on the first follows the analogy of the Latin or the German as they here coincide. Other similar examples are *Kárneval*, *Lieútenant*, *O'cean*, *Schárlatan*. In such words as *Adjectív*, *Infinitív*, *Kaval-*

lerie the accent is sometimes heard on the first and sometimes on the last syllable. The same can be said of the dissyllables *Bureau, Diner, Souper*, the tendency in North Germany being to accent the final and in South Germany the radical syllable. In Switzerland one may even hear *Cóusine, Hôtel, Párterre*. It may be stated as a general truth that more attention is paid in the North to correct pronunciation than in the South. For this reason, the foreign, which is the correct, pronunciation of these and like words, is retained as nearly as possible. The actual result however comes far short of what is aimed at, for the heavy stress placed on the final syllable of French words, by the North Germans, is as far from the intonation of the native French as the misplaced accent of the South Germans. When one learns a foreign language from the printed page, that is by sight rather than by ear, he is likely to pronounce a letter or combination of letters as they are pronounced in his own language. Hence the Germans frequently pronounce *Toast* as a dissyllable, because *oa* does not occur as a digraph in their language, though it is common in English. Most languages have sounds peculiar to themselves which can only be learned by long practice begun when the vocal organs are still in a plastic condition. It is a rare thing for an adult to learn correctly the pronunciation of any other tongue besides his vernacular, but the ability to hear and reproduce foreign sounds accurately differs considerably in different individuals, and is not wholly a matter of education and training.

NOTE.—One of the most careful observers in this field lays down the following propositions:
1. "Whenever a foreign language is perfectly acquired, there are peculiar family conditions. The person has either married a person of the other nation or is of mixed blood.
2. When a foreign language has been acquired (there are instances of this) in quite absolute perfection, there is almost always some loss

in the native tongue. Either the native tongue is not spoken correctly or it is not spoken with perfect ease.

3. A man sometimes speaks two languages correctly—his father's and his mother's, or his own and his wife's—but never three.

4. Children can speak several languages exactly like natives, but in succession, never simultaneously. They forget the first in acquiring the second, and so on.

5. A language can not be learned by an adult without five years' residence in the country where it is spoken, and without habits of close observation a residence of twenty years is insufficient."—*P. G. Hamerton.*

The effort to produce the sounds of a foreign language generally results in giving the native sound that approaches most closely to it—in the uneducated this is always the case. For example the Latin 'feria' becomes *vira* in the earlier German, in the later *Feier;* 'creta' became *crida* then *Kreide*. The same procedure may still be observed. The mute e of the French is generally represented by the German e, in spite of the fact that the sounds of the two letters differ considerably. The French nasal sound is often represented by a simple n or m, or by ng, as in *Mansarde, Rang, Tambur.* This is true both of German and English. Both nations have great difficulty in producing graphically as well as phonetically the French liquid sounds. In German we generally find gn represented by nj and so pronounced. The German l often stands as the representative of the French liquid l, so that in South Germany *bouteille* is pronounced *Budél* or *Búdel* and *fauteuil Fotöhl.* Sometimes lch performs the same office in North Germany and we get *Budelch* and *Fotölch.* The final -il in *detail, email* is pronounced in South Germany so as to rhyme with *Heil* and *Teil.*

Notwithstanding these variations, it is possible in most instances to discover what particular sound of the foreign tongue is represented in a loan-word, and therefore, to determine at what stage of development, speaking broadly, the foreign word was taken into the German. By a comparison of sounds it is usually not difficult to decide at about what time the borrowing must have been done. The Latin c, for example, before e and i was pronounced like k until about the seventh century of our era; subsequently it gradually took the sound of z (ts). Hence we know that the German words *Keller* (cellarium), *Kerbel* (cærefolium), *Kirsche* (cerasus), *Kiste* (cista) are loan-words of earlier date than *Kreuz* (crucem) and *Zins* (census). Such words as *Panier* and *Rappier* must have come into the German at a time anterior to *Bariere* and *Lisiere* because the French pronunciation -*ière* was preceded by -*iere*, i. e., the accent shifted one syllable nearer to the end of the word. Sometimes we may draw conclusions as to the mode of inflection in a foreign language from the form loan-words have taken in German. These words shaped themselves according to the analogy of the native words which they most nearly resembled and with especial reference to the current inflectional endings. When substantives, they generally took the gender of the class that occasioned their change of form. In this way the Latin words ending in -*arium* were classed with the German words ending in -*ari* and incorrectly became masculines. *Kellari* (O. H. G. chëllari) is the oldest known form of *Keller* and *wiari* (vivarium) of *weiher*, and correspond in form and gender with such words as *lêrari* (Lehrer), *scribari* (Schreiber), etc. The French words *le groupe*, *le rôle*, and all substantives in -*age*, however, became feminine in German after the analogy of *Bitte*, *Gabe* and their congeners. It is therefore ridiculous pedantry to insist on *der Rhone*, as some teachers do, simply because the Latin *Rhodanus* is masculine. But not merely the formal analogy between loan words and native words has had an important influence upon the former: the relation between the concepts has likewise been a determining factor. *Kadaver*, though neuter in Latin is masculine in German because *Leichnam* is of this gender. *Mauer* and *Nummer* are feminine while the Latin *murus* and *numerus* are masculine because *Wand* and *Zahl* are masculine. *Libell* takes the gender of *Buch*, *Pferd* (late Latin *paraveredus*) that of *Ross*. In Vienna *Tramway* is feminine for the reason that *Pferdebahn* is. In a number of cases, however, there were no words in the German that corresponded exactly to the loan-word. This led to an uncertainty in the gender and it is not easy to discover any definite rule of procedure. In fact there is a rather long list of words that have different genders in the different Germanic dialects. The French noun, in spite of the fact that it is generally attended by the article, has not always decided the gender of nouns lent to its eastern neighbors. During the M. H. G. period the masculine is represented more frequently than in later times. Compare, for example, *Harnisch* (harnais), *Palast* (palace), *Preis* (prix), etc., with the modern *Bankett*, *Bataillon*, *Banquett*, *Dejeuner*, *Filet* and many others, all of which are masculine in French and neuter in German. Some difficulty was probably experienced by the Germans, who were accustomed to a language with three genders, in grasping the genius of a language which like the French has but two. This difficulty would be the greater when both languages were written but little and their contact chiefly oral. In later times, especially among the lettered class, the reason may be assumed to have played a part denied to it in the earlier periods when the growth of languages is chiefly instinctive. Though the originals of *Bankett*, *Bataillon*, *Journal* and *Palais* are masculine, they designate neuter objects and would naturally be assigned to that gender if the judgment had any part in the decision, which unfortunately it has not in the German nor in some other languages.

A number of words are of two genders. *Chor* is both masculine and neuter, as are likewise *Konsulat* and *Patriarchat*, though in the latter cases it is the result of scholastic pedantry. The German language in its instinctive stage made all words ending in -at neuter, according to the analogy of the Latin words the stems of which ended with the same letters. As soon as loan-words became thoroughly naturalized in the German they were subjected to the same phonetic laws as native words. They underwent the same phonetic variations, and by a careful study of this fact we obtain some chronological aid in determining the date of incorporation. The Latin 'parochus,' 'planta,' 'porta' appear in German as *Pfarrer*, *Pflanze* and *Pforte*. These words have, therefore, undergone the second stage of consonantal shifting and must have been borrowed before it took place. On the other hand *Pech* (picem), *Pein* (pœna), *Pilgrim* (peregrinus), came into German subsequent to this change. It is evident from many German words that those who used them frequently modified their form in order to bring them into closer harmony with the genius of the language; that is, they exhibit the effects of an evident effort so to change their structure as to draw them into etymological relation to other and more familiar words, for the purpose of making them more easily intelligible. This is the case in *Bibelbuch*, *Dammhirsch*, *Grenzmark*, *Maulesel* and their like, where the two parts of the compound mean substantially the same thing. In other cases, what may be called a folk-etymology has brought about the entire transformation of a word, so that *Arcubalista* became *Armbrust*, *Agrimonia Odermennig*, and *cold cream*, *Gold creme*.

This tendency of the human mind has brought about a transformation of a large number of place-names and given rise to many local legends. Familiar instances are the change from Pileatus to Pilatus, the latter name then becoming the nucleus about which grew the legend of the sojourn and death of the well known Roman governor upon this mountain; the metamorphosis of the name Mautturm into Mausturm and the story of bishop Hatto who was devoured by swarms of rats and mice; and the change of the name of Martyrerkapelle near Bonn into Mordkapelle.

It will be readily understood that the meanings no less than the forms of words undergo a change, a statement that is equally true of native and loan-words. 'Dictare' and *Dichten* are related to each other as ancestor and descendant, but they are far from signifying the same thing. The same may be said of 'poena' and *Pein*, 'puteus' and *Pfütze*, etc.

The best English work known to me on popular etymologies is, Folk-Etymology, by Rev. A. S. Palmer, London, 1882. Taylor's Words and Places contains some interesting matter of the same subject.

SPECIAL PART.

THE NEW HIGH GERMAN ORTHOGRAPHY.

IN ORDER to represent adequately, by means of graphic signs, all the sounds of a language there would be necessary as many characters as there are sounds. Each sign would need to stand for one and the same sound, at all times and for no other. The German language is a considerable distance from such an ideal, though it approaches more nearly thereto than the English does. Different letters and diphthongs are used to designate the same sound: for example, (*Sie*) *waren* is pronounced exactly like (*die*) *Wahren* and (*die*) *Waaren*, or *Waren*. *Voll* has the same initial sound with its primitive *füllen*, and so has *vor* with the related *für*. On the other hand, the same graphic sign or signs represent different sounds. For example, *ch* in *Bach, Loch, erlaucht,* must not be sounded as in *Bäche, Löcher, erleuchtet, Milch, mancher;* after *a, o* and *u* it is formed further back in the throat than after *e, i, ö, ü* and consonants. In words like *Wachs, Dachs, sechs,* the *ch* is pronounced like *k*. The combination *ch* is also evidence of the fact that in some cases two letters are employed to designate a single sound. The same is true in those instances where *ie* is used to represent the simple long *i*, while *ng* in *lang, Gang,* and *sch,* are always used as simple sounds. The converse is likewise found. The single letters *z* and *x* each represents the double sounds *t+s* and *k+s*. It will be evident from what has just been said that it is important to distinguish between the letters of a language and the sounds for which they stand.

The lack of congruity between the letters and sounds of the German language arises from the manner in which the latter came to be graphically represented. Every person learns to write from another who in turn has learnt the art from a third; and so on. In this way the orthography of a language gains a considerable degree of fixedness while the spoken language undergoes changes. A person may therefore write as his father or his grandfather wrote, but he will talk like his contemporaries. In a century the changes are generally few and unimportant, and usually affect but a small number of words; but in the course of several hundred years the divergence is sometimes quite marked. The invention of printing was an important event not only in so far as it affected German orthography but that of all modern languages. By means of the printing press it was in the main fixed, as it now stands, three or four centuries ago notwithstanding the fact that during this period many phonetic changes have crept into the language. The Germans write *ei* and pronounce *ai* or rather *ae*. In such words as *lieb*, *Dieb*, the *e* was originally pronounced though it is now silent except in some dialects. Such words as *steif* and *spitz* are no longer pronounced as written, but *schteif* and *schpitz*. The graphic change did not keep pace with the change in pronunciation. In the words *Ratte*, *Vetter*, *Himmel*, *Donner*, and their kind, a double consonant is written and a single one pronounced. This is easily verified by an experiment that any one can make. Because double letters are hardly ever necessary the advocates of spelling reform discard them in most cases. The reason of the doubling is as follows: in the M. H. G. there were real double consonants, or rather, consonants pronounced long, as is still the case in modern Italian. During the transition from the M. H. G. to the N. H. G. nearly all short sounds were lengthened where they stood before single consonants, but the vowels before double consonants remained short. In the spoken language the double consonants were in many cases dropped, but retained in writing, and the impression gradually prevailed that a short vowel was necessarily associated with a double consonant. The result was that consonants were frequently duplicated in writing where they had never been so pronounced, if a short vowel happened to be conserved before a single consonant. Thus the M. H. G. *hĭmel* and *dŏner* came to be written *Himmel* and *Donner*, because the older *stimme* and *sonne* are now pronounced *Stĭme* and *Sŏne*.

These defects of the N. H. G. orthography are not without significance for the language. Written speech reacts, among the educated, upon the spoken language and modifies it. Many persons see a radical difference between the words *stets*, *bestätigen*, *leer*, *schwer*, *erklären*, *gefährlich* and their like, when, in truth, the diphthong *æ* is common to them all. The Esthonian Germans pronounce *Haide*, *Kaiser*, *Maid*, as diphthongs of which the first part is an *a*, but *Heide*, *Keiner*, *Meineid*, with a distinct *e* in the same place. In the M. H. G. all these words had *ei* as the radical vowels, but in contemporary German dialects no distinction is made between them.

THE ACCENT OR INTONATION OF THE GERMAN.

The syllables that constitute a word or a sentence may be distinguished from one another in one of two ways: a difference may be made in the pitch of the tones, or in the force with which they are uttered. As regards the former, the variation in a single word is but slight, and therefore unimportant; but the case is different when we take into account an entire sentence. There is a wide difference in the manner in which affirmative, interrogative and hortatory sentences are uttered. In a simple, affirmative sentence the inflection is, in general, the falling. If we were to set *Er geht fort* to the notes of the musical scale we should place the last word on about the fifth below the key-note. In interrogative and hortatory sentences the melody naturally rises,—in the former usually to the extent of an octave. In the sentence *Er geht fort?* the last word would thus be placed on the eighth note above the other two, while in *Er geht fort!* (go away, betake yourself off!) it would be placed in the fourth above. When a sentence is incomplete in form or sense by reason of something yet to follow that is not expressed it ends with the rising inflection. The first part of a compound or complex sentence usually closes with the rising inflection. It can hardly be said that the cause of these various inflections is as yet well understood, but it probably lies in the general character of the tones themselves. However, as this is not a question that concerns the German alone, but is treated in every Manual of Elocution it need not detain us further here.

In the second place, the tones that enter into a sentence are distinguished from each other dynamically; and it is to this distinction that we have reference when we speak of accent. It is well to remember, too, that accent in a word and emphasis in a sentence are not two radically distinct things. The Germans speak of *Hochton* (high tone) and designate syllables as *hochbetont* as if accent was concerned only with the pitch or elevation of sounds and not with their force. The reason of this is that the force or stress with which a tone is uttered generally has some connection with its pitch, not only in German but in most other languages. The different words of a sentence are usually uttered with a stress proportioned to their importance in it, viewed from the standpoint of logic. It is also true to a considerable extent that the most important syllable of a word is pronounced with the greatest stress. In accordance with this principle, almost any syllable of a word may receive the accent under particular circumstances. We might say of a person, *er ist bekléidet, nicht bemált;* or, *er ist békleidet, nicht éntkleidet; bekleidét, nicht bekleidénd.* Except in cases of marked antithesis the German, like the English, in distinction from the Latin and especially the Greek, has the accent on the same syllable of a word under all circumstances, a fact that has already been briefly adverted to. For example, *ein, einig, Einigkeit, Einigkeitsbestrebungen* all have the accent on the first syllable, though the words differ greatly in length. The syllable that regularly takes the accent is in all simple words the radical or first syllable. The apparent exceptions offered by such words as *Jägerei, Büberei, hantieren, stolzieren* have been caused by French influence. These and other similar words are not pure German. See also page 191.

But, as we have seen, there is a tendency to change the accent of foreign words to the first syllable during the process of naturalization in German. The English language, too, furnishes many examples of this gradual recession of the accent. In compound words the rule for the accent is not so simple. Of great importance in such cases is the logical relation which the first part of the compound bears to the second.

In the majority of examples the first member of the compound defines or limits the second. When in such cases the first member is a noun, adjective, or verb,—that is, a word that expresses a complete concept, the accent falls upon it, as *Móndschein, Grünspecht, Trétrad* (tread-wheel). This rule also holds good for those cases where adjectives, prepositions, or particles are used to form compounds with nouns or adjectives, as *Wiedertäufer, Antwort, Ueberflusz, Vórlaut, Missetat* (misdeed).

When compounds are constituted of a particle and a verb they may be combined in one of two ways: if the prefix is inseparable the radical portion of the verb takes the accent, but if it is separable the accent falls upon the prefix. It is thus that we get *beléhren* (instruct), *entnéhmen* (take from), *erfáhren, misfállen* (displease), *verráthen* (betray), *zerréiszen* (tear in pieces); but *béistehen* (assist), *fórtfallen*, *wéggehen*. A considerable number of particles may be either separable or inseparable parts of a compound: the two words though spelled alike do not have the same meaning and are pronounced differently, as *dúrchbrechen* (intrans.) and *durchbréchen* (trans.), *híntertreiben* (drive behind) and *hintertreiben* (thwart), *übersetzen* (cross) and *übersétzen* (translate), *úmgehen* (deal with) and *umgéhen* (avoid).

The laws governing the accentuation of words that are compounded with particles as prefixes, as above enunciated, seem in a number of cases to conflict with each other.

Such words as *Beschéid* (advice), *Eróberung* (conquest), *Verléger* (publisher), seem at first sight to have a prepositional prefix; which according to the rule above laid down would require the accent. In fact, however, there are no such words as *Scheid*, *Oberung*, and *Léger;* their apparent compounds are not formed of prefix and substantive but are derivatives of *beschéiden*, *eróbern*, and *verlégen*. They, therefore, rightly receive the accent of verbal composites. On the other hand words like *ántworten*, *úrkunden* and *úrtheilen* are not at variance with the rule for the reason that they are derived from *Antwort*, *Urkunde* and *Urtheil* (judgment).

But it sometimes occurs that the second member of a compound is not materially, or not at all, changed in meaning by its prepositional or adverbial prefix. In such cases the second member receives the accent, or the accent oscillates between the first and second member of the composite. Such is the case with the prefix *ge-* in *leiten* and *geleiten*, *streng* and *gestreng*, *Wasser* and *Gewässer*, between which couplets there is but a slight shade of difference. The same is true as to the prefix *voll-* in *vollenden*, *vollführen* ; as to *all-* in *allgütig*, *allmächtig*, and others. Sometimes the prefix in composites merely intensifies the radical meaning of the word as in *groszmächtig*, *kleinwinzig*, *mittendrínn*, &c.

The German also possesses a number of words which when occupying the place of prefix, may either cause a change of meaning or be merely intensive: compare *stéinreich* (stony) with *steinréich* ("mighty" rich) *blutárm* (very poor) with *blútarm* (exanguious), *bómbenfest* and *bombenfést*. It is to be noted, however, that both compounds are sometimes accented alike, in which case the sense must determine which of the two is meant.

Of still less importance is the first member of a compound when the speaker is not conscious of the relation existing between its two parts. This is usually the case when the second member no longer has a separate existence. *Notwendig* is sometimes pronounced with the chief stress on the first syllable and sometimes on the second, because there is no such word as *wendig*. The same remark applies to *léibhaftig*, and *leibháftig*, *wíllkommen* and *willkómmen*, *wáhrscheinlich* and *wahrschéinlich*, with a number of others. This fact will also explain the pronunciation of *Forélle* (trout) and *lebéndig* (living). In the M. H. G. these words were accented on the first syllable and were simply derivatives. But as there are in the N. H. G. no analogous words with the termination *-endig* and *-elle*, these vocables came to be regarded as compounds and to be accented according to the rule applicable in such cases. In adjective compounds that have the prefix *un-* the accent rests on this when the second part also exists as an independent word; when not, then the accent is upon the second part of the word. We say *schön* and *únschön*, *fréundlich* and *únfreundlich*, *frúchtbar* and *únfruchtbar*, but *unbeschréiblich*, *unermészlich*, *unsäglich*, *unzählich*, because there are no such words as *beschreiblich, ermeszlich*, etc. In the examination of compound words it is likewise of importance to note the syllable that has the so-called secondary accent. It is true, in general, that this accent would falls upon that syllable of the simple word that enters into the compound if it stands independently. We say *Sómmerarbeit, hínterlìstig, Unèinigkeit,* placing the secondary stress on -*ar-*, -*list-*, and -*ein-*, because the words *Arbeit, listig* and *Einigkeit,* when standing alone, have the accent on these syllables. This rule, while true in general, is however subject to two exceptions: if the first member of the compound is a monosyllable with a strong secondary accent, and if the second member, a syllable with a strong secondary stress, follows directly upon that having the primary accent, there is an evident tendency to conform to a general law of the N. H. G., namely, to pronounce successive syllables with an alternating strong and weak accent. By pronouncing the words that constitute a sentence in this way, the sentence itself moves forward with a sort of rhythmic or wave-like motion that gives pleasure to the ear. For this reason we say *únabsìchtlich, únvorsìchtig,* in spite of the fact that *absichtlich* and *vórsichtig* are correct. In the same category fall such words as *Amtsmisbrauch, Vóranzeige, Vórurtheil, únfruchtbar,* etc.

THE DOCTRINE OF SOUNDS IN GERMAN.

A knowledge of the laws of accent is not only important in itself, but also for the additional reason that the relation of accented to unaccented syllables in a word has much influence upon its form. The changes which in process of time take place in strongly accented syllables are usually of a quite different kind from those occurring in syllables that are habitually uttered with but a slight stress. When, therefore, it is proposed to consider the morphology of the German vowels it is important to distinguish carefully between those that are accented and those that are unaccented. It is in the former, as has been before indicated, that the most important changes have taken place, and here lies the chief difference between the Old and the New German. First and foremost, attention needs to be called to the long M. H. G. vowels i, u and ü (written iu) which appear in the N. H. G. as ei, au and eu, that is, as diphthongs. This transformation began in the Bavaro-Austrian dialect and appears as early as the twelfth century. In its progress it gradually embraced the dialects of Central Germany, South and East Franconia and Swabia; but the Alemanian and Low German remained unaffected. We find, therefore, that the N. H. G. *mein, dein* and *sein* are represented by the Alemanian, Low German and M. H. G. *mīn, dīn* and *sīn*. The M. H. G. *hūs, mūs, hiule* correspond to the N. H. G. *Haus, Maus, heute*. In unaccented syllables the original simple vowel has in some cases remained, probably for the reason that it had been shortened before diphthongs began to appear in the language. Consequently we have *reich* alongside of *Heinrich, Friedrich, Gänserich* together with *Leiche, Leichnam* and their derivatives in *-lich*. See p. 176. The N. H. G., however, contains a tolerably long list of words with a single vowel in the place of a former diphthong. These are, for the most part, loan-words from the Old German, the Low German and the Alemanian. For this reason we have both *Schweiz* and *Schwyz, Neid* and *Nithart, Auerochs* and *Ur, raunen* and *Runen, Gertrud* and *traut, Bruno* and *braun, Hune* and *Heune*.

The three phonetic tendencies above pointed out are all due to the same law,—they indicate the influence of the vowel sound represented by the letter a: in fact Germans even to-day pronounce *mein* and *heute* as if written *main* and *haüte*. The same tendency began to manifest itself in the three diphthongs that existed in the Old German; the M. H. G. *ei* also passed into *ai*, so that *keiser*, for example, became *Kaiser* in Modern German; the M. H. G. *ou* passed into *au*, so that for *boum* we now have *Baum*; and the M. H. G. *öu* likewise was changed into *äu (-aü)*, that is, *böume* into N. H. G. *Bäume*. It will be seen that the N. H. G. *ei* pronounced, and occasionally written, *ai*, represents an older *î* and *ei*, that is, the N. H. G. *aü* in sound, but written *eu* and *äu*, and *au* have each absorbed two sounds of the M. H. G. The process may be represented thus:

N. H. G. *ei* = M. H. G. *î* and *ei*,
N. H. G. *eu* = M. H. G. *iu* and *öu*,
N. H. G. *au* = M. H. G. *û* and *ou*.

The pronunciation is, however, not quite uniform throughout Germany. The Middle and Low Germans, when speaking the N. H. G., no longer make a distinction, but the South Germans make a slight difference either in the character or in the length of the tones. The M. H. G. *wîde* (willow) becomes *Weide* and *wîse* (manner), *Weise;* as the M. H. G. *weide* and *weise* became *Waide* and *Waise* (a+i), and the M. H. G. *tûbe* is pronounced *Taube*, but *taub* (deaf) represents the M. H. G. *toube*. In like manner *reuen* (pronounced *raüen*) represents an older *riuwen* and *streuen* (pronounced *straüen*) an earlier *ströuwen*. To repeat in other words what has been said above: in South Germany the diphthong *ei* has two slightly different sounds; and the statement is true of *au* and *eu*, while in Middle and North Germany, the two couplets of sounds are alike. This is to be explained by the fact that the people of the former section maintain in pronunciation though not in print a distinction that formerly existed throughout Germany, while those of the latter have lost it. But there is likewise a tendency in the German to separate the old single vowels into diphthongs. The M. H. G. sounds represented by *ie*, *uo*, and *üe* appear in Modern German as *i*, *u*, and *ü*, that is, *liëf* becomes *lief*, *guot* becomes *gut* and *grüezen* becomes *grüszen*. This process of simplification begins to show itself at the close of the M. H. G. period and seems to have started in Central Germany. The Bavarian and the Alemanian, however, retain the old diphthongs to the present day, with here and there a slight change in the second vowel, though the variation is not quite the same in the two dialects. In the Alemanian the words *Bube, Blut, Gut, Hut,* of the N. H. G. are *Bueb, Bluet, Guet,* and *Huet,* but in the Bavarian, usually, *Buab, Bluat,* etc. In view of the fact that the long i-sound of the Modern German generally originated from *ie,* it is easy to understand how this diphthong comes to be written for every long *i*, including even those cases where it has a different origin. Such instances are numerous. It is easy to observe that in the same word the radical vowel sound is sometimes pronounced long and sometimes short, either because certain words exhibit a long, others a short vowel; or because the same vowel is at one time pronounced short and at another, long. We have, for example, *wir nehmen, ihr nehmt,* but *er nimmt, du nimmst, nimm,* where the double consonant is the sign of a short vowel; *geben, wir geben,* but *du gibst, er gibt, gib* or *giebst, giebt, gieb.* The pronunciation of *des Glāses, des Tāges, des Wēges* is universal; but the South Germans say *Glās, Tāg, Wēg,* while in North Germany one often hears *Glăs, Tăg* and *Wĕg.* In like manner we get *Herzŏg* and *Herzōg, jĕnseits* and *jēnseits.* How are these variations to be explained? The reply is that where the same word exists in two forms that have but a single signification it is probable that one represents the regular process of phonetic development, but that the other is due to the force of analogy, a process that has been briefly explained on p. 122. Applying these principles to the cases just cited we find that the North German pronunciation exhibits the original, that is, *das Glăs, des Glăses.* Going back to the M. H. G. we find *glăs, glăses,* in conformity with a law according to which a short vowel in the M. H. G. always appears long in the N. H. G. when it stands before a single consonant followed by another vowel. In closed syllables the radical vowel remains short except that the presence of an *r* makes an exception to this rule. This lengthening process first appears in Middle Germany and in the M. H. G. period. In the case of closed syllables that contain a long vowel contrary to the law here laid down, the phenomenon is to be attributed to the influence of those forms which contained an open radical syllable: that is, the reflex influence of *Glāses* produced *Glās* and of *wir gāben* modified *er găp* into *er gāb*. In the same manner the primitive *wĕg* became *Wēg* through influence of *Wēges;* the adverbial *wĕg* (away) is simply the accusative of this noun which has maintained its original short vowel because its connection with the substantive ceased to be felt. It is true there are exceptions to the law that the vowel of an open syllable is always long. If the simple consonant following the radical vowel is in turn followed by *e+l*, *e+n* or *e+r* the radical vowel may be either long or short. We accordingly find both *Măkel* and *Mākel, gesŏtten*, M. H. G. *gesōten*, but *gebōten* though the M. H. G. is *gebŏten, wĭder*, the M. H. G. form also, and *wieder*, besides *Vater*, with the dialect form *Vătter* and its derivative *Vĕtter*. These apparent irregularities have not yet been satisfactorily explained.

The same vowel sounds that have in some cases remained short have in others become short though originally long. We find *nie* alongside of *nimmer*, the old form being *niemer*, that is, *nie mêr*. That *Fŭtter* and *Mŭtter* were once *Fūter* and *Mūter* is shown by the Alemanian and Bavarian forms *Fūeter* and *Mūeter*. That the ancestors of *Blatter* and *Jammer* are *blâter* and *jâmer* is proven by the wide spread dialectic forms *Blōter* and *Jōmer*; for in many dialects still current the vowel *ō* represents not only the *ō* of older words, but is not unfrequently a development of an original *a*. The literary High German contains a number of words taken from different dialects that exhibit this change from long *a* to long *o*. Thus, we find existing alongside of each other *Atem* and *Odem*, *Wahn* and *Argwohn*, *Magsamen* and *Mohn*, etc. *Mond* is *māne* in M. H. G. and the ancestor of *Wage* is *wāc*. Further back in the history of the German language than all these variations we find the process taking place which the Germans call Umlaut. This is a modification of the radical or root vowel. It is thus that *Kräfte* is formed from *kraft*, *möchte* from *mochte*, *Häuser* from *haus*, *träumt* from *traum*, *führe* from *fuhr*. In all cases the unmodified vowel is the original. It will thus be seen that the same root, though not the same form of it, contains both the shorter and less open vowels *a*, *o* and *u*, as well as their variants *ä*, *ö* and *ü*. Now it can be shown by the history of the German as well as by that of other languages that *a* is more primitive than *ä*, *o*, than *ö*, etc. The N. H. G. furnishes some hints on the origin of the unmodified vowels: we have, for example, *Kraft* and *kräftig*, *Rom* and *römisch*, *Thor* and *thöricht*, *Ruhm* and *rühmlich*, *kosten* and *köstlich*, *Graf* and *gräfin*, with a host of others. It will be seen that in all these instances the modified vowel is followed by an i in the next syllable; and the fact is that as long ago as the O. H. G. period it was this i that brought about the change in the preceding vowel: for even those words from which it has now disappeared once had it. In the O. H. G. period *krafti* corresponded to the modern *Kräfte*, *mochti* to *möchte*, *hūsir* to *Häuser*, *troumit* to *träumt*, *fuori* to *führe*. We may, therefore, define Umlaut as the modification of a vowel by the influence of a subsequent i.

There are some words in German which seem to have a modified vowel in the root form and a primitive vowel in some of the derivative forms. This is sometimes called *Rückumlaut* on the supposition that the second change is simply a return to the original form. Examples are *brennen*, preterite *brannte; rennen*, preterite *rannte; senden*, preterite *sandte; schon* and *schön*, *fast* and *fest*. In fact, however, appearances are here deceptive. It is the custom of grammarians to designate certain words or syllables as radical, or primitive, and others as derivative. The base of the verb is usually found in the present tense, that of the noun in the singular number, and that of the adverb in the adjective. But the theory does not always correspond with the facts, and does not in the above examples, since *brannte*, *schon* and *fast* exhibit the primitive, unmodified vowel, while *brennen* is derived from *brannian*, *fest* from *fasti*, and *schön* from *sconi*.

The sound represented by *e* in the N. H. G., of which the ancestor is *a*, is written in two ways, either as *ä* or *e;* in like manner the Umlaut of *au*, as *äu* or *eu*. The modified *a* (*ä*) is employed when there is a real or fancied connection between it and the original or radical *a*, as *Band* and *Bänder*, *Wahl* and *wählen*, *Haus* and *Häuser*, *Traum träumen;* on the other hand, *e* is used where the connection has been forgotten, as *streng*, O. H. G. *strangi;* *leugnen*, M. H. G. *lougnen*, O. H. G. *louginon*. These are cases in which the same radical vowel exist in a number of derivatives, in some of which it is felt and in others not. For example, *fahre* is the ancestor not only of *Fährte* and *Fährmann*, but also of *Ferge* (ferry-man) and *fertig;* to *Schlacht* belong not only *Schlächter*, but also *Geschlecht*, which originally meant the same with *Schlag*, as may be seen in *Menschenschlag* (race, type of men).

In the study of these and similar phenomena the reader needs to keep constantly in mind that the spoken language preceded the written by a long interval, and that even after writing had come into vogue to some extent there were thousands who used their native speech orally only. When words began to be put on parchment and paper their pronunciation had been in the main fixed, and could rarely be modified. Besides, most languages are written a long time before the etymological relations of words are understood, and the efforts of scholars, where they have tried to represent these relations, have for the most part remained without permanent results.

Different from, and yet closely related to the umlaut, is the breaking or *splitting* of a vowel. In many cases the same radical vowel contains both *e* (*ä*) and *i*, as in *gebären* and *gebiert, Erde* and *irden, Herde* and *Hirte*. These changes have likewise been wrought by the influence of the final vowel. In the O. H. G. the words above given were phonetically represented by *gaberan gabirit, erda irdin, herta hirti*. In all cases the radical vowel of the stem is *e*, as may be seen in the corresponding Latin and Greek words fero and φέρω; the *e* remained when followed by *a*, but was changed to *i* when succeded by the same letter. This law has been deduced by the examination of so large a number of words that it is safe to assume when, for instance, we find *Gebirge* existing alongside of *Berg*, and *Gefilde* alongside of *Feld*, that we have in *Feld* and *Berg* the influence of an *a*. This modification of *e* before *i* into the latter took place in prehistoric times. Until recently philologists were generally of the opinion that the original vowel was *i*, and that this letter had passed (or broken) into *e*. This *e* corresponds to the primitive Indo-European *e*, and should be carefully distinguished from the same letter when it is the representative of a modified *a*. Several German dialects have preserved, in their pronunciation, the distinction between the two sounds. Here, as in many other cases, the Alemanian and Swabian have adhered most tenaciously to the archaic forms, the broken *e* being pronounced somewhat like *a*, and the modified *e* with a nearer approach to *i*.

The views regarding the influence of the a-sound upon *e* and *i* which have proved to be erroneous, are correct with reference to *u* and *o*, or rather *ü* and *ö*, since the old *u* was modified in the O. H. G. period by a subsequent *i*. The forms *wir wurden* and *geworden, ich würfe* and *geworfen, für* and *vor* take us back to the O. H. G. *wurdun-gawordan, wurfi-gaworfan, furi-fora*. Here the original *u* persisted before *i* and *u* in the final syllable; in other words when it occurred before *i* it afterward changed into *ü*; but it was later broken to *o* by the influence of a subsequent *a*,—a phenomenon which likewise took place in the General Germanic stage of the language. This breaking did not take place when *u* was followed by a nasal consonant; so that we have *gefunden, gesungen*, in spite of the fact that the O. H. G. forms were *gafundan, gasungan*. It will be readily seen that if the law had been universal in its application we should have *gefonden* and *gesongen*, just as we have *geworfen* and *geworden*. This *u* has not only undergone the breaking process when it stood alone but also when it formed a diphthong with *i*, that is *iu*. In the older N. H. G. we find the inflections *du fleugst, er fleugt, ihr flieget*, to which correspond the M. H. G. in older forms *du fliugest, er fliuget, ihr flieget*, and the O. H. G. or still older *du fliugist, er fliugit, ihr fliogat*. We see, therefore, that *iu* stands in the same relation to *io* that *u* does to *o*. It will thus be evident that we have here in the change from *u* to *o* and from *iu* to *io* (*ie*) the data for determining with almost absolute certainty what the final syllable must have been originally. *Fülle* alongside of *voll* points to an older *fulli*, and *voll* must have lost a final *a*; similarly *siech* and *Seuche* are evidence of an older *siuhhi*, the intermediary M. H. G. being *siuche* (sick). The M. G. dialects exhibit some apparent examples of breaking which are, however, not genuine, *u* being sometimes modified to *o*, and *ü* to *ö*, which is not due to the influence of a succeeding *a*. For example, the N. H. G. *Sommer* and *Sohn* are in the M. H. G. *sümer* and *sün*. Other examples are *Sonne* and *sunne, König* and *künic, Mönch* and *münch*.

To the phenomena of umlaut and breaking are largely due the variety exhibited by German phonology. Aside from these two factors all the variations are referable to ablaut (or vowel gradation). This influence may be noticed in *Grab, Grube* (M. H. G. *gruobe*), *grübeln* (O. H. G. *grubilon*); *Binde, Band, Bund; Sitz, Satzung; Brecher, Brachland, Bruch; Schneide, Schnitt; flieszen, Flosz, Flusz*. This variation of the radical vowel is wholly independent of the subsequent vowel and was fully developed in the far distant prehistoric period of the Indo-European language. To the English reader his own language will readily suggest many examples; and they are equally numerous in Latin and Greek. Cf. pello, pulsus; tollo, tuli; sēmen, sătus ; ἄγω, ἦγον; τρέπω, τρόπος; λείπω, ἔλιπον, λοιπός; φεύγω, φυγή.

At the basis of these changes lie the general principles of vocalization common to the entire stock of Indo-European languages: the accented syllables have for the most part stronger vowels and the unaccented weaker and thinner vowels. The underlying causes we do not understand, and they will doubtless remain forever impenetrable. All we can say is that human thought and feeling are wont to manifest themselves through speech in this way. There is in man an inherent dislike of monotony, and variety is produced by running up and down, or by touching now this and now that note of the vowel scale. In order to avoid repetition the general subject of vowel gradation will be more fully discussed in the chapter which treats of the inflection of the verb.

When we compare German substantives and adjectives with their cognates in Latin we at once notice the absence of endings in the former compared with the latter. We have *Halm* but *calamus*, *Wind* but *ventus*, *Fisch* but *piscis*, *Haut* (M. H. G. *hût*) but *cutis*, *Joch* (Gothic *juk*) but *jugum*, *Hals* but *collum*, *collus* and *colsum*, *Horn* but *cornu*. This difference did not exist in the remotest times; but after the general Germanic tongue had broken up into its various branches, we find, even earlier than the existence of any literary monuments, a tendency to neglect, in pronunciation, the final syllables. First final s and m began to be dropped; and later the vowels shared the same fate.

We have already mentioned that the weakening of the ultimate syllables characterizes the transition from the O. H. G. to the M. H. G. Similar phenomena are again observable in the development of the N. H. G. from the

M. H. G. We have *des Tages* or *des Tags*, *dem Tage* or *Tag*, *Werkes* or *Werks*, *Werke* or *Werk;* but usually *des Landtags*, *dem Landtag*, *Handwerks* and *Handwerk*, but not *Landtages* or *Handwerke*. *Des Königs*, *dem König* are used in preference to *des Königes*, *dem Könige*. Alongside of *Friede* we have its derivative *friedlich;* alongside of *Heide*, *nieder* and *Himmel*, the relative words *heidnisch*, *niedrig* and *himmlisch*. In nearly all cases we observe apocope of final e in unaccented syllables. In those words where this letter has been suppressed in the middle of a word it was likewise unaccented. The German present participles are almost always traceable to fuller forms, as, for example, *lebend* to *lebende*. *Wirtinn* represents the M. H. G. *wirtinne*, *Weisung* M. H. G. *wīsunge*, *Herzog herzoge*, *Häuslin hiuselin*. In N. H. G. dissyllables an unaccented e is sometimes retained, and sometimes suppressed or apocopated, a fact that may be explained by the place of this letter in connected discourse. As a further illustration of the tendency to abbreviate, it may be stated that in the German dialects which have not attained the dignity of literary rank many words are still more abbreviated than in the written speech. Nearly all those words which have come from the A.-S. into English have been shortened unless they were monosyllables, where abbreviation was impossible. In like manner the French, which is hardly more than corrupt Latin, is almost entirely made up of words that have lost one or more syllables in their passage from the ancient to the modern language.

In some cases syllables that were originally but feebly accented suffered mutilation even when their vowel was full-toned. *Jungfer* and *Junker* are referable to older *Jungfrau* and *Jungherr;* *Nachbar* (neighbor) may be traced to the M. H. G. *nâchbūre*, one who abides near, the modern German words *Bauer* and *bauen* having developed a somewhat different signification. The doubles *Schultze* and *Schultheisz* take us back to the M. H. G. *schultheize*. Zwei-

tel, Drittel contain the word *Teil* in the final syllable, while *Urteil* and *Vorteil* are also found as *Urthel* and *Vorthel*. These last double forms resulted either from their receiving a heavier or lighter accent, as the case might be, in connected discourse; or they for a time followed the general law above enunciated until with the spread of intelligence it began to be perceived that *-thel* is really a separate word, when it was restored to its original form. The latter is the most probable explanation, as illiterate persons still use the lighter syllable. In general the dialects, especially those of South Germany, carry the process of abbreviation and lightening farther than the literary language. Hebel, a native of Basel, who wrote largely in the Alemanian uses *Arfel, Hampfel, Mumpfel,* for *Armvoll, Handvoll* and *Mundvoll.* *Wingert* signifies *Weingarten,* while *Rechnig* and *Zitig* mean *Rechnung* and *Zeitung.* The most important phenomenon noticeable among the consonants is due to what is known as the law of the rotation of mutes. We have been constrained to examine this part of our subject earlier because the division of the German language into its various dialects is chiefly dependent thereon. Apart from this single fact the changes which the consonants have undergone are far less important and far reaching than those through which the vowels have passed. The influence of this law may be traced back to that early stage of the language when it had not yet broken up into its various dialects. Here, for instance, we find that *t* can stand only after a spirant. In this way we can explain the relation of *mögen* to *Macht,* of *pflegen* to *Pflich',* of *tragen* to *Tracht,* of *geben* to *Gift* (originally the same as *Gabe,* as may be seen in *Mitgift.* Cf. for a similar development of meaning our word dose, from δόσις) and of *treibe* to *Trift.* It is true we have *klagte, sagte, liebte* and *lobte,* but this is owing to the fact that in former times there was a vowel between the *g* and the *t,* which was dropped long after the law had ceased to be operative. In the earliest Germanic period, when the language was still in a stage of which no records have come down to us, there was in force a law which did not permit the use of a *w* at the end of a word. Where this letter happened to be final it was changed into *o*, rarely *u*. The nominative *milo* (Eng. meal) makes its genitive *melwes*. The final vowel was first weakened to *e* and this was in some cases dropped, but medial *w* was changed to *b* after *l* and *r*. In this way we get *Mehl* alongside of *Milbe* (older form *milwe*, the insect that makes meal) and *Melberei*, the Bavarian designation of a flour-store; likewise *gar* with *gerben* which originally meant 'to make ready.' Sometimes medial *l* was transferred to the end of a word, in which cases we have usually doublets, as *fahl* and *falb*, or *gelb* alongside of the dialectic *gehl*. The O. H. G. forms were *falo*, Gen. *falwes*, *gelo* Gen. *gelwes*, the Eng. equivalents being 'fallow' and 'yellow.' In the M. H. G. we meet with many cases where the consonant is different according as it stands in the middle or at the end of a word. In the N. H. G. the influence of analogy has generally obliterated these differences, but some isolated instances remain which show the effects of the law. In the first place, every medial sonant in M. H. G. is changed into a final surd: *tac* has for its genitive *tages*, *sanc sanges*, *liet liedes*, *lop lobes*. In the N. H. G. the medial consonant is transferred to the end, that is, we have, by the force of analogy *Tag*, *Lied*, *Lob*, because the genitives have the form above given. When we examine the endings *-ng* and *-nk* we find that in Northern Germany the old forms have to some extent persisted, which gives such pronunciations as *Gesank*, though written *Gesang, Gesanges, ich gink, wir gingen*. In isolated cases the final letter or letters of a word have taken the place of the medial. We have, for instance, the N. H. G. *Mark Markes* while the M. H. G. is *marc marges*, and in *ausmergeln* the original *g* is retained. *Der Wert, des Wertes* belongs to the same category with *wurde* and was *wert* *werdes* in the M. H. G. In like manner *Welt Welten* points to M. H. G. *werlt werlde*. In those cases where in the Low German initial *g* was pronounced as a spirant it was changed into final *ch*, and it is by this law that we can explain such forms as *Menge* alongside of *manch mancher* for the older *manech maneger*, M. H. G. *manec maneger*.

In the second place, medial *h* of M. H. G. corresponds to *ch* final, as *sehen, ich sach, schuoch schuoches*. But in the N. H. G. this *h* has taken the place of *ch* so that we find not only *sehen*, but also *ich sah* and *der Schuh*. The older relation remains only in *hoch höher am höchsten*, and partly in *nah* with the superlative *nächst* and in the adverb *nach*. Alongside of *schmähen* we have *Schmach;* the M. H. G. form of *rauh* was *ruch* which persists in the modern *Rauchwerk*, a collection of furs. The old nominative is maintained in the proper name *Schuchardt*, which in M. H. G. was *schuoch worhte*, that is, 'shoe-worker.' There is evident in the M. H. G. as in the N. H. G. a tendency to pronounce contiguous consonants with the same vocal organs, or rather, with the vocal organs in the same position, in order to greater ease of utterance. In this way the two consonants are brought as near together as possible. In ordinary conversation we do not say *anbeiszen* or *einbrechen*, but *ambeiszen* and *eimbrechen;* but in deliberate discourse generally, and almost always in spelling, this phonetic tendency is neutralized by the influence of analogy in words whose prefixes are maintained in their integrity, as, for instance, *anhalten, anlaufen, anstoszen, einatmen, einlegen, eintränken*, etc. Assimilation, however, takes place in some cases where the etymological relation of the prefix has been forgotten. For this reason *empfangen* and *empfinden* used for *entfangen* and *entfinden; empfehlen* for *entfehlen, Imbisz* for *Inbisz, Himbeere* for *Hindbeere* (berries which the hind likes), *Homburg* for *Hohenburg, Schaumberg* for *Schauenberg, Wimper* for *Windbraue* (the brow that moves), cf. the Eng. wend, move, turn about. Complete assimilation has taken place in *Eilant* for *Einland* (the land that is alone); in *Grummet* for *Grünmahd* (grass that is mowed while green, aftermath); in *Hoffahrt* for *Hochfahrt*, and in some other instances. The law of assimilation as we see it exemplified in German is of wide-spread application. In Latin and Greek a number of prepositional prefixes are accommodated to the initial sound of the word with which they are joined, among them the same prefix 'in' or ἐν we have been considering above. There are two other phonetic peculiarities of the German that are to be noted. First, final *r* was dropped before a consonant and presisted before a vowel. We have thus *da* but *darin* and *darum;* *wo*, but *worin* and *warum* (dialectic *worum*), and alongside of *ehe* and *hie* we find *eher* and *hier*. This final *r* is retained in the English cognates there, where and ere, the A.-S. equivalents being *aer*, *hwaer* and *thaer* respectively. Second, the combination *ag* and *eg* are sometimes changed to *ei*. In the M. H. G. occur both *Magd* and *Maid*, *Vogt* and *Voit*, *Hag* and *Hain*. *Getreide* is related to *tragen* and signifies that which is carried, clothing, baggage, etc. (M. H. G. *getregede*). *Verteidigen* is derived from the M. H. G. *tagedinc* (*Gerichtstag*), its older form being *vertagedingen*, to bring before a court of justice or arbitration. *Reinhard* and *Reinecke* have no connection with the adjective *rein*, but the first syllable is a shortened form of *regin*, an old Germanic word which was nearly equivalent to *Rat*. Partly in the M. H. G. and partly in the N. H. G. we find a tendency in *n* and *s*, when at the end of a syllable, to generate a succeeding *d* which under some circumstances is changed into *t*. Though we have *gelegen* and *offen* we say *gelegentlich* and *öffentlich; entzwei* and *entlang* are traceable to *enzwei* and *enlang*, which are simply *in zwei* and *in lang*, or 'in two' or 'along.' *Jemand* and *Niemand* are in full *je*(*ein*)*Mann*, and *nie*(*ein*) *Mann; zusammt* is equal to *zusament* which in turn is *zusamen; einst*, *mittelst* and *selbst* represent an older *eines*, *mittels* and *selbes*, and are adverbial genitives of *ein*, *Mittel* and *selb*. *Papst* is in M. H. G. *babes* from the Greek παπᾶς, while the dialectic *jez*(*ie ze*) corresponds to the H. G. *jetzt*. Another phonetic change that began in the M. H. G. stage of the language in Middle and Lower (or Northern) Germany and afterward spread over Upper Germany is the disappearance of an *h* between two vowels which then coalesced. It is owing to this phenomenon that *h* came to be used to lengthen the preceding vowel. The Germans write *Stahl*, *zehen*, *Bühl*, because M. H. G. exhibits *stahel*, *zehen* and *bühel*. The change of an older *rs* into *rsch* is confined to the H. G. The Low German *Bars* is represented by the South or H. G. *Barsch*, Eng. *barse* or *bass*. The Lombard word *verza*, a kind of cabbage, reappears in the modern German *Wirsching*. A peculiarity of the L. G. is the assimilation of *h* before *s*, so that *Ochsen* becomes *Ossen*, while *Fuchs* and *wachsen* are pronounced *Vosz* and *wassen*. The M. H. G. *tw* was sometimes doubled. In South Germany it appears as *zw* and in Middle Germany as *kw* or *qu*. *Quer* reappears in *Zwerchfell* and in *überzwerch*, M. H. G. *twerch*; *quängeln* is related to *zwingen*, M. H. G. *twingen*.

THE INFLECTIONS OF THE NEW HIGH GERMAN.

THE SUBSTANTIVES.

The N. H. G. noun exhibits great variety in its inflections. This is particularly noticeable in the cases of the singular and in the relation that exists between the singular and the plural. The latter is, on the other hand, subject to but little variation: either its cases are all alike, or the nominative corresponds to the genitive and accusative and the dative takes an additional -*n*. In the first category belong those words that form the nominative plural in -*n* or -*en*, such as *Drachen, Ochsen, Bauern, Wurzeln*, etc.; in the second such words as Nom. Plur. *die Tage,* Dat. *den Tagen; die Wörter,* Dat. *den Wörtern.* Taking the genitive singular and the plural as bases we have, in modern German, the following types:

1. The genitive singular ends in -*es* or -*s*, the plural ending in -*e:*
    (a). *Der Tag, die Tage,*
    (b). *Der Gast, die Gäste,*
    (c). *Das Ding, die Dinge;*
       or in -*er*,
    (d.) *Das Huhn, die Hühner;*
       or in -*n*,
    (e.) *Das Ende, die Enden;*
       or is without a characteristic ending,
    (f). *Der Eber, die Eber; der Wagen, die Wägen,*
    (g). *Der Käse, die Käse,*
    (h). *Das Gebirge, die Gebirge.*

2. The genitive has no inflection, as in all feminines, the plural ending in -*e:*
    (a). *Die Kraft, die Kräfte; die Kuh, die Kühe;*
       or in -*n* or -*en*,
    (b). *Die Klage, die Klagen; die Katze, die Katzen,*
    (c). *Die Saat, die Saaten; die Insel, die Inseln;*
       or is without a characteristic ending,
    (d). *Die Mutter, die Mütter, die Tochter, die Töchter.*

3. All other cases of the singular and plural have an additional -*n* as compared with the nominative singular:
    (a). *Der Bote, die Boten; der Knabe, die Knaben,*
    (b). *Der Graf, die Grafen; der Mensch, die Menschen.*

These paradigms differ from those of the M. H. G. in two respects: first, the N. H. G. exhibits a greater variety of forms; and, second, diverse forms have coalesced into one. The types marked above 1. (a), (b), (d), (g), (h); 2. (a), and 3. (a), are the only ones represented in the older language. It will be seen that the modern forms are twice as numerous as the more ancient.

The types represented by *Tag* and *Gast* date from the M. H. G. stage, and we have before stated the reason why words of one syllable and words of more than one are differently inflected. But when we go back to the O. H. G. stage we find a divergence in the plurals. The words *tac* or *tag* (day) and *gast* (guest) are thus declined in the plural: Nom. *taga, gesti*,
Gen. *tago, gestio*,
Dat. *tagum, gestim*,
Acc. *taga, gesti*.

Here the forms of the second word show the reason of the umlaut in the plural of *Gast*. In a still older stage of the language, one of which no monuments have come down to us, but about which many conclusions may be drawn by inference, there was also a difference in the endings of the singular. *Der Tag, den Tag* were once *tagos* and *tagom; der Gast, den Gast* were *gastis* and *gastim*, where we have terminations corresponding to the Latin 'lupus' and 'lupum,' 'turris' and 'turrim.' It may be well to call attention to the fact that in the above examples only -s and -m can properly be regarded as case-endings. What remains after the removal of these is the stem (or root), and since one of them ends in -o and the other in -i they belong to the class of vowel stems. They may be still further differentiated by being classed as o-stems and i-stems. It is also to be observed that the Latin 'lupus' was 'lupos' in an earlier stage of the language, just as the German *tagum* was *tagom* and *taga* was *tagons*. Moreover, the final o of the German stems was pronounced with a close approximation to a; indeed, it may have passed entirely into the sound of this letter before it dropped off.

Now, since the two types had become alike in the M. H. G. stage, except the stem vowel of the plural, it is easy to see that the paradigms would sometimes be confused.

It has happened that the M. H. G. umlaut was dropped in the N. H. G., as where *lehse* and *lühse* have become *Lachse* and *Luchse*. A great majority of the o-stems have followed the same course with the word *Gast Gäste*. *Hof Höfe* was in M. H. G. *hof hove*, and in O. H. G. *hof hova;* the old form without umlaut is latent in the names of places like *Adelshofen* and *Königshofen*, which are in fact datives plural. The same is true of the names ending in *-kon*, occurring so frequently in the the vicinity of Lake Zurich, such as *Pfäffikon, Sissikon, Zetzikon*, where the final syllable is a contraction of *-ichofen*. Doublets like *Schachte* and *Schächte, Drucke* and *Abdrücke* and *Eindrücke*, are due to the permanence of an older form and the creation of a corresponding modernized new one. In some instances the dialects exhibit forms with umlaut where the literary language has retained the vowel without change, as, for instance, the Alemanian *Arm* for *Arme*, and Franconian *Däg* for *Tage*. The type *der Eber die Eber* is in a sense a transformation of the type represented by *Tag Tage*. The older forms of the latter word *tac tages*, Plur. *tage*, represents the M. H. G. declension of *eber eberes*, Plur. *die ebere; himel, himeles*, Plur. *die himele; wagen wagenes*, Plur. *die wagene*. But since in these words the final was preceded by an unaccented syllable, its vowel was suppressed in the N. H. G. in accordance with a phonetic law explained on p. 232, and the older forms were shortened into *Eber Ebers*, Plur. *die Eber*. Since, now, the nominative and accusative plural had become identical with the same cases in the singular it was natural to make a distinction in some way. This was done by introducing the umlaut which was a characteristic of the i-stems. Compare *Hafen Häfen, Hammer Hämmer, Nagel Nägel, Ofen Ofen, Vater Väter, Vogel Vögel* with the older *havene, nagele*, etc. In this category we have likewise both old and new forms still existing alongside of each other, but only among words terminating in *-en*, as *die Bogen* and *die Bögen*, *die Laden* and *die Läden*, *die Wagen* and *die Wägen*. In the older language the type represented by the neuter *das Ding die Dinge* was closely related to the masculine o-stems represented by *der Tag die Tage*. The only points of divergence were in the nominative and accusative plural where one had *die tage* and the other *diu dinc*—in other words, the neuter lacked final e. A tendency to bring these two types into harmony begins to manifest itself in the M. H. G. stage, and by the time the language has reached the N. H. G. period but very few words remained unaffected: such are *Lot*, *Masz*, *Pfund*, *Stück*, and others used in connection with numbers. This usage became a type to which both masculines and feminines in the course of time conformed. Accordingly we not only say *zwanzig Pfund*, *zwanzig Stück*, but also *zwanzig Fusz*, *zwanzig Zoll*, *zwanzig Ohm* (Eng. aam, awm) or *Saum* and *Last*. As we have shown above, some neuters form their plurals in *-er:* the M. H. G. of *huon* is *hüener*. In the older language this type embraced a smaller number of examples than now come under it. Many of its modern representatives belonged to other categories in the O. H. G., or at least had the alternate ending without *-er;* for example, *Haupt* had the M. H. G. plural *diu houbet* only, but the modern form is *Häupter*. The older form survives in proper names, such as *Berghaupten* and *Roshaupten*, both datives plural. The same statement applies to *Feld*, Plur. *die Felder*, but in the M. H. G. *diu velt* is represented by such modern names as *Degerfelden* and *Rheinfelden*. *Die Häuser* corresponds to M. H G. *diu hiuser* and *diu hus*. It is represented in names of places like *Rheinhausen*, *Schaffhausen*, *Sangershausen*, etc. An occasional word has retained a double plural to the present day, but in every case it is evident that the ending *-er* is regarded as preferable; the other is either archaic or belongs to the elevated style. Compare, e. g. *Bande* and *Bänder*, *Dinge* and *Dinger*, *Lande* and *Länder*, *Worte* and *Wörter*. A few masculines have taken the termination -*er* in the plural of the N. H. G. Examples are *der Geist die Geister*, *der Leib die Leiber*, *der Wald die Wälder*, of which we have the archaic form in *Unterwalden*, i. e., 'unter den Wäldern.' Some additional plurals similar in form are found in several dialects. The primitive Germanic neuter in the singular was represented by *thingom* or *wordom*, which latter corresponds to Latin 'verbum,' older 'verbom' for verbhom. In this case the true termination is -m, and as it is preceded by -o- these words must be classed among the o-stems. Just as the Latin exhibits words of which 'odium' and 'exordium' are a type, so there are in German words in which the final o of the stem was preceded by an i. This type is represented above by *das Gebirge die Gebirge*, which has remained unchanged from the M. H. G. stage, the O. H. G. being *daz gabirgi diu gabirgi*, and before the loss of the final letter *gabirgiom-gabirgio*. It is thus, evidently, an io-stem. In the N. H. G. but few nouns belong to this class, and all are composites with the prefix *ge-*, such as *Gefilde*, *Gebilde*, *Gefüge*, *Gewölbe*. As they are all to a greater or less extent collective nouns, it was of small importance to distinguish the singular from the plural. The two words, *Gelage*, older form *gelac*, and *Gestade*, older form *gestat*, have been drawn into this class by the force of analogy, in spite of the fact that they belong to the a-stems. The absence of the umlaut is sufficient evidence that there was never an i in the final syllable.

A large number of words belonging to this class have been confounded with that represented by *Ding* since the two paradigms correspond externally except in the nominative and accusative singular. In the older N. H. G. a considerable number of the original forms in -e are retained and are still occasionally used. We find both *Glück* and *Glücke*, *Gemüte* and *Gemüt*, *Kreuze* and *Kreuz*, *Stücke* and *Stück*. The plural of *Gemüt* follows the type represented by *Hühner* and is *Gemüter;* the dialectic plural *Stücker* is common. The latter plural is not used in the familiar phrase "*ein Stücker sechs*" in the sense of "*etwa sechs*," but is a mutilated contraction of "*ein Stuck oder sechs*." In the earlier stages of the language there were a few masculine stems ending in -io, but of these only a single one still exists in the modern German, viz., *der Käse die Käse* (A.-S. cēse, Eng. cheese). It is, however, not originally a Germanic word, but is a modification of the Latin 'caseus.' All the rest have taken their places under other types. A different kind of stems from those hitherto considered is represented by type 3. (a) *der Bote die Boten*, above. The M. H. G. inflection corresponds exactly with the N. H. G. which is Sing. Plur. The O. H. G. was Sing. Plur.

Nom.	*Bote*	*Boten*	*boto*	*botun*
Gen.	*Boten*	*Boten*	*botin*	*botōno*
Dat.	*Boten*	*Boten*	*botin*	*botun*
Acc.	*Boten*	*Boten*	*botun*	*botun*.

But before the force of the phonetic law had wrought comparative uniformity in the final syllables the paradigm was probably as follows:

Sing. Nom. *boto*, Gen. *botonis*, Dat. *botoni;* Plur. Nom. *botones*, Acc. *botonas;* which corresponds pretty closely to the inflection of homo, hominis, homini, etc., in Latin. If we remove the terminations -is, -i, etc., there remains a series of stems ending in the consonant -n, which gives a paradigm closely akin to our number 3, above. These n-stems are often spoken of by grammarians as representing the weak declension as distinguished from those ending with a vowel which is called strong. In the N. H. G. the type represented by *Bote* split into two general classes, the final e of the nominative falling off in some cases. This took place in accordance with a phonetic law already set forth, after an unaccented syllable, in such M. H. G. words as *schultheisze, steinmetze, truhsaeze* which became in N.

H. G. *Schultheisz, Steinmetz, Truchsesz.* Words employed as titles of honor were often used before the proper name of persons bearing them and, therefore, but slightly accented. Thus it came about that final *e* was generally dropped even when it came after an accented syllable. *Fürst, Graf, Herr* were in M. H. G. *fürste, grave, herre;* whence arose our type 3. (b). The number of nouns belonging to this class is considerably smaller than in the older language. The type represented by *Graf* formerly corresponded with those represented by *Tag* and *Gast;* which resulted in confounding the two and the vowel stems taking the place of the consonant stems in the paradigms. In some cases double forms are equally correct, and we may say *des Bauers* or *des Bauern,* Plur. *die Bauern; des Nachbars* or *des Nachbarn,* Plur. *die Nachbarn.* We find *des Märzes, dem März,* alongside of the archaic *des Märzen, im Märzen,* the latter form also appearing in such compounds as *Märzenbier, Märzenschnee, Märzenstaub.* Some words have, however, passed completely from one class to the other, as *der Herzog des Herzogs,* Plur. *die Herzöge; der Mond des Mondes,* Plur. *die Monde; der Schwan des Schwans,* Plur. *die Schwäne.* The old genitives corresponding to the nominatives *herzoge, mâne* and *swane* may be still seen in the compounds *Herzogenbuchsee, Herzogenstand, Mondenschein, Schwanenhals.* To the type represented by *Wagen* that represented by *Boten* corresponds in all its parts except the nominative and genitive singular. Compare

     Nom. Gen. Dat. Acc.
  Sing. *Wagen Wagens Wagen Wagen* Plur. *Wägen*
with Sing. *Bote Boten Boten Boten* Plur. *Boten.*
This general similarity led to a confusion of the two types and they were made alike in all the cases, the nominative in -*e* receiving an additional -*n,* and the genitive in -*en* an additional -*s.* Consequently, many words that originally belonged to class 3. (a) (*Bote*) passed into the

class represented by *Wagen*. *Der Balken, der Bogen, der Braten, der Brunnen, der Daumen, der Garten*, were in M. H. G. *balke des balken, boge des bogen, brate, brunne, dume* (thumb), *garte*. In many compounds the old forms have, however, been conserved: *Wildbret* (M. H. G. *wildbrat*) is simply *Wildbraten;* the South German *Wingert* (M. H. G. *wingarte*) means *Weingarten*, and in *Schönbrunn* (a royal villa near Vienna) we have an older form of *Brunnen*. Three modern doublets *Franken Frank, Lumpen Lump, Tropfen Tropfe* are peculiar for the reason that they have arisen from the M. H. G. forms *franke, lumpe* and *tropfe*. The three former have the characteristic in common that they designate things while the latter are applied to living beings. We have thus three words signifying respectively a coin (franc), a rag, and a drop having the same origin with words signifying a Frank, a good-for-nothing fellow, and a poor devil (as in *armer Tropf*). The peculiar fact here noted is of pretty wide application. In all cases where the modern nominative ends with -en it relates to things, while, on the other hand, almost all words where this case without -n persists they designate persons or animals without reason such as *Affe, Ahne, Bote, Buhle, Bürge, Jude, Fink* or *Finke, Falke, Hase*, etc. A probable explanation of this fact is that one class has been used as a subject-nominative much oftener than the other; and the more frequently a word is used the more it is exposed to mutilation through the influence of analogy. As a compensation for the losses which type 3, has sustained in favor of type 1. (f), it has also received various increments. Many words represented by the types *Tag* and *Gast* have, besides their original plurals in -e, another plural like the type represented by *Graf Grafen*. To this class belong *die Maste die Masten, die Sinne die Sinnen, die Stiefel die Stiefeln*, and alongside of *Männer*, which forms its plural like *das Wort die Worte*, we find *die Mannen*. *Der Hirte* belonged originally to the type represented by *Käse*—its form was *hirti*. Many words in -o, or -io have transiently belonged to type 3, and subsequently passed into the type represented by *Eber* or *Wagen*. *Der Rücken* is in M. H. G. *der rücke des rückes*, which is the type represented by *Käse;* the next step was *der Rücke des Rücken*, then the present form. The original is preserved in *Hundsrück* (a plateau in western Germany) and also in *hinterrücks, zurück,* archaic *zurücke*. In like manner *Nutzen* comes from the M. H. G. *der nutz des nutzes*, the old inflection being preserved in *Eigennutz, sich zu Nutze machen, zu Nutz und Frommen* (for use and advantage). The consonant stems were not originally confined to masculine nouns but were spread over the neuter and feminine n-stems as well. To the first belonged, in the M. H. G., *das herze, das ōre, das ouge,* the last of which was declined, in the four cases of the singular, *das ouge, des ougen, dem ougen, das ouge,* Nom. Plur. *diu ougen,* Dat. *den ougen.* This paradigm corresponded in part with that of *Gebirge* and ran thus, e. g. with such words as *Ende, Erbe* or *Hemde: daz ende, des endes, dem ende, daz ende,* Plur. *diu ende,* Dat *den enden*. The result was that a number of inflections grew up like the modern *das Auge des Auges,* Plur. *die Augen; das Ende, des Endes,* Plur. Dat. *den Enden. Herz* has retained the old dative form, but makes its genitive like *Wagen*.

We come next to the consideration of the feminine consonant stems. The word *die Zunge* (tongue) was declined in M. H. G. with final *-en* in all cases except the nominative singular, but in O. H. G. it ran as follows:

	Nom.	Gen.	Dat.	Acc.
Sing.	*zunga*	*zungun*	*zungun*	*zungun*
Plur.	*zungun*	*zungōno*	*zungon*	*zungun*

But even here the real case-endings have nearly all dropped off and *-un* represents the stem-ending. Alongside of this there was another feminine, as follows:

	Nom.	Gen.	Dat.	Acc.
Sing.	*klaga*	*klagâ*	*klagu*	*klaga*
Plur.	*klaga*	*klagôno*	*klagôn* (*m*)	*klaga*

Here, as may be easily seen, we are dealing with a vowel stem, and it will be noticed that it corresponded to the Latin mensa and the Greek χώρα. In the M. H. G. these two paradigms corresponded in several points, as may be readily seen on placing them side by side:

	Nom.	Gen.	Dat.	Acc.
Sing.	*zunge*	*zungen*	*zungen*	*zungen*
Sing.	*klage*	*klage*	*klage*	*klage*
Plur.	*zungen*	*zungen*	*zungen*	*zungen*
Plur.	*klage*	*klagen*	*klagen*	*klage;*

whence resulted the modern declension of *Klage Klagen*. That the forms of *Klage* have persisted in the singular but not those of *Zunge* is easily understood when we notice that they exhibited a difference between the genitive and dative and the corresponding forms of the plural. On the other hand, the forms of *klage* in the singular were yielded in favor of *zungen* because *klage* was the form of the nominative and accusative in the singular. Remnants of the consonant declension of the feminine are still frequently met with, as "*unser lieben Frauen*," "*Festgemauert in der Erden*" (Schiller's Song of the Bell), *Erdenleben*, *Erdensohn*, *Gassenbube*, *Harfenton*, *Höllenthal*, *Mühlenbach*, *Sonnenlicht*. In view of the fact that two older types have united in the one represented by *Klage* it has become very copious. But it has been still further enlarged from various other sources. One has been those words whose nominative likewise ended in e. This type is represented in our list by *Gebirge*. Old forms were *daz grütze*, *das wette*, *das rippe*. We may still hear the phrase, "*das alte Ripp*" (the old rip), to designate a contentious woman. Another has been the masculine stems in n belonging to the type *Bote;* the M. H. G. was *der grille*, *der imbe* (die Imme), *der slange*, etc. In many words the South German spoken language still retains the masculine gender where the literary language together with the Central and North German dialects have yielded to the force of analogy and changed to the feminine. Hence have arisen the doublets in gender *der Backen* and *die Backe*, *der Schneck* and *die Schnecke*, *der Trauben* and *die Traube*, and *der Zacken* and *die Zacke*, *der Butter* and *die Butter*, *der Schurz* and *die Schürze*, together with many others. Even in the literary language we find *der Schnupfen* alongside of *die (Stern) schnuppe*, the latter a survival from the Low German: it being assumed that the stars snuff themselves. But further, the masculine vowel-stems also end in e; *die Tage* is exactly parallel with *die Klage*. Such plurals were accordingly treated like the singular of the feminine and a new plural in -n created: to take the place of the M. H. G. *der slâf* we now find *die Schläfe*, the old form being not yet wholly obsolete. *Die Socke* was in M. H. G. *der soc*, in South Germany, *der Socken*; *die Tücke* is the M. H. G. *der tuc*, and the South Germans still say, "*einem einen Tuck anthun*," "*sich einen Tuck thun*" (to injure another or one's self). *Die Woge* is the M. H. G. *der wâc*. In addition to those words that have been transferred from one gender and from one declension to another because of their similarity in the nominative singular, there are others where a transfer was brought about by the likeness of the plurals, *die Wagen*, e. g., corresponding exactly to *die Klagen*. The modern *die Waffe* (weapon) was in the M. H. G. *daz wâfen;* "*ein gute Wehr und Waffen*" occurs in Luther's famous hymn, and *das Wappen* (coat-of-arms) is a survival of the Low German.

It yet remains to consider the types 2. (a) and (c), *Kraft Kräfte* and *Saat Saaten*. The former only is primitive and its modern inflection is found in the M. H. G. The plural in the O. H. G. is declined thus: *krefti, kreftio, kreftin, krefti*. In the M. H. G. there are alternate forms of the genitive and dative singular, viz., *der kraft* and *der krefte*, but only one nominative, *kraft*. In the O. H. G. *krefti* is the sole form. How, then, are we to explain the M. H. G.? The Germanic originally possessed not only consonant stems ending in *n*, but also in other letters. Among the most common of these was the word *Nacht*. In the O. H. G. it inflected as follows: Sing. *naht, naht, naht, naht*, all the cases being alike; Plur. *naht, nahto, nahtun, naht*, where only the genitive and dative vary from the singular form. Compare with this the four cases of the Latin nox, noct-is, noct-i, noct-em. *Diu naht*, Gen. *der naht* came to be taken as patterns for the genitive and dative of *diu kraft, der kraft* in the singular; and, conversely, a plural, *die Nächte*, came into use after the model of *die krefte*. Eventually *der kraft* was employed to the exclusion of *der krefte*, doubtless because the latter was exactly like the plural and could not easily be distinguished from it when unaccompanied by the article; but even with the article this was not possible in the genitive of both numbers. Remnants of the e-forms are seen in *Bräutigam* for *Bräutegam* (bride-g(r)oom, man of the bride), M. H. G. *der briute;* in *Bürgemeister* the archaic form of *Bürgermeister*, and in *Mägdesprung*. *Behende* is the modern form of M. H. G. *bî hende*, at hand, although *Hand* did not originally belong to the i-stems, as may be seen in the datives plural without the umlaut, *zu Handen, von Handen gehen, abhanden kommen, vorhanden* (*vor den Handen*), but was an u-stem. That *Nacht* was not originally an i-stem may be seen in the current *Weihnachten, zu den wîhen nahten* (in the holy nights). The type *Kraft* exhibits points of contact with that of *Klage*. In the case of some words belonging to the latter, final e had dropped off. For example, *Frau Frauen* corresponded in the singular with words like *Kraft*, and plurals were formed in -*en*, as *Burgen* M. H. G. *die bürge, Fahrten* M. H. G. *die verte*,

Thaten M. H. G. *die taete.* But plurals in *-en* might arise from two forms of the singular, one with e and the other without e. In consequence of this, the type *Kraft*, *Burg* was sometimes confounded with that of *Klage*. E. g., the modern *Blüte* was *bluot* in the M. H. G., and *Eiche*, *Leiche*, *Stute* were respectively *eich*, *līch*, *stuot*.

The type 2. (d) is solitary, for to it belong only the two words above given. These were originally consonant stems and had the same endings as *Bote;* that is, they were without umlaut. By a false analogy they were classed with words like *Acker Aecker*, *Bruder Brüder*, etc.

THE PRONOUN.

Pronouns differ from nouns not only in their endings but also in several other respects. In the primitive Indo-European language there were three numbers, the singular, the dual, and the plural. The ancient Greek affords the most familiar instance of the frequent use of the dual number. In the general Germanic the dual forms of the nouns early became extinct; but they were preserved in the pronouns after this had split up into several dialects. 'We two' is *wit*, 'ye two' *git*, in the Old-Saxon poem called the Heliand (composed probably in the ninth century). The corresponding words in the O. H. G. were probably *wiz*, *iz*. In the Old-Saxon, 'to us two' is *unk* and 'to you two,' *ink*, the Dat. and Acc. being alike. The dual of the second person plural is still in use in the modern Bavarian and has even displaced the regular plural, *es* or *ös* taking the place of *ihr* and *enk* that of *euch*. The German pronoun like the English, the Greek and the Latin, forms the singular and the plural in great measure from different stems. Compare *meiner*, *mir* (my, me) with *wir*, *unser* (we, our), and *deiner*, *dir* (thy, thee) with *ir* (*ihr*), *euer* (you, your). But the language in the course of its development tended more and more to obliterate these distinctions. We accordingly find in widely divergent dialects *mir* and *mer* alongside of *wir*, as likewise *dir* and *der* alongside of *ihr*. Here again we see the influence of analogy: the initial sounds of *meiner*, *mir*, *mich* and *diener*, *dir*, *dich* were transferred to the plural number. In some cases the final syllables are made alike. *Meiner*, *deiner* are formed, at least in part, after the pattern of *unser*, *euer*, the older words being *mein*, *dein*. These, though archaic, are by no means obsolete. After *mein* and *dein* had assumed the additional syllable, *sein* followed suit and became *seiner*. The German pronoun exhibits the somewhat remarkable phenomenon of having in part obliterated the distinction between the dative and the accusative. In English, on the other hand, the dative has displaced the accusative entirely. As long ago as its earliest stages the Low German had but a single form each for the dative and accusative plural of the two persons: *uns* representing both nobis and nos, while *iu* is either vobis or vos. The dative singular is *mi* and *thi*, corresponding to the current *mir* and *dir*, where the final r is a development of s which dropped off in Low German; this branch of the Teutonic being in nearly all cases nearer the English than the German proper. The accusative was probably *mik* and *thik*. This distinction was obliterated very early: in some dialects of the L. G. *mi* and *thi*, in others *mik* and *thik* are employed for both cases, these following the analogy of the plural and becoming alike. Owing to the habit of neglecting to make a distinction between the two cases it is easy to understand why the native Low German constantly fails to distinguish between *mir* and *mich*, *dir* and *dich* when he uses a H. G. dialect. The influence of analogy extended yet farther. After it had become a matter of usage to make no distinction between the first and second person, it was natural to follow the same course with the third, and accordingly we find the dative *ihm*, *em* used for the accusative *ihn*. While in the M. H. G. we still have the dative and accusative *uns*, but dative *iu*, accusative *iuch*, we find that in the N. H. G. the accusative *euch* has completely displaced the dative. Owing to this coalescence of the two cases the illiterate frequently make a curious blunder in the language of civility: as *Sie* has no existence in any dialect they are unable to distinguish between the dative and the accusative of the third person. We, accordingly, hear such expressions as, "*ich habe Ihnen (Sie) ja gar nicht erkannt,*" and "*Se (Ihnen) kann dat goa (gar) nicht fehlen.*" But even the modern *sich* was originally an accusative like *mich* and *dich*, the older language using in its stead the regular personal pronoun. Luther says, "*unser keiner lebt ihm selber, unser keiner stirbt ihm selber,*" where in modern German we should use *sich selber* or *sich selbst* for *ihm selber*. It may be remarked that in general the distinction between the reflexive and the non-reflexive pronoun is not carefully observed. The Germans say *gedenke sein, geniesze sein,* where the older language possessed a genitive *es* for the nominatives *er* and *es* (M. H. G. *ez*). Traces of this fact are still found in certain stereotyped formulas like "*ich bin es satt, ich bin es zufrieden,*" for, as is well known, the verb *sein* can not take an accusative after it.

It remains yet to consider a few peculiar isolated forms of the pronoun. Alongside of *ihr* the N. H. G. exhibits the archaic *ihro*, which corresponds exactly with the O. H. G. *iro*. It is used almost exclusively in addressing royal personages and other members of the nobility. That the modern German has two words where the older language had but one is doubtless due to the difference in accentuation in the latter: *iro* naturally becomes *ir* and *iró* remained unchanged. The same remark holds good as to the relation of *dero* to *der*. As to the pronouns *er*, *der* and *wer*, we generally find two forms in current usage, *dessen* and *des*, *deren* and *der*, *denen* and *den*. The shorter forms are the only ones existing in the M. H. G. as may be seen in *deshalb, deswegen,* " *Wes Brod ich ess, des Lied ich sing.*" The possessive pronoun *ihr* was originally a variant of the personal pronoun—the genitive singular of the feminine, or the genitive plural of all genders. It accordingly forms a doublet with the later *ihrer* and corresponds to the French d'elle, d'eux, d'elles (of her, of them). The younger forms probably developed under the influence of the dissyllabic pronouns like *dieser, jener,* and similar adjectives may have aided their growth.

THE ADJECTIVE.

When we come to consider the adjectives we find that some are inflected and some entirely without endings. Of the latter such as *gut, öde,* and their like, correspond exactly to the nominatives and accusatives of nouns having vowel stems: compare *Tag, Käse,* etc. In both cases the primitive ending dropped off, the German *lang* having once been precisely equivalent to the Latin 'longus.' The inflected adjectives have, in their turn, a two-fold set of endings—one used with the definite article, the other without. The former, *der gute, des guten, dem guten, den guten,* show consonant stems. The masculine, in this case, is exactly like the substantive declension represented by the type *Bote, Boten,* above. In the feminine and neuter of the adjective the O. G. types of the consonant declension are preserved, which have been lost in the M H. G. substantive. The modern *die gute, der guten,* are exactly like M. H. G. *die zunge, der zungen;* and *das gute, des guten,* like M. H. G. *das ouge, des ougen.* Thus far there is, accordingly, no radical difference between the adjective and the substantive. This likewise represents the primitive relation of these two parts of speech to each other in the original Indo-European, as may be seen by an examination of the Latin and Greek. But the German adds inflectional terminations when the adjective is not preceded by a word that clearly marks the case, as *guter Wein, gutes Weines, gutem Weine, guten Wein*, etc.; but *der gute Wein, des guten Weines, dem guten Weine, den guten Wein*.

The former mode of inflection grew out of the tendency to make it conform to that of pronouns of the third person singular. Compare, e. g., the O. H. G. paradigms of the two classes of words:

MASCULINE.

	Nom.	Gen.	Dat.	Acc.
Sing.	der	des	demu	den
Plur.	die	dero	dem	die (diu)

FEMININE.

Sing.	diu	dera	deru	die (dia)
Plur.	dio(a)	dero	dem	die (dia)

NEUTER.

Sing.	daz	des	demu	daz
Plur.	diu	dero	dem	diu

MASCULINE.

Sing.	guoter	guotes	guotemu	guotan(en)
Plur.	guote	guotero	guotem	guote

FEMININE.

Sing.	guotiu	guotera	guoteru	guota
Plur.	guoto	guotero	guotem	guoto

NEUTER.

Sing.	guotaz	guotes	guotemu	guotaz
Plur.	guotiu	guotero	guotem	guotiu

There are but few points of divergence except the weakening of all unaccented vowels to e, and the changes which the pronoun has undergone since the O. H. G. period have been steadily followed by similar changes in the adjective. The nominative of the Fem. Sing. *diu guotin*, which would regularly have become *den guten* in accordance with German phonetic laws, has been displaced by the Acc. *die gute;* and in like manner the Plur. of the neuter *diu guotiu* has been superseded by the corresponding form of the Mas. and Fem. *die gute.*

Jacob Grimm (born 1785), who published the first scientific grammar of the Germanic languages, designated the pronominal declension of the adjective as "strong;" the other, as also that of the substantive, he called "weak." His reasons were purely fanciful, but the terms have been retained by all subsequent grammarians on account of their brevity and convenience.

THE VERB.

In German, as in English, verbs are usually divided into two classes distinguished from each other by their mode of forming the preterit (or imperfect) tense. The one class makes the preterit by means of final *-te,* the other by a change in the vowel or vowels of the radical syllable,—in other words by means of vowel-gradation. For example, *ich lehre, ich lehrte,* corresponding in the main to the English 'I learn,' 'I learned,' may be compared with *ich gebe, ich gab* and ' I give,' ' I gave.' The first class which requires external aid in order to express the past has been called "weak," by J. Grimm and the latter, which requires no such aid, he called "strong." It will be readily seen that the weak verbs correspond to the regular verbs of the ordinary English grammar, and the strong verbs to the irregular. English grammars are however coming more and more to adopt the German terminology. A suffix is also a characteristic of the past participle; in the weak verbs *-t* or *-et,* in the strong *-en.* Here again the English furnishes parallel forms in ' learned ' and ' given.' The weak verbs in German as in English comprise much the largest class and their mode of inflection is the simpler of the two. The radical vowel of the present tense undergoes no change in any part of the verb, the apparent exception in *frage* *frägst frägt*, alongside of *frage fragst fragt* being due to the influence of the strong verb, and both *frug* and *fragte* are correct preterits. There is a slight difference in the preterits of the weak verbs, some having final -*ete* and others -*te* only—for example *lehrte*, *liebte*, *fragte*, but *bildete*, *fürchtete*. In general -*ete* is attached to all stems that end in a *t*-sound. The M. H. G. likewise exhibits both forms, but the longer would in obedience to a phonetic law previously explained, be shortened to -*te* by the suppression of the unaccented medial *e*. In the case of words like *bild-te*, *fürch-te*, that is, where the final sound of the stem is substantially identical with the initial sound of the suffix, it would be difficult to pronounce both without the intervention of another vowel. But the parallel forms, -*te* and -*ete*, of the M. H. G. have a different origin. In place of the monotonous uniformity exhibited by the weak verbs a greater variety prevailed. The O. H. G. possessed three classes of weak verbs, distinguished from each other by the final -*ô*, or -*ê*, or -*i*, of the stem. To illustrate by examples, there were *salbôn* which has become *salben*, *fragēn* which is now *fragen*, and *legian* or *lerian* that are still in use as *legen* and *lehren*. Similarly we have in Latin ' amāre,' tacēre ' and ' andire.' The preterits of *salbôn* and *fragēn* were *salbôta* and *fragēta*, which in the M. H. G. became *salbete* and *fragete*. A distinction must be made in the case of the i-stems between those in which this stem was short and in which it was long. In the case of the former the stem-ending in the preterit remains; the O. H. G. *legita* became *legete* in the M. H. G. In case of the long stems, the i of the preterit was suppressed in obedience to a phonetic law that need not be considered here, while in the present tense it remained somewhat longer: *lerian*, *lerta* became M. H. G. *lerte*. In consequence of this difference between the i-stems with long syllables, a difference also arose between the present and the preterit tenses, which does not occur in the other groups of verbs. If the stems of verbs contained an a or an o or an u, these vowels would necessarily take the umlaut in course of time in the present tense where an i followed in the next syllable; but in the preterit they would remain unchanged. For example, *brannian*, *branta* becomes *brennen*, *branta* and later *brante*. Besides this verb the German contains *kannte*, *nannte*, *rannte*, *sandte* and *wandte*, that appear to have been modified by umlaut, but which were in fact not so modified, as has been pointed out on a preceding page. In like manner we have *gebrannt*, *gekannt*, etc., because substantially the same phonetic changes took place in the preterit participle which the preterit of the verb proper underwent. In the M. H. G. what the German grammarians call Rückumlaut—a sort of reversed umlaut—affected a much larger number of words than it does at present. Compare *decken dacte, smecken smacte, beswaeren beswarte, loesen loste, hoeren horte* with the modern preterits *deckte, schmeckte, löste, hörte*, etc.

In these and a number of other examples the radical vowel of the preterit has been modified so as to conform to that of the present, and only a few participial adjectives remain as evidence of the former state of affairs: for example, *die gedackten Pfeifen der Orgel* simply means *die gedeckten*, etc; *getrost* is an old participle of *trösten;* *wohlbestallt* recalls *bestelle, bestalte, bestalt*. In the last series we have an example of a new verb formed under the influence of the participle, viz., *bestallen*. Similarly *erboesen erboste erbost* has led to the formation of a new verb *sich erbosen* (grow angry). A like relation exists between *lehren* and *gelahrt*, and *durchläucht, erlaucht* and *durchleuchten, erleuchten*. The singular feature of this change of the principal vowel lies in the fact that the participle, though derived from the verb, afterward brought about a modification of the latter; or to use a slightly mixed metaphor, but which answers the purpose very well here, the ancestral type was conformed to that of the descendant.

We find in the strong verbs a greater variety of vowel changes than in the weak; here we see exhibited the effects of the three phonetic influences before designated as Umlaut, Brechung (breaking) and Ablaut (vowel-gradation). In the weak verbs the stem of the present tense always ended with the same vowel and it could not therefore effect any change in the radical vowel. But in the strong verbs different vowels immediately followed the final consonant of the radical syllable, and it was these that characterized the various subclasses. For example, the indicative present of *tragen* in the most ancient O. H. G. was thus inflected: Sing. 1. *tragu*, 2. *tragis*, 3. *tragit*, Plur. 1. *tragames*, 2. *traget*, 3. *tragant*. In the natural course of development of the language the a of the second and third person singular would receive the umlaut, thus becoming ä. This is the present state of all similar verbs excepting *du haust, er haut* and *du kommst, er kommt*, though even here we find the variants *du kömmst, er kömmt*. A considerable number of the dialects have however dropped the umlaut under the influence of the verbs that never had it, as *trage tragsch, tragt; laufe, laufsch, lauft*, etc.

The diversity of endings which produced umlaut is likewise the cause of breaking in so far as it applies to the verb. We find a uniform interchange between the vowels e and i; the latter occuring in those verbs that are capable of taking the umlaut, the former in those which are not. Accordingly, we have *wir geben, ihr gebt, sie geben;* e also occurs regurlarly in the subjunctive, the infinitive and the present participle. But the second and third persons of the singular are *giebst, giebt*, (or *gibst* and *gibt*) and the imperative is *gieb*. In the first person singular where the H. G. has *ich gebe*, the South German dialects exhibit *ich gib, ich lis (lese), ich nimm (nehme)*, and so on. This represents the status of both the O. G. H. and M. H. G. i. e. *gibu, lisu, nimu*. These forms, however, point to the earlier existence of *gebu, nemu, lesu;*

but the first person was changed to conform to the second and third. In the N. H. G. the original status has unconsciously been restored: under the influence of the first person Plur. *geben*, the M. H. G. *ich gibe* has become *ich gebe*, and similarly *giebst, giebt* was made to conform to the type *trage, trägst, trägt*. But here again the South and Middle German dialects have gone still farther, so that we find *du gebsch, er gebt; du nemsch, er nemmt*. The interchange between e and i does not occur in verbs whose stem ends in a double nasal or in a nasal in combination with a mute. In such cases e had been changed to i in prehistoric times even when an a followed. We have, accordingly, *ich beginne, wir beginnen; ich finde, wir finden*. Exactly parallel with this interchange between e and i is that between iu and ie in the M. H. G., or iu and io of the O. H. G. which has already been pointed out. The M. H. G. has *ich fliuge, du fliugest, er fliuget,* but *wir fliegen, ir flieget, sie fliegent*. The German of Luther's Bible conserves many remnants of unbroken verbal forms, such as *fleucht, kreucht, leugt, zeucht;* but in the current literary language the unbroken forms have carried the day everywhere, so that we have *ich fliege* like *wir fliegen*. The archaic forms are still occasionally used in poetry. The perfect tense of the strong verbs was originally formed in two ways. The first was by means of a reduplicating syllable prefixed to the stem: in other words a syllable was formed by means of the initial consonant or consonants together with the vowel e, and placed before the word as a prefix. In the second, vowel-gradation was employed. Reduplication is a familiar phenomenon in Greek and Latin, as may be seen in such examples as τρέφω, τέτροφα; pello, pepuli. The examples, however, in which these two processes are plainly evident in the Germanic languages are very few. Even in the Gothic traces of reduplication are rare and in the majority of cases vowel-gradation has been obscured or wholly obliterated by the influence of phonetic laws. We find in *lētan* (let) *lelōt*, both reduplication and vowel-gradation, but *haldan, hehald; haitan, hehait; hlaupan, hehlaup*. In consequence of contraction and other transformations these perfects were so changed that they uniformly exhibit the diphthong ie in the M. H. G. and i (or ie) in the N. H. G. no matter what the vowel of the present tense may have been. The preterit participle, which in the strong verb is generally subject to vowel-gradation, has the same vowel as the present in most of these reduplicated verbs. Compare, e. g., the Latin pello pulsus, vello vulsus, sero satus. The following types of N. H. G. verbs belong to this class:

(1) *halten   hielt   gehalten* and *fallen   fiel   gefallen*,
(2) *blasen   blies   geblasen*,
(3) *rufen   rief   gerufen*,
(4) *heiszen hiesz   geheiszen*,
(5) *laufen   lief   gelaufen* and *hauen   hieb   gehauen*.

Very few Germanic verbs show reduplication proper even in the oldest forms accessible to modern research; but, perhaps, owing to this fact vowel-gradation has been the more fully developed, and is, therefore, the more clearly marked. Many verbs exhibit not merely two tones or letters of the vowel scale, but even three, though the latter are greatly in the minority. Or, to illustrate the statement by modern examples, we have about four times as often the gradation *bleiben blieb geblieben* as *singen sang gesungen*. In the latter case we always find in the O. G. a different vowel in the preterit singular from that in the plural of the same tense. This variation is not accidental, and not every vowel can be substituted for any other. An *a*, e. g., may not occur in the same stem with certain others, *ei* for instance. Those vowels that regularly succeed each other in the same stem constitute what is known as a gradation series (*Ablautsreihe*). This series is in the M. H. G. as follows:

Class I., containing a in the present tense,

Pres.	Pret. Sing.	Pret. Plur.	Pret. Part.
trage	*truoc*	*truogen*	*getragen*

Class II., containing e or i in the present tense, sub-class (a),

Pres.	Pret. Sing.	Pret. Plur.	Pret. Part.
ich binde	*bant*	*bunden*	*gebunden*
wir binden			
ich wirfe	*warf*	*wurfen*	*geworfen*
wir werfen			

On the change from e to i, or from u to o, see page 230. This class no longer exists in its purity in the N. H. G., the variation between the different forms of the preterit having been suppressed. In a majority of cases the singular has gained the mastery: compare *fand fanden, gelang gelangen, half halfen, sprang sprangen,* but which were in M. H. G. *fant funden, half hulfen,* etc. Alongside of *sangen* an older form has been preserved in the familiar proverb,   *Wie die Alten sungen,*
   So zwitschern die Jungen,
through the influence of the rime demanded by *Jungen*. In other cases the vowel of the plural remains, though not in its M. H. G. form as *u*, but in its M. G. transformation as *o*. See ante p. 230. Examples are *ich glomm wir glommen, schwoll schwollen, schmolz schmolzen,* which were M. H. G. *glam glummen, swal swullen, smalz smulzen*. In a single case only does the modern German exhibit *a* and *u* in parallel forms, *ich ward* and *ich wurde wir wurden,* M. H. G. *wart wurden*. The reason of this exception is not clear.

Class II., sub-class (b), in which the stem-vowel is followed either by a liquid or a nasal or the combination of a stopped consonant with a liquid,

ich nime	*nam*	*nāmen*	*genomen*
wir nemen			
ich spriche	*sprach*	*sprāchen*	*gesprochen*
wir sprechen			

To this type a few verbs of the older language conform whose stem contains no liquid, as *fichte gefochten* following *flihte geflohten, stechen gestochen* following *brechen gebrochen* and *sprechen gesprochen*. In the N. H. G. the diversity which formerly existed between the singular and the plural has been eliminated, so that the older *ich sprăch, wir sprechen* has become *ich sprāch, wir sprāchen*. In a considerable number of verbs even the difference between the preterit tense and the preterit participle has disappeared, as may be seen in

	ich schere	schor	schoren	geschoren
M. H. G.	ich schire	schar	scharen	geschoren
	ich pflege	pflog	pflogen	gepflogen
M. H. G.	ich pflige	pflăc	pflāgen	gepflogen

In the N. H. G. *schwören* has conformed to the type *scheren* and *heben* to that of *pflegen*. Both verbs originally belonged to the type *tragen*.

| ich swere | swuor | geswaren |
| ich hebe | huop | gehaben |

The anomalous present tense is due to the fact that their historical antecedents were *swariu* and *habiu;* there was, therefore, an external correspondence to the present tense of the i-class. See ante p. 256. We still have in the adjective *erhaben* an old participle of the *erheben*, which was subsequently displaced by the analogical form *erhoben*.

Class II., sub-class (c) in which e (i) is followed by a single consonant which is neither a liquid nor a nasal, provided no combination of such a consonant with others precedes.

Pres.	Pret. Sing.	Pret. Plur.	Pret. Part.
ich gibe	găp	gaben	gegeben
wir geben			

The M. H. G. *găp găben* has become *gāb gāben*, but the L. G. has in many cases conserved the original quantity. The verbs *bewegen* and *weben* now follow the type of *pflegen, heben* though originally they were inflected like *geben.*

| ich bewige | bewac | bewâgen | bewegen |
| ich wibe | wap | wâben | geweben. |

Class III., containing long i in the present tense.

| Pres. | Pret. Sing. | Pret. Plur. | Pret. Part. |
| ich schribe | schreip | schriben | geschriben |

The diphthong in the preterit singular of the N. H. G. has been dropped entirely and its place taken by the vowel of the preterit plural and the past participle. To this class belong also the modern verb *scheiden* which was originally inflected like the reduplicating verbs, M. H. G. *scheide, schiet, gescheiden*. The adjective *bescheiden* is a remnant of the older inflection, it being a participle of *bescheiden*.

Class IV., interchanging *iu* with *ie* in the present tense.

Pres.	Pret. Sing.	Pret. Plur.	Pret. Part.
ich fliuge	flouc	flugen	geflogen
wir fliegen			

The N. H. G. development of this series corresponds throughout with the preceding except that as in Class II. (a), the *u* of the preterit plural does not prevail but appears as *o*. To this class belongs also *saufen soff, saugen sog*, of which the present tense was different from that of *fliuge* in the earliest period of the language, though the other forms were similar. Closely connected with the variations produced by means of vowel-gradation, a number of verbs exhibit a change of consonants due ultimately to a difference in accent. It has been previously shown, when speaking of Verner's Law, that the accent determines whether an Indo-European tenuis shall be represented in the Germanic by a spirant or a medial mute,—whether h or g, e. g., should take the place of primitive k, and th or d that of t. Thus the root 'duk' (Lat. duc) would give in the O. H. G. the verb *ziohan* (Eng. tug and tow), in the M. H. G. *ziehen* and *ich ziuhe, wir zugen, gezogen*, N. H. G. *ziehen, zog, gezogen*. Similarly *snide, sniten, gesniten* gives *schneiden, schnitt, geschnitten.* This shift has also been preserved in the N. H. G. *leiden* and *sieden*, where we find *leiden, litt, gelitten* and *sieden, sott, gesotten*, respectively. In the M. H. G. we likewise find *slahe, sluogen, geslagen;* but the N. H. G. has assimilated this verb to the type represented by *tragen* and formed a new present, *schlagen, ich schlage.* The M. H. G. has also *ich gedīhe (gedeihe), wir gedigen, gedigen;* but the N. H. G. adjective *gediegen* is the only part of the verb that has been able to resist the leveling process, and we have now only *ich gedeihe.* In some of the dialects g has occasionally displaced h and we find *ziege* instead of *ziehen.*

Parallel with the substitution h:g and d:t is that of s:r. This is shown in the N. H. G. *erkiese, erkor, erkoren,* and *war, waren, gewesen.* We find it too in the M. H. G. *friuse, wir fruren, gefroren,* and *verliuse, wir verluren, verloren.* With these examples we may compare the Eng. 'lose' and 'forlorn.' A few other German words still retain the original s. The tendency of s to become r is seen in other Indo-European languages. In Eng. we have 'I was' but 'we were;' throughout this verb the interchange of s and r is traceable to the Anglo-Saxon period. Similarly in Latin we have es, est, esses, esset, but eras, erat, eris, erit. The weak verbs, likewise, show some instances of interchange between consonants; which have, however, no connection with those just set forth. We find, e. g., *bringen, brachte* and *denken, dachte* in accordance with a phonetic law previously set forth: viz, that in German only a spirant can stand before *t.* The *n* occurring before the spirant *h* was dropped. The M. H. G. exhibits the forms *mich dünket, mich duhte* (methinks, methought). Here too there has been assimilation or leveling. In the first place the umlaut of the present was carried over to the preterit which became *däuchte.* Subsequently a new preterit *dünkte* was created for the present *dünken,* and for the preterit *däuchte* a new present *däucht* and even *däuchtet.* The O. H. G.

predecessor of *dünken* is *dunchan*, and that of *denken* is *denchan*, the two words being represented in A.-S. by 'thencan' and 'thincan' respectively. Both have become blended in the modern English 'to think,' a process that had already begun in the A.-S. period. A reminiscence of the original difference is preserved in the archaic 'methinks,' but 'seem' has almost entirely usurped its functions.

In German, as in English, a number of verbs have both the strong and the weak inflection. For example, *ich salze, ich salzte* has for its participle *gesalzen* (not *gesalzt*). This mixture does not exist in the earliest stage of the verbs, and may have been brought about by one of several causes. Some strong verbs may have followed the analogy of weak verbs in the imperfect or the participle, or both. In the M. H. G. we find *ich salze, ich sielz, gesalzen*, and instead of the modern *ich spalte, ich spaltete, gespaltet* or *gespalten* only *ich spalte, ich spielt, gespalten. Fallen* and *schaben* shared a similar fate, as evidences of which the adjectives *gefallen* and *abgeschaben* remain. The influence of the strong system of inflection upon the weak is much more extensive than vice versa, and many verbs originally weak have become strong. Thus *fragte* is older than *frug*, which has doubtless been influenced by the type *tragen trug, schlagen schlug. Ich steckte* is more primitive than *ich stack*, which now conforms to the type *erschrecken erschrack*. The same is true of *dingen gedingt* as related to *dang gedungen*, which has yielded to the influence of *singen sang* or *springen sprang*. The dialects exhibit many more examples of transition from weak to the strong conjugation. A number of older verbs had both strong and weak inflections, and two or more of these being often nearly alike in the present, came in the course of time to be confounded. It occurred quite frequently that a strong verb with intransitive and a weak verb with transitive signification were developed from the same stem. The M. H. G. contained two verbs, *leschen* or *erleschen* (to cease to burn) and *loschen* (to extinguish). Of the former the imperfect was *erlasch*, of the latter *erlaschte*. But the N. H. G. has made of the one *erlische erlosch erloschen*, and of the other *erlöschen erlöschte erlöscht*. Similar doubles are *erschrecken erschrack erschrocken* (be frightened) and *erschrecken erschreckte erschreckt* (frighten) and *schwellen schwoll geschwollen* and *schwellen schwellte geschwellt*. The plural number of the present tense of both verbs, as also the subjunctive together with the infinitive present, have always the vowel e in the M. H. G., with this difference, however, that this e in the strong verbs, which sometimes appears as i, was a broken vowel, while in the weak it was modified (*umgelautet*), and, therefore, differently pronounced. The older N. H. G. possessed two imperfects, *lud* and *ladete*, that are often taken to be interchangeable. In this case two verbs have been confounded which were originally identical neither in form or meaning. In the O. H. G. *hladan hluod gehladan* meant 'load,' and *ladon ladota giladot* 'invite.' A singular mixture of strong and weak inflections is exhibited by the auxiliaries *ich musz, ich kann, ich darf, ich mag, ich soll, ich weisz*, though they do not all, strictly speaking, perform the same office in German as in English. It is noticeable, in the first place, that they lack the endings in the first and third person of the singular of the present tense which all the other verbs have. This occurs elsewhere only in the preterit of the strong verbs; and this fact furnishes us the key to the solution of the enigma: these six verbs now used as presents were originally preterits and are accordingly called preterit-presents. The loss from disuse of the present tense of verbs and the substitution of the perfect with a present signification is met with in both Greek and Latin and in other languages. E. g. coepi (I begin), novi (I know), odi and οἶδα are verbs of this type. The German *weisz* corresponds exactly to the Greek. *Weisz* at first, doubtless, meant 'I have seen,' and is probably referable to a present *ich wize* of type III. ante. It is the only remnant of the old preterits of this ablaut-series since *meit, treip, schreib*, etc., have been displaced by analogous forms, viz., *mied, trieb, schrieb*. *Ich musz*, M. H. G. *muoz*, belongs to the type *tragen*. We are probably correct in assuming the former existence of presents *kinnan, derfan, megan, skelan*, to which the modern *ich kann, darf, mag, soll* (O. H. G. *skal*, A.-S. sceal, Eng. shall) are preterits according to our types II. (b) and (c). When the original signification as a past tense had been forgotten, from whatever cause, and these forms had come to be used for present time a new series of imperfects was formed after the pattern of the weak verbs.

The L. G. *gahn* and *stahn* are explained by the long a, as also the South German *goh* and *stoh*. The preterit of *gehen* is formed as if from a present *gangen* (cf. *fangen, fieng*), which in fact once existed and is conserved in some of the dialects, not only of Germany but also of England and Scotland. The mediæval preterit of *stên* was *stuont*, which is likewise referable to a still current dialectic *standen*. It followed the type *trage, truoc*. *Ich stund, wir stunden* is occasionally used, but is archaic. It was first inflected after the type *bant bunden* and became *ich stand wir stunden;* when, subsequently, the plural of this series was modified to conform to the singular in the preterit *ich stand, wir stunden* followed suit and became *ich stand wir standen*. On L. G. territory the influence of analogy produced a different phonetic change: *stan stunt* became the pattern after which the imperfects *gung* and *fung* were formed to *gan* and *fangen*. The case of *thun, that* is somewhat different. The O. H. G. preterit of *tuon* was *teta*. Here *te* is a reduplication of *ta*, both the preterit and the present stem having probably once been identical. The difference, doubtless, grew out of the fact that in the preterit the stem was unaccented and its vowel accordingly weakened. The O. H. G. *teta* appears in M. H. G. as *tete*, which is virtually the *thät*, met with in popular songs and in the poems of Uhland, a Swabian. The plural of *teta* is *tatun*, a verb-form hard to explain, which became N. H. G. *thaten*. The singular number *that* is a new creation after the model of the plural. The German verb *sein*, like the verb 'to be,' is made up of three different roots or stems. The first had an initial b which is represented by the Latin f in 'fui,' 'fore,' 'futurum esse,' that is *ich bin du bist*, which is also found in the Eng. 'be' 'been' 'being.' The second is 'es' and occurs in Lat. 'est' 'eram' for 'esam,' i. e., *er ist* (he is, etc.). An abbreviated form of this same root occurs in the subjunctive *er sei*, the indicative *sind*, and in the Lat. 'sunt' 'sim.' The third is 'wes,' Eng. 'was,' 'were,' which has no corresponding form in Latin. Here belongs the M. H. G. preterit *ich was, wir waren*, the infinitive *Wesen* now used only as a substantive, and the old participle found in *abwesend, anwesend*, etc.

It yet remains to consider one point in the structure of the preterit participle. We find both *gezeugt* and *bezeugt, er ist alt geworden*, but *er ist geschlagen worden*, how shall we explain this prefix *ge-?* The participle had originally no prefix, as may be seen in the Gothic *binda* (I bind) *bundans* (*gebunden*). But the older Germanic possessed a large number of verbs in pairs formed from the same stem, one of which had the prefix *ge*, while the other was without it. To this class belong *bieten* and *gebieten, brauchen* and *gebrauchen, leiten* and *geleiten*. The difference in meaning was hardly more than one of degree, the prefix serving merely to intensify or to designate the completion of the action. From the nature of the case the composite form would be frequently used as a preterite participle, and the syllable *ge-* came in the course of time to be regarded as the essential characteristic of this part of the verb. A long list of verbs, however, remained free from this prefix owing to the fact that they were already provided with an inseparable prefix. The German is naturally averse to the use of a second prefix before a word that is already provided with one, and we could hardly expect to find *gebeleben* alongside of *beleben*, *geverstehen* and *verstehen*, or *gezerreiszen* and *zerreiszen*. Plainly, then, there would be no such participles as *gebelebt* or *geverstanden*. But few uncompounded verbs form their participle without *ge-* except *worden*, which has already been mentioned. Among these we find *rechtschaffen* as well as *geschaffen*, *trunken* as well as *getrunken*, and also *lassen* alongside of *gelassen*. In these instances the old participle, owing to the absence of the prefix *ge-*, is commonly regarded as an infinitive. In the folk-speech of some parts of South Germany the omission of *ge-* is still common.

WHAT IS ANALOGY IN LANGUAGE?

Owing to the fact that the law of analogy plays a very important part in the morphology of all the languages of the Indo-European stock it may be well to consider this part of our subject a little more fully. It is a well known fact that all these languages exhibit the fullest and most varied vowel system in the oldest specimens that have been preserved. Ante-classical Latin had a number of diphthongs that were subsequently fused into single vowels, and this process went still farther in its derivatives the Romance languages. Modern Greek gives the same sound to a number of vowels and diphthongs that were differently pronounced in the ancient Greek, η, ι, υ, ει, οι, and υι all being sounded like the long *e* (or *i* as in machine) in English. The Gothic of which we possess long specimens by several centuries older than any other Germanic dialect has a much more fully developed vowel system than the later German. In short there is a universal tendency toward simplification, both in vowels and consonants. A sound that was frequently used began to modify others until in the course of time several sounds were blended into one and the same sound, or a certain form of the noun or verb was taken as a general type and all similar words used in the same sense conformed to this type. In Latin, for example, the nominative plural of words ended in -ae, or -i, or -es, or -us. But in the French nearly all plurals end in -s or an s-sound. A large number of words from the first, second, and fourth declension of the Latin passed into the French, yet their plurals nearly all end like the plurals of the third. It is evident that the plurals of this declension became the type of all plurals in French and words that originally formed their plurals differently were made by analogy to conform to it. The A.-S. had also a number of different endings for the Nom. Plur. and the Gen. Sing. The former with few exceptions have become -s or -es and the latter 's which is our modern English possessive case. In other words, the prevalent type in the course of time became almost universal. The Italian for various causes was less simplified than the French, yet even here some of the Latin plurals were given up and the ending -e became the general type for feminine plurals and -i for the masculine. The influence of analogy may be daily observed in the speech of children and uneducated persons. At a certain stage in its mental development the child will form the incorrect preterit " I thinked " and the like, because many preterits are formed in this way and it is misled by analogy. The incorrect " brung " is formed after the analogy of ' sing,' ' sung.' For the same reason we hear persons say " sheeps," " memorandums," " cherubims," because they have not observed that these and many similar words have a peculiar plural and they are misled by the general law of English plurals. It will be readily seen from these few examples that at a period when languages have not yet acquired a degree of stableness by being embodied in a

written literature such changes might in a comparatively
short period of time effect a complete revolution in this
phonetic system.

THE SYNTAX OF THE NEW HIGH GERMAN.

The syntax of a language, except so far as it relates to
the order of words and the arrangement of sentences or
parts of sentences, is, in the last analysis, nothing more
nor less than a department of the general subject of the
meaning of verbal signs, or sematology. What case is to
be used with a preposition depends upon the significance
of the case. Whether I am to use 'in' with the accusative in Latin or German, with the dative in German or
the ablative in Latin must be determined by the meaning
I intend to convey to the hearer or reader. Whether the
indicative or the subjunctive mood is to be used in a subordinate sentence depends upon the difference in meaning
between these two forms of the verb. That the Germans
say *eine fromme Frau* and not *eine frommer Frau* is solely
due to the fact that they have from time immemorial been
accustomed to associate the notion of masculinity with the
nominative *frommer*. The signification of the different
forms of the same word varies according to its endings;
it would not therefore be much amiss to designate that
part of grammar which is usually called syntax, the doctrine of the meaning of the flectional syllables. In this
book we have thus far discussed hardly any changes in the
meaning of words, except those that have taken place in
the radical syllables. But even here we are, at least in part,
within the domain of syntax so far as it concerns those
variations in the signification of words, which take them
out of the class to which they naturally belong in a grammatical system. When an adjective is used as a noun, as
when, for example, the word *Fürst*, which is simply the
superlative of *vor* (Eng. fore) and literally means the first

or foremost, is used to designate a prince, the procedure is exactly parallel to the use of *Korn* (corn) to designate a particular cereal. We do not generally think of a nobleman as a noble man, nor of a gentleman as a gentle man, any more than the uneducated German sees any necessary connection between *ein Edelmann* and *ein edler Mann*, yet we have here the assumption, by a particular class, as a sort of mental escutcheon, of an attribute that is equally applicable to some men in all classes. The indefinite *man* is no more nor less than a faded and generalized *Mann*, just as the French 'on' is a remnant of the Latin 'homo:' both are used in the same sense. Here we have a process analogous to that through which *scheinen* passed; for while it is cognate with 'shine' and meant originally to emit rays of light it is now frequently used in the sense of 'seem.'

THE PARTS OF SPEECH.

All the primitive words in a language are divisible into four classes and four only: nouns and adjectives, numerals, verbs, and pronouns. Our present knowledge does not justify a further reduction, though it is maintained by some writers on language that all parts of speech were originally derived from two—the verb and the pronoun. Nouns, or substantives, and adjectives form but one class; for at first every noun designated but a single quality of an object. New nouns are still frequently formed from adjectives. The converse process, that is, the formation of adjectives from substantives, is of much rarer occurrence. The substantival origin is plainly recognizable in the few examples found in the N. H. G—*feind, noth, schade, schuld*—from the fact that they can not be used attributively and do not admit of comparison. There seems to have been no transition from the verbal class into any of the other three classes, nor vice versa. It is probable, however, that a few pronouns are derived from other parts of speech; *man* has already been cited; *jemand* and *niemand* are compounds of the adverbs *je* and *nie* with the same word. *Jeglicher* is a combination of *je* and the adjective *gleich*. In the earlier N. H. G. the adverb *so* is often used as a relative pronoun. Not all pronouns proper are equally primitive: *welcher*, *wer*, and *was* have an indefinite as well as an interrogative meaning, and are equivalent to *etwelcher*, *etwas*. Both the Greek τίς and the Latin 'quis,' as well as the English 'who' can be used in either sense. There are reasons for believing that these words acquired an interrogative signification sometime after they had been otherwise used. If we address a person with *du suchst etwas* (lit. thou seekest something), we plainly indicate to him that we should like to be informed as to the object of his search; and we use an interrogative sentence. Neither are relative pronouns traceable to the roots of languages. In the ordinary speech of every-day life comparatively few subordinate sentences are used; the information to be communicated is conveyed to the hearer in a succession of independent, co-ordinate sentences. This is a characteristic of speech in its most primitive stage, and it is safe to assume that all words now used to connect sentences were originally employed for a different purpose. The relative pronoun *der*, *die*, *das*, was at first purely demonstrative. Such a sentence as "*es war der, der gepredigt hat*" was in O. H. G. *iz was, der bredigota*, and in a still earlier stage of the language it must have been *es war der—er hat gepredigt*. In that stage of the language when the pronoun was not regarded as a necessary accompanist of the verb we would have had, *das war der—hat gebredigt*, *iz was der—bredigota*, for the pronoun must have been placed originally at the end of the first and not at the beginning of the second sentence. Subsequently, when it had become necessary to express the subject of the verb, it looked as if *der* belonged to the following verb. A sentence like *das ist der Mensch, der mich geschlagen hat*, must at one stage of the language have been used in the form, *das ist der Mensch, der hat mich geschlagen*. In Eng. this would be equivalent to 'this is the person, this one has beaten me.' Here, it is plain, the relative pronoun belonged in the first instance to the sentence in which we now find it, and we have accordingly to assume two points of origin for the relative *der*. In a somewhat different way the relative pronouns *wer*, *was* and *welcher* have been developed from the interrogative pronouns during the N. H. G. period.

The adverbs are, in so far as they can be traced to their source, for the most part fossilized or stereotyped case-forms, and in many instances they have conserved such significations as no longer attach to these cases in the nouns and pronouns as at present employed. There is a concealed genitive of way and manner in *einst;* in the M. H. G. it is *eines*, the regular genitive of *ein*. *Flugs* (quick) is properly *fluges, im Fluge; mittelst* takes the place of *mittels*, and is, therefore, the genitive of *Mittel*. The form of the dative plural is latent in *allenthalben* i. e. *allenhalben*, the substantive portion of this compound being the O. H. G. *halba, die Seite* (side), and occurs in the Eng. be-half. *Weiland* is traceable to the older form *wilen*, the Dat. Plur. of *wile* (time), and is the same word as the Eng. while (a little while, between whiles), of which the older authors have the dative whilom, whilome, with the exact meaning of *weiland*. We have in 'whilst' the excrescent *t* found in *mittelst, allen-t-halben*, etc. *Je* and *nie* are concealed accusatives, the O. H. G. forms being *io* and *nio* from *ni-io*, of which *io* (older *eo*) corresponds to a Gothic *aiw*, the Acc. Sing. of *aiws* (time, Eng. aye). Compare the Gr. αἰώ'ν and Lat. aevum. The German *nicht*, O. H. G. *niowiht*, is compounded of *nio* and the accusative (or nominative) *wiht* (Eng. wight). A trace of the substantival character of *niht* is preserved in the phrase, *hier ist seines Bleibens nicht*, in which *Bleibens* is an old partitive genitive. The history of 'naught' has several points in common with that of *nicht;* its older form is 'nawiht,' i. e., no whit, no thing. It is still further contracted in ' not,' the o of which has led to the spelling ' nought.'

Closely connected with the adverbs are the prepositions; and it is probably true that "all prepositions were originally adverbs." The German, like the English, has a long list of words that belong to both of these parts of speech : for example, *durch, hindurch, durchgegangen; um, darum, umgefallen; wider, dawider, widerreden*, etc. If we trace backward the course of development of these words we find that the adverbial signification is always the most primitive. In the earliest periods of the Indo-European languages there was no need of prepositions: the case-endings were in themselves sufficient to indicate the different relations in which words were used. A transition stage between adverb and preposition is preserved is such expressions as *den Tag über, die Nacht durch*. The current forms of many prepositions still bear evident traces of their origin in other forms of speech. The preposition *zu* was in the ninth century used exclusively as an adverb. *Kraft, laut, wegen* and others have developed their adverbial uses since the M. H. G. period, the starting point being such datives as *in Kraft, nach Laut, von — Wegen*, the last being the dative plural of *der Weg*. On the other hand, many prepositions have, in combination with certain case-forms, aided to form adverbs. *Entlang, entzwei* were originally *in lang, in zwei; neben* is *in eben; überall* is equivalent to *über Alles*, and *sintemal* takes us back to *sint dem mal*, i. e., *seit dem Mal, seit der Zeit*.

The introduction of the class of words now known as conjunctions was likewise a gradual process ; in the earliest stage of the language no need of them was felt. Even at the present day the illiterate have comparatively little use for this part of speech. The same may be said of poetry and of language intended to produce lively emotion, which is by a sort of atavism a partial recurrence to the primitive type of speech. The modern German *Sie stand und weinte* could be expressed in O. H. G. *stuont, weinota*. Cæsar's famous "veni, vidi, vici" is a good example of the effect produced by a series of sentences uttered in rapid succession without connecting words.

Those conjunctions that stand at the head of subordinate sentences have been developed from pronouns or adverbs. Their office is either to introduce the sentence which is to follow or refer back to a preceding sentence. Many conjunctions perform both of these functions. *So* is a word of this class. When we say, "*So ist die Sache vor sich gegangen*" we may intend to speak of an occurrence yet to be related or of one that has already been told. The pronouns *der, dieser* and *jener* have, likewise, this character. Their original use was to designate objects to which attention could be called by a gesture; now they are often employed to refer mentally either to what precedes or to what follows. Some particles point both forwards and backwards at the same time; for example, those that imply concession or contradiction or limitation. All these are words that in the first place conveyed the idea of acquiescence or solemn assurance, such as *gewisz, allerdings, ja, wohl, freilich, ja freilich* and *zwar*, M. H. G. *ze ware*, i. e., *in Wahrheit*. *Entweder* and *weder* refer only to what follows: the former is developed from *ein weder*, 'one of two.' If we say, "*er wollte entweder siegen oder sterben*," we imply a choice between victory or death. *Weder* is referable to *ne-weder:* "*weder heisz noch kalt*" originally signified 'neither of the two, hot or cold.' The third personal pronoun, *er, sie, es*, refers exclusively to what has gone before; in German its office is always conjunctive except when it takes the place and performs the functions of the first and second personal pronoun. *Aber* and *sondern* also point in the same direction. The former originally meant *nochmals*. It often occurs when one person repeats the act of another or when he speaks after another has spoken, that he is moved by the spirit of opposition. This idea is prominent in a number of words and phrases; *entgegnen* (go against or toward) is equivalent to *antworten*; *Wortwechsel* (exchange of words) is simply *Zank*. Similarly, we sometimes hear the remark in English, "I do not wish to have any words with you," meaning, "I do not wish to quarrel with you," while altercate and altercation differ little etymologically from alternate and alternation. *Sondern* is plainly related to *besonders* and signifies *ausgenommen*, which is precisely 'excepted,' i. e., except. It is probable that these words did not originally indicate opposition or contradiction in its full sense, but rather a denial of the general validity of a judgment, while admitting its applicability to certain cases: *nur das ist richtig* (only this is correct) and *das aber ist richtig* (but this is correct) mean about the same thing. It is, accordingly, from words of this class that the great majority of subordinate conjunctions has been gradually evolved. If we trace *dasz* to its origin we shall find that it primarily belongs, not to the subordinate sentence which it introduces but to the principal sentence to which it is attached. *Ich weisz dasz er lebt* really means *Ich weisz dasz: er lebt*. Putting this into English, 'I know that he lives' is equivalent to 'I know that: he lives;' so the fact above given is equally true of both languages. The conjunction *ehe* was originally used as a reflexive adverb in subordinate clauses, at least when it follows a negative clause. *Ich kehre nicht heim ehe ich ihn finde* points to an earlier stage of the language when this expression meant, *ich kehre nicht heim: ehe (vorher) finde ich ihn* (lit. I return not : ere I shall find him). The situation is somewhat different in the case of an affirmative sentence. In the older language it was followed by a subordinate clause having its verb in the subjunctive. Christ's address to Peter is *du lougenst min, e danne der han kraeje* (*du verleugnest mich, ehe dann*, etc.). Subordinating one sentence to the other we should probably have *du verleugnest mich vorher, dann wird* (or *dann mag*) *der Hahn krähen*. We have already called attention to the fact that it is reasonable to assume a twofold origin for the relative pronoun *der*. The transformation of independent sentences into subordinate ones will be more readily understood if we bear in mind that the order of words now characteristic of the latter was, at one time, also admissible in the former. The development of certain conjunctions can not be comprehended if we start from sentences consisting of two members; they must have required three or more. "*Da Herodes sah, dasz er betrogen war, ward er zornig*," (Matt. ii., 16) would have been stated co-ordinately, *da sah Herodes, dasz er betrogen war; er ward zornig*, in which case *da* at the beginning pointed to what had just previously been related. The causal *nun* may be similarly explained. *Nun dem so ist, so wollen wir*, must have originally been *nun ist dem so, so wollen wir;* in which case *nun* must have been preceded by another sentence. A similar origin must be assigned to *seit, indem, nachdem*, the last two having been evolved so recently as the N. H. G. period.

There is, nevertheless, a class of conjunctions now used to introduce subordinate sentences that were never used with such as were co-ordinate. In fact they can hardly be called conjunctions at all and perform the office of connectives owing to the somewhat fortuitous circumstance that they were used to introduce sentences that were afterward relegated to a subordinate relation. Here belong primarily the pronouns employed to introduce subordinate clauses. *Er fragt was vorgeht* has grown out of *er fragt: was geht vor*. The conjunction *ob* (Eng. ef, if) was employed in the older German, not only to introduce an interrogative clause, but also in the sense of *wenn*. Both meanings have been developed from the same primary concept: *ob* was, probably, in the first place an adverb with the sense of *vielleicht, etwa*. *Wenn du Gott bist, so sage es uns* (M. H. G. *obe du got bist*) is substantially equivalent to *vielleicht bist du Gott; so sage es uns*, which in turn does not differ much from, *sage uns, ob du Gott bist* (tell us if thou art God). On the other hand *ob* in the compounds *obgleich, obschon, obwohl* do not refer directly to the meaning of the adverb, but their concessive signification has been gradually evolved out of the conditional. A similar course of development can be traced in *auch wenn, wenn auch, wenn gleich* and *wenn schon*. The conjunction *geschweige dass* is unique. *Geschweige* is, in the first instance, an entire sentence represented by the first person singular of the obsolete verb *geschweigen* and *ich schweige davon, dass*, etc. (lit. I am silent thereof that). In like manner we hear the colloquial " let alone " used, as, " I am not able to keep myself, let alone pay my debts."

The latest of all the parts of speech to develop its current use was the article. During the Indo-Eur. period it had no existence ; nor is it found in the Latin, or the older Greek, or the Anglo-Saxon. The Gothic has a definite but no indefinite article, or rather, the demonstrative pronoun is often used as a definite article ; and we see here as in the Greek the intimate relation between the two classes of words. The O. H. G. uses the indefinite article, but it does not occur earlier. *Der Mann* was at first equivalent to *jener Mann* (iste homo) who was either spoken of before or who is soon to be mentioned. Gradually it came to be used to designate some object well known to the hearer or reader. The indefinite article is no more and no less than the numeral *ein* and does not differ much from it in usage. There is one sense, however, in which the article came, in the course of time, to be employed which it did not have originally, and that is as a disjunction, if it be admissible to coin a word upon the model of conjunction and meaning its opposite. It often indicates that the object to which it relates has no connection with what has just preceded.

Grammarians usually place the interjection last on the list of the parts of speech. They are, in fact, not so much single words as entire sentences. *Au!* means ' you hurt me' and *ah!* is equivalent to ' how fine that is.' Interjections are, accordingly, to be regarded as on a par with certain important words which are often taken out of a sentence to represent the whole sentence. This is done when the remainder may easily be supplied. *Endlich, still, traun* (M. H. G. *'triuwen, in treuen, in Wahrheit*), *ja* and *nein* are of this kind. *Ja* (Eng. yea) probably meant at first nothing more than *das* (*ist so*), just like the Provençal oc, an abbreviation of the Latin hoc, which is used in the same way. *Nein* is equal to *ni ein* (not one), a compound the first part of which is widely represented in the Indo-Eur. languages with substantially the same meaning it has in German.

THE NOUN.

The Indo-European language had the four cases which at present belong to the German, but in addition to these a vocative and ablative, still existing in the Latin, a locative and an instrumental. The two last disappeared during the primitive Teutonic stage and the remaining cases assumed their functions. The instrumental, though not found in the Gothic, has left some traces in the singular number of the West Germanic dialects. When this case also disappeared the remainder had to bear an additional burden. Of these, however, none were put on the accusative; the genitive may have received a small portion of the ablative; but the dative became a sort of huge reservoir in which a great variety of meanings collected. An original dative exists in "*einem etwas geben;*" it has taken the place of an earlier ablative after the prepositions *aus* and *von;* that of the locative in connection with *auf* and *bei*, and that of the instrumental, which was originally used with *mit*. But while the functions of some of the cases were enlarged in one direction they were curtailed in another. The greatest vicissitudes befell the dative and accusative. By means of the dative it was possible during the Indo-European stage to express various local relations without other auxiliary words. But as the several relations indicated by the cases became more numerous, and therefore more liable to confusion, it was found necessary to employ local adverbs in connection with them in order to mark their significance more sharply; and these adverbs in the course of time became prepositions. In the oldest accessible records of the German language this process was nearly completed, the instrumental being virtually the only case that could be used without the aid of a preposition. We find, for example, in the Heliand (see p. 250) the phrases *frostu bifangen* (with frost encircled), and *thurstu endi hungru bithwungen* (with thirst and hunger overcome). The accusative occasionally serves a similar purpose. We find so late as the M. H. G. *er fuor wald unde berc* (fared through forest and mountain). So far as we are able to follow the phenomenon in existing records, it is chiefly the genitive that has suffered curtailment of its functions. The genitive of way and manner fell into desuetude and left only a few traces in certain adverbial phrases that have already been spoken of. While in Luther's time it was still correct to say "*gebet dem Kaiser was des Kaiser's ist, und Gott was Gottes ist*" (Matt. xxii., 21), we should now have to render the same passage with *was dem Kaiser, was Gott zukommt, gehört;* but the older phraseology is preserved in such expressions as " *sind Sie des Teufels?*" Another remnant of an earlier stage of the language is conserved in " *sich Rats erholen*," and in poetry

19

this construction is still now and then found, as, *"es schenkte der Böhme des perlenden Weins,"* where the genitive is used partitively. We recognize an archaic coloring in the use of the genitive after *ermangeln* (lack), *erwähnen* (mention), *genieszen* (partake of, enjoy), instead of the accusative. In current usage the German says *ein Glass Wasser, ein Stück Brod* (or *Brot*), but the M. H. G., almost like the Eng of to-day, has *ein glas wassers, ein stück brotes* (a piece of bread, though we cannot say a piece bread's). The older Eng. is like the N. H. G. and we find in Chaucer, "Gif us a busshel whet, or malt, or reye." In both these cases the syntactic transition may be traced to a well marked cause, as has already, in part, been explained. The modern pronoun *es* was once *ez*. Its genitive was *es*, so that *ich bin es Satt, es müde* (tired of it) corresponded exactly to the current Eng. usage. In like manner *etwas gutes, nichts gutes*, represent a genitive construction, the M. H. G. being *etewaz guotes, niht schoenes*, the nominative being *guotez* and *schoenez*. Toward the close of this period the two sounds *s* and *z* coalesced in pronunciation. The genitive and accusative cases looked and sounded alike, besides being identical with the nominative which led to their ultimately being regarded as one. There were other circumstances under which the genitive could not be distinguished in form from the nominative and accusative. It thus came about that such formulas as *es genieszen*, where the verb seemed to require an accusative after it, were taken as models for *das Glück genieszen*, while *etwas Brod, ein Stück Brod* followed *etwas gutes*.

The genitive has almost disappeared from the modern German dialects. The most important remnant is preserved in the apparent plurals occurring in such expressions as *Pfarrers* or *'s Pfarrers, Müllers* or *'s Müllers*, meaning the family of the pastor, the miller or Müller. In Eng. we likewise use proper names in the possessive case, the word 'house' or 'residence' being understood.

Here belong also the apparent adjectives in such phrases as *Basler Leckerli, Münchner Kindl, Wiener Würste*. These are old personal genitives plural, and the above named objects are in reality *die Leckerli* (dainties) *der Basler, das Kindl der Münchener, die Würste der Wiener.*

These combinations take us back to a time when it was admissible to place a word in the genitive case without the article before the substantive which it limited. The place of this Gen. has in most cases been taken by the Dat. with the preposition *von*. This circumlocution, examples of which occur as early as the O. H. G., probably has its origin in the partitive genitive. *Er izzet des brōtes* and *er izzet von dem brōte* differ but slightly, if at all. After usage had come to regard the expressions as equivalent the latter not only gradually displaced the former, but the ablative mode came into vogue even where no action was implied, as in the examples cited at the beginning of this paragraph. The general tendency of all languages toward the analytic construction may also have had its influence. The genitive was further displaced by a kind of possessive dative like *meinem Vater sein Haus*, which hardly differs from the English, " B. D. his book." This is a genuine old dative, and it was originally placed close to the verb, not the noun. Instead of *"meines Vaters Haus hat er gekauft"* it is proper to say *" meinem Vater hat er sein Haus abgekauft;"* or with a change in the order of words, *" er hat meinem Vater sein Haus abgekauft,"* in which case the dative stands in close relation to the following substantive, because the collocation *"meines Vaters Haus"* is in the mind of the speaker before he begins the sentence. After the same model, then, such expressions as *''er hat meinem Vater sein Haus gekauft"* were formed, where the dative has no longer any relation to the verb.

Within the territory of the L. G. dialects there is evident a slight tendency to displace the dative and put in its place the accusative with *an*. This is common in the

Dutch, and regular in the Romance languages, where the case-endings of the noun have all been lost and their place taken by a modification of the Latin ' ad.'

If we regard the endings of the noun with reference to their case meanings there is no difference between the substantive and the adjective. In the latter, however, not only do the different endings correspond to the different cases, but they also indicate certain special shades of difference in signification which are foreign to the noun. The terminations of the adjective are divided into two classes which, like those of the noun, are designated as strong and weak respectively: besides which they are also used without inflection. The weak endings have a definite signification—in other words they assign the quality or property which they imply, to a definite object; they are accordingly preceded by the definite article or some related pronoun. The strong endings, on the other hand, designate qualities appertaining to an object which is not definitely limited, and they are, therefore, used with the indefinite article or some similar word. *Guter Wein* (good wine), means wine possessing a certain quality, but leaves it unlimited in every other way. "*Du hast den guten Wein bisher behalten,*" makes the quality or property of the wine prominent in contrast with other wine then and there present. The uninflected form is neuter and can be used in either sense. At present it is only used as a predicate. But this has not always been the case, and there was a stage of the German language when the uninflected adjective might be employed attributively: it could be placed after the noun as is still done in archaisms like *Röslein rot*, or between the article and the substantive, as *ein guot kind, ein wilt swīn.* This fact will explain why the German language contains so many composites of which the first member is an adjective, such as *Gelbschnabel, Grünspecht, Rundkopf,* etc. Conversely, the strong form of declension was also used in the predicate during the O. H.

G. period, as *das glas ist vollez*, (*das Glas ist voll*), and as an attributive when it followed the noun : *ein Glas voll Wasser* might be put *ein glas vollez wazzers* in the M. H. G. This condition of things seems to explain the singular M. H. G. phrase, *eine schüssel voller kirschen*, and the like. Here *voller* is the original nominative of the masculine singular, so that it would have been quite correct to say *ein tisch voller kirschen* (plenus cerisiaram). When this postposition was no longer admissible, the idea began to prevail that such words as *voller* in combinations of this kind were genitives and they are accordingly at present used after substantives of all genders, and in both the singular and the plural. The same fate befell the old nomitives *halber* and *selber*, both of which are now employed adverbially in nearly all cases.

THE VERB.

When we come to a study of the forms of the verb we find the most important to be those which designate the time and mode of action or being. We discover here the same phenomena to which we called attention in the discussion of the noun : expansion and contraction of meaning go hand in hand in the two parts of speech. The Indo-European tongue had not less than four or five different tense-forms, present, future (or imperfect), aorist, and perfect. The German, however, has and always had but two tenses to represent the variety exhibited in the parent speech, the present and the preterit. In its earliest stage the present united the significations of the present and the future ; though it could not, as is now the case, be employed in historical narration. As early as the O. H. G. period the need began to be felt of some method by which the future could be more distinctly marked. The verb *sollen* in connection with the infinitive was accordingly employed for this purpose : *ich scal lesen* being equivalent to *ich werde lesen*. This mode of indicating futurity is still used in the English which has retained it from Anglo-Saxon times where *ic sceal lesen* is the exact formal equivalent of 'I shall read.' An event that was about to happen was designated by a mode of speech that indicated its desirability; as a rule the cause was put for the anticipated effect. At the close of the M. H. G. period there came into use another circumlocution that, to some extent, embodies the element of futurity, that is, *werden* was used in connection with the participle. It was just as proper to say *er wirt sehende* as *er wirt alt*. Hence arose the modern mode of speech. But it did not grow out of abscission of the participial ending, for other conditions had led to the belief that the participial and the infinitive could properly be employed, one for the other. There is hardly a distinguishable difference between *er gāt suochende* or *er kumt bitende* and *er gāt suochen* or *er kumt biten* (he goes, comes to seek, in order to seek, for the purpose of seeking). When the present tense, after passing through this course of development, had come to be somewhat familiarly employed to designate futurity, it was easy to extend its newly gained elasticity still further and use it in reference to past events. We, accordingly, find it in the service of historical narration from the fifth century onward, when the writer's object is to bring an occurrence before the mind of the hearer with the greatest possible vividness. And it may be remarked that the German shares this use of the present in common with most other cultivated languages. The preterit, which in respect of form, corresponded to the Indo-European perfect, represented in the earliest stage the imperfect, the aorist and the perfect of the Indo-European. But ever since the earliest period it began to lose the signification which it had originally, and combinations of *sein* and *haben* with the preterit participle are used to designate the present perfect, i. e., the completion of an action. The circumlocution with *sein* is entirely clear: *ich bin gekommen* (I am come) is equivalent to *ich bin ein gekommener* (I am one who has come). That with *haben*, as we find it to-day, is not in all cases equally primitive. At first *haben* could only be used with verbs that might be put in the passive voice. *Er hat ihn gefunden* meant *er hat ihn, besitzt ihn als ein gefundener* (he has him, possesses him as one who has been found)—the reason of the possession being generally an antecedent act of finding. It thus came about that *er hat gefunden* might be regarded as substantially equivalent to *er fand* and upon this model might be framed *er hat geschlafen* like *er schlief*. Modern German dialects have still further limited the use of the preterit: in all those belonging to South Germany it is found only in the subjunctive mood. In the indicative the compound forms with *sein* and *haben* are exclusively employed. Accordingly, the illiterate do not say *ich ging* but *ich bin gegangen*, nor *ich asz* but *ich habe gegessen*. The beginning of this usage is about coeval with that of the historical present and must be assigned to the second half of the fifteenth century. So far as the use of the different tense-forms is concerned it makes no difference whether the verb is in the principal or the subordinate clause. But the case is different when we come to consider the moods of the verbs as they are at present employed. It will be remembered that the subordination of one sentence to another is, in a sense, a modern innovation and that in the primitive state of language co-ordination alone prevailed. It would accordingly be supposed that the signification of a mood would be the same in either the principal or the subordinate clause. The facts are, however, against this theory. In the first place, certain usages that prevailed in independent sentences have passed out of currency in dependent sentences; and in the second, we find that now, as always, a certain mood may be used in a dependent sentence where it was never employed in independent sentences. It is probably owing to the force of analogy that the subjunctive was sometimes used as a sign of formal dependence in cases where the intent of the sentence intrinsically required the indicative. Strictly speaking, the German language has but two moods, the indicative and the subjunctive; for the imperative ought properly to be classed with interjections while the infinitive and the participle are nouns. (See, for a full treatment of this part of Grammar, Jolly, Gesch. des Infinitivs). The subjunctive corresponds formally to the Greek optative: *er grabe* is *grabai* in Gothic, and γράφοι in Greek; but it embraces in its application both the Greek subjunctive and optative. As, however, the Indo-European optative had two different significations, one of wishing and one of supposition or expectation, the German subjunctive may properly be said to have three. The optative of wishing, however, corresponds very nearly to the hortative subjunctive and may be regarded as one with it, more especially as in German a well defined line of separation between the two can not be drawn. Over against this we may place as distinctly marked the optative of supposition. The hortatory subjunctive and the subjunctive of wishing may stand either in dependent or independent sentences: *er gehe* (let him go), *gebe Gott* (God grant), *käme er doch* (O that he would come). Its most frequent use is with verbs of wishing and commanding, *ich befehle, dasz er gehe*. Its use in such cases was originally imperative without exception. Now, however, the indicative is frequently used, especially in the present tense, *ich wünsche, dasz er geht; ich wünschte, dasz er ginge*. We see here the influence of analogy as exhibited in such constructions as *ich höre, sehe, weisz, dasz er kommt*. We have shown how combinations like *ich wünsche, dasz er gehe*, where one sentence is subordinated to the other, have been developed from two sentences that were originally co-ordinate: i. e., from *ich wünsche das—er gehe* (I wish that—what? he would go). Again, those forms of construction that are without the conjunction may be traced to the subjunctive of wishing or exhortation. *Käme er, er wäre willkommen* points to an earlier combination, *käme er (doch): er wäre willkommen* (would he but come, he would be welcome). We have also seen that conditional sentences are nearly related to concessive as, *sei dem auch so, ich bleibe dabei*, an expression that might be divided into, *sei dem auch so, ich bleibe dabei* (even if that be so, I stick to my statement). A remarkable fact is thrust under our notice in the study of these examples, viz., the slight difference existing between the meaning of the subjunctive present and the subjunctive past. One would naturally expect to find, in the first case, some distinct reference to the present, and in the second, to the past. But it seems probable that neither in the Indo-European, nor in the Germanic was such a distinction of time made, between the present subjunctive (or optative) and the perfect. The presumptive signification of the potential optative is clearly seen in hypothetical sentences. Here we find regularly the subjunctive preterit with distinct reference to present time, not only in the principal, but also in the subordinate sentence, as, *ich könnte es thun; ich weisz, dasz er es thun könnte*. Curiously enough we find the hypothetical subjunctive also used occasionally in sentences that contain no element of the conditional. For example, the German will say, upon arriving at a certain place, "*da wären wir.*" In such cases the underlying thought seems to be, "*da sind wir; es wäre schön, wenn wir schon weiter wären;*" nevertheless it must be confessed that this explanation is not entirely satisfactory. The sentence in its entirety being in the mind of the speaker or writer before he begins to express it, the conditional part presses forward, as we may say, for utterance, thus making its impress on the strictly affirmative portion. We may notice a similar phenomenon in such English expressions as "I don't think he will do it; He is not expected to live," where the thought plainly is, I think he will not do it; He is expected not to live.

The potential subjunctive in the present tense is now employed only in conditional expressions—in dependent affirmative and interrogative sentences. *Er glaubt dasz es heisz sei; er fragt ob es heisz sei* may be traced to, *er glaubt, es sei wohl heisz*; *er fragt—ist es vielleicht heisz?* In the oldest German *er sei* might be used in independent sentences with the meaning, *er ist wohl* (he probably is). We, however, find the subjunctive of the present tense used indiscriminately with that of the preterit without difference of meaning. In the High German, the subjunctive of the present is on the whole to be preferred: though that of the preterit is always to be preferred where the present subjunctive is not plainly to be distinguished from the indicative, as is the case in all the forms of the plural. We accordingly find *er sagt* or *sagte, sie hätten das Fieber*, but *er habe das Fieber*, more rarely *er hätte das Fieber*. This variation is not found in the dialects, the Low and Middle German, as well as the Franconian and the Austrian using the preterit subjunctive; the Alemanian and the Bavarian, the present. Both the variations in High German and the more consistent usage of the dialects are to be traced to an older invariable rule, the so-called CONSECUTIO TEMPORUM which we still find in the Latin: when the principal sentence is in the present tense the subordinate sentence should be in the same tense, but if the principal sentence is in the preterit the subordinate sentence should be in the same—*er waenet, ez si*, but, *er wänte, ez waere* (putat sit, putavit esset). In order to fully comprehend this rule one should keep in mind the origin of independent sentences in general. What is called ORATIO OBLIQUA has no existence in popular speech. The unlettered rustic relates an occurrence reported to him by another as if it were matter of his own observation. And this is true not only of the German but probably of all languages. When Paris is represented in the Iliad as declaring his willingness to restore all the treasures which he carried away from Argos, the message which announces this to the Achæans reads: " Priam directs me to announce to you the decision of Paris; he will restore everything that he has brought with him from Argos." If we take a sentence like the following: *er bringt Botschaft, der Kaiser sei tot,* in M. H. G. it would read, *er bringet maere, daz der keiser tot sī.* Translated into more primitive German we should have, *er bringt Botschaft; der Kaiser ist tot,* putting the whole into past time, *er brahte maere, er waere tot* (*er brachte Botschaft; der Kaiser war tot*). When, then, the content of the message was expressed in suppositional form, the potential optative took the place of the indicative present, which as we have seen might be used in independent sentences. After the pattern *er bringet maere, er sī tot,* the subjunctive would naturally, in the course of time, assume the notion of past time and *er brahte maere, er was tot* would become *er brahte maere, er waere tot.* Such being evidently the origin of dependent sentences we are also furnished with an explanation of the somewhat peculiar shifting of the person as exhibited in the pronouns of these sentences. Take, e. g., the statement *er wuszte, ich bin krank,* which becomes *er wuszte, er waere krank* and this in turn may be traced to *er wuszte es, er war krank.* This fact may even be stated, *er war krank; er wuszte es.* The old German rule for the sequence of tenses was in vogue until the fifteenth century. The irregularity in its use was caused by the historical present which came into currency about the same time. Viewed externally, the present must needs be here employed, but intrinsically the preterit alone was correct. Though originating with the historical present this variation in usage gradually passed over to the ordinary present and from this again to the historical preterit.

PROPER NAMES.

From the stand-point of pure theory the subject of proper names has no claim to a separate chapter in the history of a language. Every proper noun was once a common substantive or adjective, and subject to the same laws of formation and change with these. Underlying the roots to which every word in the Indo-European language can be traced are general concepts of which they are the visible expression. By combination and by means of various relational suffixes these roots have undergone a continual limitation of meaning, and this process is still in operation. While the number of general ideas which the human mind is capable of conceiving has increased little, if it all, since the earliest period of language the number of words is increasing rapidly. It is evident, therefore, each new word has a more limited and therefore a more definite meaning than any that existed before. It is estimated by competent authorities that the half a million names found on the map of Germany have been formed from about 500 roots by combinations in various ways. The common noun in its transition to a proper noun simply undergoes a restrictive process like that explained on p. 156. But in the practical application of these principles there are, however, certain peculiarities that are more or less inherent in the nature of proper names and which entitle them to be considered as a special part of our subject.

NAMES OF PERSONS.

The modern custom of giving each person at least two names, or rather of assigning to him a name in addition to that which he gets by inheritance, is relatively recent. The ancient Germans, as a rule, had but a single name; and this was somewhat peculiarly constituted in that it was always a compound of two parts. This custom prevailed among the ancient Greeks and may be safely assumed to have originated during the Indo-European period. Those qualities that were considered desirable in a man or that graced a woman were given to the child shortly after birth as a sort of amulet which it was to wear through after life. Thus Albert or Albrecht, in its O. H. G. form Adalbrecht, is, he who is conspicuous for nobility; Gerbert, designates one who is brilliant with the spear; Eckehart, him who is hard with the edge of the sword, *ecke* meaning edge or sword. Friedrich means one who is powerful in peace or in making peace; Gottschalk, God's knight or servant, and Notburga is the citadel, the protection in time of need. We have here an expression of the aspiration of parents and friends similar to that recorded in the earlier Old Testament names; as when, for instance, Jacob changed the name of his latest born, called by his dying mother Ben-oni (son of my sorrow), to Benjamin (son of my right hand). The names of Abram, Sarai and Jacob are also exchanged for or transformed into such as were of better omen. For we find the belief widely prevalent in ancient times that the name borne by an individual had more or less influence upon his subsequent destiny, a belief that the Romans embodied the alliterative phrase "bonum nomen, bonum omen."

A certain class of persons profess to experience great delight in discovering the vigor and poetic ring concealed in many of the old German names. Yet it is doubtful whether the Germans themselves were in any considerable number of instances conscious of the poetry in their names—in fact it is well nigh certain that such could not have been the case. Generally the words that became component parts of names had already gone out of use in current speech and could therefore have no significance for the nomenclator. What was the meaning of the first part of *Ingeborg* or of *Ingraban* was as much of a mystery to the Germans of historic times as it to us; nor did they know that the part of such names as *Anselm*, *Ansgar*, *Oswald* concealed the word "god." They were in precisely the same relation that most persons of the present day are to such names as Isra-el, Samu-el, Dani-el, Hanni-bal, in which the name of the deity is never suspected. On the whole it must be said, however, that the ancient Germans were concerned to apply their names with some reference to their sense.

The mode of procedure was probably similar to that recorded as employed by the ancient Hebrews, where such proper names as Eve (Chavah), Seth, Moses, and many others, are said to have been given with direct reference to the ordinary significance of these words in the vocabulary of the language. In German names, however, which, unlike the Hebrew, are always compounds, we find one part generally significant; and the obscure portion is much oftener in the first part of the composite than in the second. The second part of a compound is always the chief bearer of its meaning. It may happen that both the component parts entering into a proper name are words still current in the living language and yet their signification be obscured by assimilation, vowel weakening, or some other change to which the simple words have not been subject. A transformation of this kind may be seen in the O. H. G. names whose first syllable is *Liut-* or *Leo-*, as *Liutpold* (*Leopold*) and *Liuthold* (*Leuthold*), in which it would not be readily noticed that they are compounded of two words, meaning respectively *volkskühn* and *volkswaltend*. Such combinations as these may properly be compared with Greek names, of which the first element is Demo-, as Demosthenes, Democritus, and others. It may happen, also, that even when the two parts of a compound are etymologically plain, their fusion will make no sense so far as we can discover. To this list belong, e. g., *Wolfram*, O. H. G. *Wolfraban*, the meaning of which would be Wolf-raven, and *Hildegunde*, of which the first part signifies *Kampf* (combat), and the second, the same thing. It is a difficult matter to discover any sense in such words. Here again we find parallel instances in Greek in such names as Lykourgos and Lykomedes. *Rutland*, that is, *Roland*, is equivalent to *Ruhmesland* and *Kunigund* signifies *Geschlectskampf;* and while the compounds do not exactly make nonsense, it is hard to see what applicability they could have to a person. The only plausible explanation rests in the fact already referred to, that the simple elements were no longer clearly understood before they were made parts of the compound. In this way no doubt the notion began to be gradually developed that it was of little importance for a name to be entirely significant, and that it was sufficient when a new-formed name contained at least one traditional term. But there was one thing more. No doubt the custom existed in many places of giving the child a name that represented in its component elements both that of the father and the mother. It might happen in this way, that the daughter of a certain *Hildebrand*, 'sword of battle or combat,' and of a woman whose name was *Gundrun* or *Gudrun*, 'sorceress of combat,' would be named *Hildegund*. Readers of Aristophanes will readily recall the scene from the clouds which may be appropriately cited here, in which the mother insisted on calling her first-born son Chanthippos or Charippos or Kallipides, while the father as stoutly held out for Pheidonides, until the controversy is ended by adopting a name made up of a portion of two, viz., Pheidippides. It is also evident from an examination of the recorded names that a certain degree of phonetic congruity was sought after in the formation of compounds, and when this was attained the necessary conditions of composition were supposed to be fulfilled. In a mediæval story a certain *Engeltrut* is said to have preferred a suitor whose name was *Engelhard* to one called *Dietrich*, for the reason that the name *Engel-*

hard and *Engeltrut* harmonized better than *Engeltrut* and *Dietrich*.

The great majority of old German names were inconvenient for daily use on account of their length. They accordingly experienced the same fate which befell nearly all words containing a considerable number of syllables. In such names as *Charlotte*, *Elise* and *Johannes* or *Nikolaus*, which in familiar usage have become *Lotte*, *Lise*, *Hans* and *Klaus*, we see only those portions retained that are made prominent by the accent. These abbreviated forms which we may call pet-names or nick-names, originated in one of two ways: sometimes one of the component parts, usually the second, was dropped entirely, the remnant then ending either with the vowel -o or -i. In this way *Ingraban* became *Ingo*, *Kuonrat Kuno*, and *Volcwart Folko*. When the first member of the name was a derivative noun the nick-name likewise lost the suffix. It is thus that *Ebarhard* becomes *Ebaro*, *Ebo*; *Irminrich* appears as *Irmino*, *Irmo*; while *Raginbald* is abbreviated to *Ragano*, *Rago*. The termination -i is still very common where the Alemanian dialect is spoken, *Conrad* (or *Konrad*), the Greek Θρασύβουλος, appearing as *Kuoni*, *Rudolf* (*hruotwolf*, *Ruhmwolf*) as *Ruodi*, both these names, together with others of similar structure occurring in Schiller's well known drama, Wilhelm Tell; and *Walther* (*Waltend-Heer*) as *Wälti*. It is not safe, however, to assert with entire confidence that the last name represents *Walther*, for the evident reason that the same nick-name may be an abbreviation of one of two or three different names. *Gero*, e. g., is a shortened form of either *Gerbert* (*speerglänzend*), or *Gerhard* (*speer-gewaltig*), or *Gernot* (*speernot*), or *Gerwig* (*speerkampf*), or *Gerwin* (*speer-freund*); but it is not always possible to discover which. The origin of nick-names formed by the second process is less ambiguous. Here the second part of the compound is represented in the abbreviation. It is thus that *Sigbald* and *Sigbert* become *Sibo* (from a longer form *Sigbo*) N. H. G. *Seib;* *Sigfried* appears as *Sigfo*, then *Siffo*, and *Sigimar* or *Sigimund* is shortened to *Simo*. Into all these compounds 'victory' enters as the principal element. On the basis of these abbreviations all sorts of derivatives are formed, most of them probably having a diminutive signification. Those having the suffix *-in* and *-ilo* are distributed all over Germany; those ending in *-iko* and *-izo* or *-zo* are confined chiefly to Lower and Upper German territory respectively. Double derivatives in *-ilin, -liko, -ikin, -zilo, -ziko,* and *-zilin,* also occur. The word *diot* meaning 'people,' 'populace,' appears in many compounds of which the most common modern representatives are *Diedel, Tilly, Tiedge, Tieck, Deecke, Dietze, Dietz,* and others. It will readily occur to the reader that many abbreviated forms of proper names are still in daily use, such as *Fritz* for *Friedrich*, *Heintz* for *Heinrich*, *Kuntz* for *Konrad*, *Utz* for *Ulrich*, and many others.

The names we have thus far considered are easily traceable to a purely German source; but with the introduction of Christianity came a flood of names of diverse origin. The appellations of the saints who appear in the calendar—and it needs to be remembered that every week day of the year was sacred to one or another of them— undergo abbreviation like all others. Sometimes they appear as diminutives, sometimes as nick-names. It thus happens that a single name becomes the ancestor of a numerous progeny, as, e. g., *Johannes*, some of the descendants of which are *Johann, John, Jan, Hannes, Hans* and *Hansel;* while *Jacob* (Latin Jacobus) is represented by *Jack, Jäggi, Jock, Jockel, Kob, Köbel* and *Köbi*. The two names *Johann Jacob* which are often borne by the same person, especially in S. Germany, are abbreviated in Basel to *Beppi*.

The custom of having but one name prevailed in Germany until the Mediæval period. The modern practice of giving two or more names is closely connected with the rise of cities, the growth of civil liberty, with the extension of trade and travel and the frequency of contracts between buyer and seller. Double names appear first in the cities, whence they spread into the surrounding country, first of all in the cities along the Rhine and in South Germany. For it will be remembered that the cities of Germany owe their existence primarily to Roman influence, the Germans themselves being naturally adverse to living in close proximity. Accordingly where this influence was but little felt the cities are of much later growth. Within the first named territory we meet with double names as early as the twelfth century, while in Middle and North Germany they do not begin to occur till the thirteenth and fourteenth centuries. In many localities the serfs seem to have been content with a single name until the sixteenth century. The Frisians, who dwell in the northern Provinces of Holland, and the Jews, were constrained by legal enactments so lately as during the present and the last century, to conform fully to modern usage in the matter of proper names. It is owing to this fact that nearly all the Jews in the United States, who are for the most part immigrants from Germany, have German and not Jewish names. When the custom of double names came into vogue the traditional German and foreign appellations were adopted as baptismal names. What we now call family names are of multifarious origin, and stand in some degree in contrast to the other, earlier names. Those are for the most part of native creation and given to the child by its relatives; these are in the main the creation of strangers. Within the family circle there is even now little need of any other than the baptismal name. The salient characteristic of family names is the fact that they are inherited from generation to generation. It is probable, however, that in former times this inheritance did not follow so much as a matter of course as is the custom in our day. Indeed, it is no uncommon thing for people to change their family names. This is of especially frequent occurrence among the Germans who settle in the United States. Sometimes the original name is translated, sometimes it is changed outright by authority of the law-making power to one more agreeable to the possessor, but more frequently it is transformed into one more easily pronounced by those accustomed only to the use of the English language.

Among the causes which contributed to make names hereditary, that of location was perhaps the most potent. In the Black Forest, for example, the possessor of an estate is sometimes known by the name it bears rather than his own. It may thus happen that two successive occupants are called by the same name, when in fact they are different. Proper names derived from locality are formed in two ways: either a preposition is prefixed to the designation of the place, or the termination *-er* is added. By the first method we get such names as *Amthor* (*an dem Thor*), *Aus' m Wörth* (*Wert* signifying island, peninsula, any low land), *Thorbeke* (equivalent to *am Bach*), *Ambach, Ueberweg, von der Tann*, etc. By the second, such names as the following are formed: *Steinberger, Bärenthaler, Sulzbacher*, etc. To this class belongs the long list of names ending in *-bacher, -hauser, -häuser, -hofer, -röder, -reuter*, and many others. These terminations are all significant in various ways, *-röder, -reiter* or *-reuter* signifying the dweller at a place where a clearing has been made, and *-hofer*, one who occupies an estate. Sometimes the designation of the locality is simply applied to the dweller in or on it, without prefix or suffix, whence come such names as *Steinthal, Berg, Stein, Bach*, etc. These have their exact equivalents in our English Hills, Vales, Brooks, Stones and many others of similar origin.

If we look at proper names with reference to their source we shall see that there may be as many different classes as there are designations of localities. One of these is easily misapprehended. It has always been the custom in Germany to mark inns and drug-stores with some sign or device by which each may be known from every other. During the Middle Ages this custom prevailed even more widely, and included dwelling-houses, as is still the rule to some extent in Switzerland. These legends were plants or animals, or some similar object. The inventor of printing bore the name *Gensfleisch* from the device on the house in which he lived or was born. A person having the name *Drach* (Eng. Drake. See p. —), or *Ochs* would not be so called because such a designation was suitable to his mental characteristics, but because his house bore the legend of a dragon or an ox, or because he was born in one so marked—for it must be remembered that in the cities the dwellings were generally large enough to contain several or more families, and built close together for purposes of defense. Another motive for transmitting a name from father to son and grandson arose from the fact that social position and occupation were likewise a heritage from generation to generation. To this category belong the names of most frequent occurrence. Such as *Meyer* (Latin major-domo), *Müller*, *Schmidt*, *Schneider*. We find the same fact in regard to the English names, the most common of which are Smith, Carpenter, Taylor, Miller and the like. Many names still survive that once designated the users of trades now no longer in existence, such as *Bogner* (Bowman), *Falkner* (Falconer), *Plattner* (a maker of laminæ for coats of mail,) and *Pfeilsticker* (one who made shafts for arrows).

But, it may be asked, how came a family to have such a name as *Bischoff* (Bishop), or *Herzog* (Duke), or Prince and Pope? To this query we may reply that these names are in part due to the devices before spoken of, and in part to mediæval dramatic performances and miracle-plays, the chief performers in which would often continue to be known during the remainder of their lives by the characters they represented. In other cases these epithets were doubtless applied to persons for purely fanciful reasons, and we find the name Rex in use among the early Romans. See also Horace, Sat. I. 7.

Viewed in the light of modern usage the son would regularly inherit the name of his father to which his own would be added. But in earlier times the new-born male child received the name of the grandfather much more frequently than that of the father, a custom that likewise prevailed in ancient Greece. In this way accordingly many of our modern baptismal names became family names. Sometimes the name of the father was given to the son, plus a suffix showing such relationship: a scion of *Matthias* would be *Matthisson*, contracted from *Matthiassohn;* of *Hans* or *Jans*, *Hansen* or *Jansen*. Or the name of the son might be put in the genitive case—*Ebers* would thus plainly be the son of one *Eber*, and *Wilken* the son of *Wilko*, O. H. G. *Williko*, a nick-name for *Wilhelm*. A similar procedure is exhibited by the large class of English names ending in -s, such as Williams, Edwards, Matthews, and the like. A large number of family names are, as before indicated, simply baptismal names become hereditary. It is thus that we get such combinations as *Robert Franz*, *Friedrich Friedrich* and *Hermann Paul*. Quite a long list of patronymics is formed by means of the suffix -*ing* or -*ung*. *Karol-ing-er*, the Karolings, are the descendants of *Karl*, and *Wäls-ung-er* are the family of *Wälse*. At present, however, it is difficult to determine how far this mode of forming derivatives was in vogue when names so constructed first came into use. For example, we can not tell whether a person bearing the name *Hartung* or *Henning* was the son of a father called *Harto* or *Henno;* or whether the parent, who may have been satisfied with a single name, already had the name *Hartung* or *Henning*. Occasionally we meet with an instance in which the son's name comes from the mother, which may have happened in the case of widows. We find the family name *Hilgard* which doubtless has such an origin, and *Lieske* was probably the son of a certain *Elisabet*.

In regard to many names it is clear that inheritance would follow as a matter of course. This statement will apply to bodily characteristics which are often transmitted and which probably account for such names as *Kraushaar* (curly-hair), *Krumbein* (Cruickshank), *Lang*, *Kurtz*, *Weisz* and *Rot(h)*. Generally, however, it is more probable that the rule fixed in other cases gave the final decision here too. It may be said in general that the principle followed in the giving of names was the same that determined the designation of other objects, and nearly all the different kinds of metaphors underlie them, often much disguised, that we find concealed or open, in other words. It needs to be kept in mind that in nearly all cases names are not given by those who bear them, but by others, and it was important that such an appellation should be chosen as would point out or fitly characterize the person to whom it was applied. Only in those instances where a person was in position to name himself would this principle be left out of sight, and he would select such a name as pleased his fancy. Such cases are most frequently met with among the Jews, when they were compelled by law to assume a second name. This is the probable source of such names as *Blumenthal*, *Rosenthal*, *Bernstein*, *Rubinstein*, *Goldmark*, *Saphir*, etc. Not a few of the older names are an uncomplimentary or even vulgar epithet, but having once been affixed to an individual he could not get rid of it, if he wished. Gradually it came to be regarded as a matter of course. The origin of it was forgotten and the appellation acquiesced in without further resistance. It is evident from what has been said that the number of possible roots from which proper names could be formed is very large and very multifarious. But there are some collateral elements that contribute to increase the variety still more. One of these is dialectic variation in the words themselves, several words meaning precisely the same thing, but differing in form. We have a familiar instance of this in the common English names Fox and Tod(d), one being of southern, the other of northern nativity. The man who exercised the potter's craft might be called either *Hafner* or *Pötter* or *Töpfer*, according to the part of Germany in which he lived; while the cooper might be named *Binder*, or *Böttcher*, or *Büttner*, or *Fasser*, or *Küfer* or *Scheffler*. Another is the peculiar relation in which proper names stand to the rest of the sentence in which they occur. We have already called attention to the fact that the hearer does not take cognizance of every sound or even of every word in a spoken sentence. It only concerns him to note so many words or such portions of longer words as will suggest to his mind what the speaker intends to convey. The attentive mind involuntarily supplies and supplements what the hearing ear has failed to catch. Now, proper names have no such mental support; they can not be used as integral parts of a sentence, nor have they any etymological relation to adjacent words, so that the hearer is unable to infer their probable form from the way in which they are used. As it is almost impossible to correctly apprehend a name by the aid of mental suggestion there is a wide field open for the play of fancy; the result is likely to be etymological vagaries of all sorts. Every one knows how difficult it is to understand a name correctly unless it be some word with which we have become familiar in other relations. While therefore we might make no mistake with such simple names as Hill or Berg, Stone or Stein, the chances are at least ten to one that we would not be equally fortutunate with Taliafero, or Mainwaring, or Bodenstedt, or Willamowitz. We accordingly find here the converse to be true of what has been mentioned before,—that names are more conservative in their development and less subject to change than the other words of a language. It is true we say *Bruno*, *Otto* and *Hugo*, though all other German final *o*'s have been changed to *e;* but these names have been artificially fixed or stereotyped with the aid of Latin documents. In popular speech they have long since been transformed into *Braun(e)*, *Hauck* and *Ott(e)*. An intentional metamorphosis of names is exhibited in the translation of those that were originally pure German into Latin or Greek, or by the affixing of termination that would make them declinable.

NOTE.—An investigation into the history of a family named *Rahmsauer* that emigrated from Germany into North Carolina some two hundred and fifty years ago revealed the fact that in about two centuries the name was found in the following forms: Ramsauer, Ramsaur, Ramsour, Ramseur, Ramser, Ramsir, Sirram, Ram, Sheep, Lamb. The United States offers a fertile field for the study of the transformation and translation of family names. The French names Du Bois, Boisvert, Boncoeur, De l'hotel, Pibaudière, Lemieux have become Wood, Greenwood, Bunker, Doolittle, Peabody and Betters, respectively. *Loewenstein* appears as Livingston, *Loeb* and *Loew* have been transformed into Lyon, *Koch* into Cook, and so on. One instance is recorded in which a German bearing the name of *Feuerstein*, who settled in turn in the French and American quarters of New Orleans, found himself called Pierre-de-feu, then Pierre, then Stone, then Flint, and finally died as Peter Gun. I have found an instance in which the modern name *Rollfuss* had undergone the following evolutionary process. Its original form was *Rudolf*, which had been abbreviated into *Rolf*. This, in turn, had been Latinized into Rolfus, then Germanized into its present form. Some years ago a German whose family name was *Pflaumbaum* applied to the legislature of his country for authority to change his name to *Blei*.' He claimed that this was the original name of his family, but that it had been translated into the Latin equivalent Plumbum. In the course of time his Low German neighbors came to look upon this as the native word *Plumbom*, and the next stage in the process was very naturally its transformation into the High German *Pflaumbaum*, which means the same thing, viz., plum-tree.

A good many names, have, like this one, a meaning in themselves, but their applicability to persons can not be discovered, at least in a majority of cases. Of this class are the following, all of which are of actual occurrence: *Jerusalem, Cæsar, Breyvogel, Süsskind, Kussmaul, Hopfensack, Teufel, Hellwald, Viehoff, Dickhaut, Rübsamen*, translated or transformed into Turnipseed or Ripsome, *Buttersack, Rothauge, Kalbfell* and *Kalbfuss*. It is by this method that *Schwarzerd* becomes *Melanchthon*, or *Hämmerlein* is transformed into *Malieolus*, while *Kurtz* and *Heinrichs* appear respectively as *Curtius* and *Henrici*. By a similar process *Schneider* became *Sartor* and *Schmidt, Faber; Fischer* and *Goldschmidt* were turned into *Piscator* and *Aurifaber* respectively; *Baumann* was translated *Agricola* and *Grossman, Megander*. *Weber* appears as *Textor*, the maiden name of Goethe's mother; *Reuchlin* as *Capnio;* and *Krachenberger* as *Gracchus Pierius*. It will be evident from what has thus far been said that names the most diverse in form frequently sprang from the same root. And it is further probable that in some cases several different roots have produced identical names. Instances are quite numerous where a name seems to be, and probably is, formed from some familiar current adjective or noun, when if the real facts were known it is a descendant of some old nickname or pet-name. The familiar *Rot(h)* may have started from the color of the hair; but it may also be a survival of *Rodo* or *Hrodo*, a nickname of *Hrodbert* and *Hrodger, hrod*, meaning 'fame.' *Baer* and *Wolf* may be Jewish names of recent date, or they may be a reminiscence of the old German *Berwald* and *Berwin* or *Wolfgang, Wolfger*, and *Wolfhard*. There is small probability that such names as *Dank, Eisen*, and *Wald* are recent; it is, however, quite likely that they take us back to O. H. G. *Danko, Iso* and *Waldo*, abbreviations of *Dankwart, Isenhard* and *Walther*. Plainly, then, the interpretation of family names is uncertain and the ground on which the investigator stands, insecure. When we have no means of knowing the history of a family and have no guide but the name in its modern form, it is generally impossible to reach any even measurably safe conclusion as to its origin. To enable one to do this written records are indispensable.

NAMES OF PLACES.

When we come to the investigation of the names of places we encounter difficulties not met with in the study of the names of persons. In many cases these are to be traced to a time when Kelts inhabited Germany, and our knowledge of the ancient language of this people is still very incomplete and fragmentary. Nor is it probable that it can ever be much increased. For this reason a large measure of uncertainty is likely always to attach to those etymologies that are presumably or possibly Keltic. The Keltic is frequent in the names of plains and running waters, less frequent in those of towns, mountains and rivers. In those countries which lie west and southwest of Germany, Keltic names are very numerous, and it is here first of all the rivers that have preserved these memorials of the earliest inhabitants. It is claimed by some writers that almost every river-name in England is of Keltic origin. Unquestionably Keltic are Rhine, Danube, Main, Isar, and the names of many smaller rivers. The root from which *Rhein* (Rhine) is derived is related to ῥέω and is also found in *Rhone, Reuss, Reinach, Rhadanau, Regen*, etc. We may also regard as Keltic *Breisach* (Brisiacum), *Mainz* (Moguntiacum), *Solothurn* (Solodurum) and *Worms* (Borbetomagus). On the other hand the investigation of place-names has an advantage that is lacking when we are dealing with the names of persons. The latter, like those compounds which we find among the old Germans, are for the most part given to children shortly after birth, and could not therefore be founded on actual, but only on hoped-for qualities. Even when proper names were founded on actual characteristics we are rarely in position to know whether they really represented the pecu-

liarities of the persons who bore them. On the other
hand, in the case of place-names we generally have the
objects themselves before our eyes and can judge what peculiar features gave rise to their designation. These designations may characterize the position of the place as
Hochhausen, *Hochheim*, or *Berghausen*, *Bergheim*, or
Thalhausen, *Thalheim*, or *Wertheim* (see *Wert*, ante),
Neckarhausen and *Rheinheim*. Or they may indicate the
natural surroundings of the place, as *Aschbach*, a place
where ash trees grow; *Birkenau*, a place abounding in
birches; *Buchenbach*, *Has(e)lau*, *Iben(Eiben)bach*, *Seligen-
stadt* or *Salweide* (O. H. G. *salacha*, willow), *Auerbach*,
Habsburg (*Habichtsburg*), *Spessart* or *Spechtswald*, *Ziegen-
hain*, etc. Or they may designate the uses to which a
place has been put. Many local names arose from mills
such as *Mühlbach*, *Molenbeck*, *Mühlhausen* and *Mühlheim;*
or from an older appellation of a mill, as *Kernbach*, *Kehren-
bach*, *Kirnbach*, the O. H. G. *quirn* meaning mill. The
large number of names ending in -*reut* and -*rode* (Eug.
root) indicate that the place occupied by them had been
cleared of forest. In many instances the ancient name is
hardly recognizable in its modern form, *Detmold* e. g. being originally *Thietmella*, a word that is made up of *thiot*,
people, and *mahal*, harangue, or place of harangue. These
three categories of names—those having reference to the
configuration of the land, to the physical features of the
region, or to the use that was made of the locality—are
about equally old: while the names themselves may have
been formed and applied at different times the principle
underlying the nomenclature is in all cases of equal antiquity. Much more recent are those names which designate the owners or inhabitants of a place; and their rise
shows us how the bond between the owner and the soil
upon which he dwelt becomes closer and closer. Here
again we encounter the Old German names *en masse*, but
in somewhat different combinations. *Bamberg* or *Baben-*

berg, the hill of a certain *Babo*, is an abbreviation of one of the common names beginning with *badu* and signifying battle ; in *Diedenhofen* we have another form of the O. H. G. *diot*, spoken of above and found also in *Detmold; Hersfeld* is the property of one *Hariulf* or *Heerwolf*, *Rudersheim*, of a *Rudolf;* while *Witgenstein* designates the stone of *Witiko*, or perhaps *Witikind*. The owner is sometimes represented by his official title only; as in *Bischofsheim*, *Herzogenhorn*, *Kaiserswörth* or *Königstein*. Sometimes the name is not a reminiscence of a single possesser or inhabitant but of several, it may be of a whole clan as *Sachsenhausen* and *Groszsachsen*. Not unfrequently a real or mythical progenitor is commemorated in a name. This is generally the case in those words ending in *-ingen* and *-ungen*. Finally some occupation or trade may give rise to a name, which is found chiefly in street designations. When we come to examine the names on the map of England we are struck with their similarity to those found in Germany, not only in general, but in particular. While it is true that Keltic influence has been less obliterated, the Teutonic stratum is very plainly marked. The second part of many compounds appearing in Germany as *-heim*, that is, home, dwelling-place, becomes *-ham* in England, while *-throp* or *-thorpe*, which is almost identical in meaning, is the German *-dorf*. Again, the suffix *-ing*, dative plural *-ingen*, so common in southwestern Germany in such names as *Reutlingen, Esslingen, Tuebingen*, appears in England in almost the same form, sometimes alone and sometimes in combination with *-ham*, as Basing, Hastings, Billingham, Issington. Town and *-ton*, meaning an enclosed place, corresponds to the German *Zaun*, which is occasionally found as a place name; its occurrence is rare, however, compared with its English equivalent. In other parts of Europe occupied at various times by Teutonic tribes but more particularly in France both *-ing* and *-ton* are of frequent occurrence on the map, under various disguises. The latter may, however, sometimes represent the Keltic 'dun,' a hill-fortress from which it is not always possible to distinguish it with certainty. The German *Burg*, used both as a separate word and as part of a place-name, e. g. *Hamburg, Magdeburg* is the A.-S. burc(g), a fortified place. Its modern English representative is '-burg,' '-bury,' '-borough,' etc., and is one of the parts entering most frequently into the names of towns. When we undertake to find the historical personage from whom the patronymics in *-ing* or *-ung* take their rise our search usually ends in disappointment. Our experience is similar to that of the historian of Rome who should undertake to trace the Julian, the Horatian, or some other noble family to a real ancestor. It is plain enough that *Reutlingen* or *Esslingen* is intended to designate the place where the *Reutlings* or the *Esslings* were settled : these names mean 'at the *Reutlings*' or 'at the *Esslings*,' but it is only in exceptional cases that we are in position to learn anything at all approaching to definiteness about these particular clans. Even in those instances like that of the Karolings and Merowings where a clan rises to distinction their origin remains obscure. It is true in general that all names of places ostensibly derived from persons generally lack a historical background. But even in the case of those names that were originally given with reference to some peculiarity of the place named we are often at a loss to discover their appropriateness; the general physical features of the locality may have undergone a change. A place near a swamp might properly be designated by some compound term ending in *-bruch*, *-moos* or *-ried;* but after the swamp had been drained and the land laid dry the appellation would be unsuitable. Examples are on record of places bearing names derived from the presence of the beech or the oak, but which are now covered with conifers; evidently here the former were displaced by the latter. Now and then the name itself may give expression to the contradiction and such designations as *Birkenäcker*, *Birkenfeld* or *Eichenäcker* and *Eschfeld*, though clearly inappropriate, at least show what kind of forest trees must at one time have covered the ground.

Many names have originated at points to which they are no longer applicable. A name at first given with special reference to some particular locality may, in course of time, have been extended to neighboring places, whence have most likely arisen the countless designations of villages compounded with -*au*, -*bach*, -*feld*, and -*wald*. The deportation might even extend to a considerable distance where new settlers wished to retain the familiar and beloved name of the place whence they emigrated. *Frankfort-on-the-Oder* has a very slender connection with the Frankish tribe. This mode of transfer is exhibited on a large scale in the names found on the map of the New World almost from the North Pole to Cape Horn.

Names are often given to places just as they are to persons, without regard to fitness or to the relation that ought to exist between the sign and the thing signified. A mere whim or fancy roaming free now and then lights upon an abstract term and applies it to a place; occasionally the first impulse is given by the motto or the superscription of a single house. There is a long list of names ending in -*lust* and -*ruhe*, and such names as *Aergernisz*, *Eintracht*, *Gelegenheit*, *Miszgunst* and *Unverzug* are not altogether unknown.

A large majority of German place-names are compounds, like the names of persons. But besides this class, single words are not rare and among them are some of the oldest names of places. In many cases, however, we are liable to be deceived by appearances as in nicknames of persons: we seem to have before us a single word, when in fact it represents a compound: just as the son of one *Dietrich* is frequently spoken of as *Dietrichs*, so his land or his residence may also be called *Dietrichs*, the second part of the compound being omitted because easily supplied. Another kind of ellipsis occurs. It is natural to regard the designation of a place as a word in the nominative case; in fact, however, this is rarely so. Where we can discover the original form of the word, it generally represents the answer to the question where? and is in the dative case, usually after the preposition *zu*. A few isolated examples of this procedure remain in such names as *Andermatt*, i. e., *an der Matt; Zermatt*, i. e., *zu der Matt*, and in proper names as already cited. The Dat. Plur. is evident in such endings as *-felden, -hausen, -hofen, -ingen -lon* O. H. G. *lohun*, Dat. Plur. of *lōh*, a copse or grove, *-stetten, -walden*, though without the preposition. The same case is seen in the names of countries, such as *Bayern, Franken, Hessen, Sachsen* and *Schwaben*, which are simply the plurals of tribal names; the full formula was *ze den Baiern, ze den Franken*, etc. Occasionally the second member of the compound is now a nominative, while the first member is still the dative of an adjective, as *Breitenfeld, Hohentwiel, Homburg* for *Hohenburg, Stolzenfels, Wittenberg*, that is, *Weiszenberg*, the L. G. for *weisz* being *witt*, Eng. ' white.' It stands to reason that the names of places like the names of persons are subject to the same phonetic laws as the remaining words of the language. Particularly frequent are the weakening and abbreviation of full compounds and the assimilation of consonants — two kinds of phenomena for which the conditions are much more rarely supplied by the ordinary material of language. In addition to these changes it often occurs that in ordinary compounds those regularly developed are in turn displaced by the influence of indepedent words. For example, an old *Ruitisrode* or *Ruotboldisrode* has become the modern *Ruperath; Markberteshusun* is now *Merkshausen;* and *Alahmuntinga* has been abbreviated to *Allmendingen*. In cases where the first part of the compound now ends in *-ers* we have before us the alternative of two different compounds of names of persons: *Herbersdorf* is the older *Heribrehtesdorf*; *Elfershausen* points to a former *Adalfrideshusum*; *Liggersdorf* is an abbreviation of *Luitcardisdorf*; *Ollersbach* is really *Adalgerisbach*; *Volkersdorf* may be traced to *Folchardesdorf*, *Einershcim* was formerly *Einheresheim*; *Drommersheim* is a shortened form of *Truhtmaresheim*; *Ballersheim* is the same as *Baldrodesheim*, *Oggersheim* the same as *Agrideshem*; and *Frankershausen* was originally *Frankwardeshusum*. The ending *-sen* of a large number of place-names is generally a weakened form of *-husen*, i. e., *hausen*, but it may also be a remnant of the termination *-es-heim*. The names ending in *-ikon*, spoken of before, represent an older *-ic-hofen*, which in turn is a contraction of *-inc-hofen*. The first member of the compound contains a patronymic in *-ing*.

Many places are known by two names, an older and a younger, one of which is the official designation, the other that in popular use. The former is generally that handed down in legal documents from remote times; but occasionally it is a mere translation of a popular name and has never had any actual existence. Dialectic differences are much more conspicuous in the names of persons than in those of places, for the reason that the latter were created on the spot and to suit the local conditions where they are used, while persons frequently migrate a long distance from home. Characteristic of the Alemanian territory, are the forms in *steten*, *weil* and *weiler;* the ending *-wang* may be either Alemanian or Bavarian. The river Lech separates the Alemanian termination *-ingen* from the Bavarian *-ing*. Names in *-lar* belong to Middle and North Germany, those in *-scheid* are Middle Franconian, while *-ungen* is generally Hessian or Thuringian. Low German territory has almost a monopoly of names ending in *-brink*, *-büttel*, *-fleth*, *-hude*, *-koog* and *-kuhl*.

A careful study of geographical names, based on accurate statistics and made with special reference to the methods according to which they are compounded, would throw much light on the connection between the different Germanic clans. A beginning has been made in this direction by Dr. Isaac Taylor in his " Words and Places," which has yielded interesting and in some cases surprising results. It can readily be seen how the study of place-names may be made subservient to that of history, as indeed language itself is often a valuable auxiliary to the historian. These are, however, questions that lie outside of the sphere of the present work.

APPENDIX.

I GIVE below four specimens of Dialect German for the purpose of exhibiting some of the most important variations from the literary language. The original of the four is by Klaus Groth, and is in the dialect of a district in Holstein. Dr. Groth has long been the foremost champion of the claims of the Low German to culture as a literary language. The humor of the poetry is well-nigh inimitable, as is often the case with similar productions; but this delicate flavor is nearly all lost by translation. To be appreciated, it must be understood in the original. Nor can the pronunciation be represented with any near approach to accuracy. Still, the reader may form some idea of the spoken tongue from what is here given. These specimens will do something toward showing how inadequate the conception most persons have of what is meant by the "German language." Not only do most foreigners have erroneous views on this subject, but the great mass of the German people themselves have little idea of the astonishing variety their vernacular presents.

What is, perhaps, the most interesting dialect to American readers, the Pennsylvania German, is not represented here, for the reason that it has received a thoroughly scientific treatment at the hands of Dr. Learned, of the Johns Hopkins University. Specimens are, therefore, easily obtainable.

MATTEN HAS'.

[In a dialect of West Holstein.]

Lütt Matten, de Has', De mak sik en Spasz,
He weer bi't Studeern, Dat Danzen to lehrn,
Un danz ganz alleen Op de achtersten Been.

Keem Reinke, de Vosz, Un dach: Das en Kost!
Un säggt: "Lüttje Matten, So flink oppe Padden?
Un danzst hier alleen Oppe achtersten Been?"

"Kumm, lat uns tosam. Ik kann as de Dam!
De Krei de spelt Fitel, Denn geit dat canditel,
Denn geit dat mal schön Op de achtersten Been!"

Lüt Matten gev Pot: De Vosz beet em dot,
Un sett sik in Schatten, Verspeis, de lütt Matten:
De Krei de kreeg een Vun de achtersten Been.

D'R HOS.
[In the dialect of Nuremberg.]

An ärtlier Hos Macht Mändla in'n Gros;]
Will e⁻* biszla schtudeiren, D's Tanzn probeiren,
Un tanzt ganz ella⁻ Af 'n hinterstn Ba⁻.

Kummt pfiffi' der Fuchs, 'r glotzt wöi e Luchs
Und sagt: "Du bist g'schwind Af'n Banen, löibs Kind!
Wos tanzst ganz ella⁻ Af dein hinterst'n Ba⁻?"

"Kumm, tanz m'r ze zweit! Ich mach dei⁻ Dam g'scheid;
Döi Kraua tout geing'ng, Döi Fidl brav schtreich'ng;
Su tanzst ganz ella⁻ Af dei hinterstn Ba⁻."

'in Hos'n g'fällt der Raut, D'r Fuchs beiszt 'n taud,
Tout—wer will's 'n wiërn? 's Hesla verziërn;
Döi Kraua kröigt's a' Su e⁻ hinteres Ba⁻.

DE HAS.
[In the dialect of Zurich, Alemanian.]

's gumpet en Has Uf em grüenige Gras,
'r ischt am Schtudire, Wott 'sch Tanze probire
Un hüppft ganz elei⁻ Uf 'm hindere Bei⁻.

De Fuchs kchunnd dezue Un lad em kei⁻ Rue,
Seid: "Tusigschöns Hasli, Wie schpringscht uf em Grasli!
Un tanzischt elei⁻ Uf em hindere Bei⁻."

"Kchum, gib mer di⁻ Hand, Mer tanzid mitenand.
I mache dir 'sch Meidli, D' Kchrä giget is weidli,
Mer tanzid Drei—elei⁻ Uf em hindere Bei⁻."

Er schtreckt em sis Kchapli, De Has gid em 's Tapli,
Hed's Tanze vergasse, De Fuchs hed en g'frasse,
Und Kchrä die fligt hei Mit eme hindere Bei⁻.

---
*The tilde⁻ represents a nasal sound.

'ES KLASLA, DER HOS.

[In the dialect of Coburg.]

'es Klasla, der Hos, Macht sich lust'g im Gros,
'r schtudirt derbei garn, Möcht's Tanz'n gelarn,
Und tanzt ganz ella Auf sei'n hinterst'n Ba.

Kümmts Füchsla abei Un denkt: Du bist mei!
Segt: "Klasla, Herrje! Wie kannsta gegeh!
Und danzst doch alla Auf dein hinterst'n Ba?"

"Kumm, ge har zu mir! Ich danz schö mit dir;
Di Kräa geigt auf, No gehts erşt hellauf—
Des sollst' emol sa Auf dein hinterşt'n Ba."

D's Klasla schlegt ei: Mei Fuchs packt'n fei,
Tregt 'n hinter e Heck Un leszt sich wohl schmeck;.
Die Kräa kriegt a So e hinteres Ba.

THE END.

www.ingramcontent.com/pod-product-compliance
Lightning Source LLC
Chambersburg PA
CBHW031901220426
43663CB00006B/717